Books by Evan S. Connell

The Anatomy Lesson
  and Other Stories
Mrs. Bridge
The Patriot
Notes from a Bottle
  Found on the Beach at Carmel
At the Crossroads
The Diary of a Rapist
Mr. Bridge
Points for a Compass Rose
The Connoisseur
Double Honeymoon
A Long Desire
The White Lantern
Saint Augustine's Pigeon
Son of the Morning Star

A
LONG
DESIRE

Evan S. Connell

NORTH POINT PRESS
San Francisco *1988*

Originally published by Holt, Rinehart and Winston,
New York; reprinted by arrangement
Portions of this book first appeared in *The Atlantic*
and *Harper's*, to whom acknowledgment is made.
Excerpts from *Richard Halliburton, His Story of
His Life's Adventure*, copyright 1940 by Bobbs-Merrill
Co., copyright renewed 1968. Reprinted by permission
of Bobbs-Merrill Co., Inc.
Excerpts from *The Alchemist* by Hans Holzer, copyright ©
1974 by Hans Holzer. Reprinted by permission of
Stein & Day Publishers.

North Point Press
850 Talbot Avenue
Berkeley, California
94706

To Ruth and Mark Costello

Contents

The soul has many motions,
many gods come and go.
            —*D. H. Lawrence*

A Long Desire

1

Various Tourists

In 1939, when Richard Halliburton tried to cross the Pacific in a Chinese junk, I was a fourteen-year-old stamp collector. Never doubting that he would make it, I paid something like $1.50 to have him deliver a commemorative envelope. It seems to me that he was supposed to initial the envelope, or hand-cancel the stamp, or otherwise authenticate each letter he was carrying. I may be wrong, it's been a while; but I clearly remember how I felt when I heard that the junk was overdue. I felt annoyed and resentful. I wanted my commemorative envelope. And when, finally, there could be no doubt that the junk was lost at sea I felt I had been swindled. I was nominally sorry for the people on the junk and I spent a little time wondering what happened, but I could not get over feeling peevish that my envelope was not going to arrive. In fact I thought there might be a chance the junk would be found and the cargo rescued. I remember being uncomfortable with this attitude, nevertheless it was so; Halliburton's life, I could not deny, meant less to me than a letter he was carrying.

Now, having had some years to reflect upon it, I find that still I am not proud of my reaction; but I have concluded also that I am no more inhuman than most. A trifle, perhaps, if you insist. But this isn't the point. The point is that when Halliburton vanished I realized for the first time that certain people do not travel the way most of us travel; not only do they sometimes choose odd vehicles, they take dangerous and unusual trips for incomprehensible reasons.

I don't think I wondered why he wanted to cross the Pacific in a tiny boat. He did such things. He climbed the Matterhorn and swam the Hellespont and slept beside the Taj Mahal and so on. That was Richard Halliburton. It was why everybody, boys especially, knew his name. *The Royal Road to Romance* was one of our classics, along with *Kidnapped, White Fang, The Call of the Wild,* and some unforgettable epics by Zane Grey which I have forgotten. So his trip made sense; it was altogether logical that he would set out on an utterly insane voyage across the world's largest ocean in a boat designed for sailing up and down the coast.

He himself had no doubts. In a letter to his parents dated September 10, 1938, he wrote: "Dad, if I could talk to you about the junk trip, I'm sure you would lose all your hesitation over it. Never was an expedition so carefully worked out for safety measures. I've a wonderful captain and engine and engineer . . ."

Two weeks later he wrote: "The name? I chose that long ago—the *Sea Dragon.* On the day of launching, the prettiest Chinese girl whom I can find will break a bottle of rice wine on the *Sea Dragon's* nose. And as the junk slides down the ways we'll beat gongs and shoot off firecrackers, in proper Chinese fashion, to drive away the demons of storm and shipwreck . . . We'll leave China

early in January and reach Treasure Island—God willing
—the middle of March."

December 12, 1938: "I have complete faith in the captain and the engineer, and feel certain that we'll arrive
without the slightest mishap—except a lot of seasickness."

January 1, 1939: "I've lost none of my enthusiasm, and
none of my confidence."

In a newspaper article he described how the ship was
painted:

> The hull is a brilliant Chinese red, edged at the rail
> with bands of white and gold. The "glance" of the eyes
> is black. On either side of the poop a Chinese artist has
> painted a ferocious red and yellow dragon twenty feet
> long, not counting the curves! Our foresail has been
> dyed yellow; the mizzensail, vermilion . . . On the *Sea
> Dragon's* stern, the central section is brilliant with a
> huge painting of a phoenix—the Chinese good-luck
> bird.
>
> We'll be twelve aboard, all American: the captain,
> engineer, radioman, seven seamen including myself, a
> cook and a cabinboy. And because one solitary mascot
> would make the total thirteen, which superstitious sea-
> men regard with horror, we're taking along *two* mascots
> —a pair of white Chinese kittens. This means that the
> *Sea Dragon* will be responsible for twelve souls and
> (counting the cats) thirty lives.

In late January came the shakedown cruise. He noti-
fied his parents that there were a few defects to be cor-
rected, and that the junk sailed slowly, very deep in the
water. He did not sound concerned.

Early in February the *Sea Dragon* left Hong Kong.

Two days out during a storm one of the crewmen fell

down a hatch and broke an ankle. Another ruptured himself. Halliburton ordered the captain, John Welch, to return to port.

This is his account of the false start: "We turned up the coast of China, as the peak above Hongkong faded behind us, as a warm twilight came, as a huge moon rose out of the sea. The northeast monsoon, which, on nine days out of ten at this season would have been blowing a gale against us, had faded to a pleasant starboard breeze . . . The *Sea Dragon*, as we wanted it to be, as we had labored hard to make it, had turned into a fantasy of a ship, a picture of a dream-junk from some ancient Chinese painting, a poetry-ship devoid of weight and substance, gliding with bright-hued sails across a silver ocean to a magic land."

On the second day, however, things looked less poetic. Black clouds swirled overhead. Waves began to mount. The radio aerial was ripped loose. Everything not fastened down was tossed about. The messboy lay in his bunk half dead from seasickness. The auxiliary engine was turned on but because of heavy seas it was necessary to close the hatch, with the result that fumes from the newly painted tanks and bulkheads almost suffocated everybody.

"At six o'clock on the second afternoon we caught sight of a lighthouse on the China coast. At six o'clock in the morning the same lighthouse was still in the same place. We had not gained an inch."

Bearded, exhausted, and dejected, they sailed into Hong Kong harbor on the sixth day. The injured crew members were taken to a hospital, then another collapsed with appendicitis, and the messboy resigned, calling the trip six days of terror.

Halliburton decided to add a fin keel because the *Sea*

Dragon rolled heavily. He expected to have this done and new crew members signed up by the end of the week.

Two weeks later he was still in Hong Kong, exasperated but optimistic.

"Mother and Dad: One more—one last—goodbye letter. We sail, again, in a few hours—far more seaworthy than before. The delay has been heart breaking, but worth it in added safety. . . . All our leaks have been plugged, and the hull tarred. Our fin-keel will keep us from rolling —so we'll be dry, comfortable and even-keeled. . . . So goodbye again. I'll radio you every few days, so you can enjoy and follow the voyage with me. Think of it as wonderful sport, and not as something hazardous and foolish."

On March 5, 1939, he left Hong Kong.

Eight days out he radioed: 1200 MILES AT SEA ALLS WELL

On March 19 he sent word that they expected to reach Midway Island by April 5 and would not be stopping at Honolulu.

This message was heard on March 24: CAPTAIN JOHN WELCH OF THE SEADRAGON TO LINER PRESIDENT COOLIDGE SOUTHERLY GALES RAIN SQUALLS LEE RAIL UNDER WATER WET BUNKS HARDTACK BULLY BEEF HAVING WONDERFUL TIME WISH YOU WERE HERE INSTEAD OF ME

The next day Halliburton's parents were told that there had been no further radio contact. "Well," his mother said, "that's it. It's all over. It's the end."

Captain Charles Jokstad, master of the liner *President Pierce*, had inspected the *Sea Dragon* in Hong Kong at Halliburton's request. Jokstad said later, "I had the awful feeling that I would never see that young man again, and I urged him not to attempt the voyage. It is my guess that the rudder snapped off in a heavy following sea, the ship broached-to in the trough, the masts went out and she broke up—probably in minutes."

Halliburton seems to have been the last great traveler. Eventually somebody may circumnavigate the world in a canoe, but it won't be the same. Now and then an eccentric in a totally inappropriate vehicle does get across the Pacific, or the Atlantic, or survives some other formidable passage, but it reminds us more of Niagara Falls in a barrel than of that sensual urge which Anatole France called "un long désir."

A number of Victorian ladies were gripped by that urge. Isabella Bird Bishop. Marianne North. Fanny Bullock Workman. May French Sheldon. Kate Marsden. Mary Kingsley. Annie Taylor. To read of their adventures leaves one feeling incredulous and puny. To look at those nineteenth-century photographs—Isabella about to inspect a Chinese village, buttoned up to the neck and wearing a pith helmet, indomitable, serene, and dumpy, posing beside a tripod camera taller than herself—well, nobody who sees that picture is going to forget Isabella Bird Bishop. Or Fanny Bullock Workman high in the Himalayas, standing truculently beside an ice ax thrust into the snow, stoutly displaying a placard headlined VOTES FOR WOMEN. Kate Marsden en route to Siberia, dressed in a coat big enough for the Cardiff Giant. Mary Kingsley, looking remarkably like Dr. Livingstone, being poled across the Ogowé River in a dugout.

And those prodigious adventurers whose names we know, who couldn't rest because of that long desire. Magellan. Columbus. Marco Polo. Ibn Batuta. Hsüan-tsang. Captain Cook. There's no end to the list, of course, because gradually it descends from such legendary individuals to ourselves when, as children, obsessed by that same urge, we got permission to sleep in the backyard.

The first of these compulsive tourists about whom we know anything is a Greek from Marseilles, Massilia it was then called, by name Pytheas—a geographer and astronomer of no small reputation. If we reach back further, beyond Pytheas, we find just what we should expect: footsteps growing less and less distinct, often obliterated, so that we must settle for allusion, reference, and conjecture. We have no idea what half-mad transients passed through Europe or Africa or Asia 5,000 years ago, though there must have been a good many, and each presumably had a name and various in-laws, and worried about snakes and alligators and avalanches just as explorers worry about such matters today. Still, some awful anxiety kept those anonymous travelers traveling: there was always a mountain or a river in the distance.

We do know of a few generals who predate Pytheas, because their expeditions are documented; but they went where they went for obvious reasons. Besides, they had thousands of companions. It is the singular person, inexplicably drawn from familiar comforts toward a nebulous goal, lured often enough to death—it is he, or she, whose peregrinations can never be thoroughly understood, who is worth noticing.

In regard to Pytheas, scholars quibble about his route. And because his own account of the trip has been lost we can only reconstruct it from various sources: long-dead writers, some of whom were very nearly his contemporaries, while others depended in turn on previous authorities. That is to say, what you believe about his tremendous voyage depends on whom you've read.

This much does seem clear. He was born in Massilia not quite 400 years before Christ and was about fifty when he set out to visit the Tin Islands—the Cornish peninsula of Britain, which was thought to be a cluster of islands. Probably he was commissioned by a group of Massiliot businessmen, because in those days Carthage controlled the Straits of Gibraltar and thus controlled sea trade out-side the Mediterranean. The businessmen of Massilia, being businessmen, naturally wanted a piece of whatever might be outside—all of it, if possible. They knew about those misty isles to the north and the adjacent mainland, and knew that besides tin there was amber to be found along the coasts, and somewhere in that faraway land there must be gold. So it is thought that these merchants commissioned Pytheas to explore the situation, to find out what the British savages wanted and what they might give in exchange.

It would seem, therefore, that he undertook the trip for commercial reasons. But he was essentially a student of the natural world rather than an employee of the com-mercial world, and when you read his report—filtered though it is through other sensibilities—you can only con-clude that Pytheas, like Halliburton, left home mostly to see what he could see.

For example, he was curious about the tides, and the deep estuaries of Britain would be a wonderful place to study this phenomenon. He suspected that the moon, of all things, had something to do with this long ebb and flow, an idea that his countrymen found hilarious. And it is too bad we don't know how he felt about being mocked, whether it pained him or exasperated him, or whether he knew how to ignore fools. What he wanted to study in addition to the tides can only be surmised; he may have wanted to map the northern constellations, examine the flowers and fish and birds and beasts, listen to primitive music, dance the jig, and get a taste of British cooking. He was that sort.

His ship—if it was typical—would have been quite sea-worthy, about 400 or 500 tons and maybe 160 feet long, larger and safer than the *Santa María*.

As to the trip, if we accept the route proposed by some historians, he sailed more than 7,000 miles, which is farther than Columbus sailed. Just why Columbus should remain a bright legend while Pytheas has been forgotten by everybody except connoisseurs of the arcane is puzzling. Time, of course; Columbus is scarcely gone. But more important, nobody followed Pytheas to verify his account. The folks at home enjoying a balmy Mediterranean climate seem to have looked upon him as the fourteenth-century Venetians looked upon Marco Polo—charming fellow, marvelous dinner companion, but an outrageous liar. After all, who could imagine a land where there's no night, where the sun spins overhead like a weathercock? Or a frozen sea? Come now!

The lesson here, of course, is that you should not strain the credulity of your audience, even if what you say is true.

In any case, the book or narrative that Pytheas wrote was titled *On the Ocean* or *About the Ocean,* and it is thought that the manuscript survived for a number of centuries, crumbling to dust in a Massiliot library. Whatever happened, it's now gone, and we must depend on such estimable authors as Pliny, Diodorus, Strabo, Polybius, Timaeus, Solinus, et al. Like more recent scribes, these gentlemen had their passions and prejudices, and sometimes rearranged things closer to the heart's desire. Consequently, you are at liberty to believe or disbelieve.

So, let's begin:

Once upon a time, one fine day, Captain Pytheas sailed westward from Massilia toward the Pillars of Hercules, which we now call the Straits of Gibraltar . . .

Or, if you like, we might begin again:

One dark and stormy night Captain Pytheas started north up the Rhône along the ancient river route . . .

His destination, though, is not disputed; and whether he slipped the Carthaginian blockade at Gibraltar, or whether he sailed up the Rhône and subsequently down the Loire to the Atlantic is unimportant. By whatever route, he reached the southwestern tip of England where he introduced himself to the Cornish tin miners and found them quite hospitable.

From Cornwall he must have sailed north through the Irish Sea to Scotland—going ashore at a number of points, but just where and to what extent we don't know. In the missing manuscript he evidently wrote that he walked all over Britain, because Polybius refers sarcastically to such a claim. Whether he walked, picking up information in the pubs, or merely paused here and there along the coast, he did learn that the island's shape was loosely triangular. He gave measurements, much too large, for its three sides —825, 1,650, and 2,200 miles—and announced that its corners were Belerium, Cantium, and Orca.

He considered the natives altogether primitive: "simple in their habits, far removed from the cunning and knavishness of modern men." The country was thickly populated, he said, with many kings and other potentates and had a disagreeable climate, so we know beyond doubt that he was in England.

He may have visited Ireland. At least he saw it, because he noted its position, which enabled the Greek geographer Eratosthenes to pin Ireland to the map.

From Scotland he sailed on up to the Shetland Islands and perhaps to Thule—Ultima Thule—the end of the world. It was his account of this fearful place that provoked the bitterest arguments. Here, "at the time of the solstice, when the sun passes through the sign of the Crab, there is no night . . ."

Greek and Roman scholars quarreled about whether or

not Pytheas was lying; modern scholars in their wisdom quarrel not about his observations but about the location of Thule.

According to Strabo, who lifted the material from Polybius, who got it almost straight from the horse's mouth, Thule is the northernmost of the British Islands, six days' sail beyond the mainland, one day's sail from the frozen sea. And around Thule is neither sea nor air, but a mixture called "sea-lung" in which both are suspended. There is a little more information about Thule, but not much. The natives "thresh their grain indoors in large barns because the climate is dull and wet. They make bread, and those who have both grain and honey brew a drink from them. Northward by the frozen zone are few animals, which all are sickly; nor do cereals flourish, except millet, though there are wild fruits, vegetables, and roots."

The principal contenders for "Thule" are Norway and Iceland, with some attention paid to Greenland.

Norway would seem to be eliminated because, of course, it is not an island, nor does it lie to the north of England. But still, geography in those days included much guesswork. Pliny, for example, refers to Scandinavia as an island. And directions were vague because the compass had not been invented, so "north" might have meant "northeast." And Norway does extend to the land of the midnight sun. And off the upper coast a clammy sea fog develops. And in the south are bees to furnish honey for mead drinkers. Some authorities believe Pytheas reached the vicinity of Trondheim.

As for Iceland and Greenland, it is tempting to think of a Mediterranean ship approaching North America thirteen centuries before the Vikings. Here again, "north" could have meant "northwest." Also, there are wild bees in Iceland, and at that high latitude the sea fog forms.

Anyway, after visiting Thule—or sailing close to it—Pytheas headed south, probably down the east coast of Britain, crossed the channel, and followed the European coastline "beyond the Rhine to Scythia . . . as far as the river Tanais." This, too, is puzzling because Tanais is the old name for the Don—which flows nowhere near the Rhine. What he took to be the Tanais must have been the Elbe or the Vistula. If it was the Vistula he was the first Mediterranean sailor to enter the Baltic. And here he either saw or heard about, among other wonders, an island called Balcia or Basilia where amber is cast up by the spring tides—"an ejectum of the curdled sea."

Then, by land or water, he started home; and all things considered, it is both marvelous and astonishing that he saw Massilia again.

As to what became of Pytheas after his tremendous trip, nobody knows, except that he was ridiculed—which does happen to storytellers. Nor can we say just why he went on such a long and perilous voyage, nor why he felt a time had come to turn around.

The same is true of Hsüan-tsang, a scholarly Buddhist monk who set out from Liang-chou near the western end of the Great Wall during the Christian year 630. That is, Hsüan-tsang had a conscious purpose, just as the American did, and the Greek. But with him, as with them, we can sketch only what is visible. In his case, we know that he decided to visit India, the fountainhead of Buddhism, because he was troubled by imperfections and discrepancies among the sacred texts.

He is said to have been highly precocious; by the age of thirteen he could remember everything in a book after it had been read to him once. But it is more engaging to learn that he was "rosy as the evening mists and round as the rising moon, sweet as the odor of cinnamon . . ."

He grew up tall and handsome, instead of fat and dis-
gusting as we might expect, "with beautiful eyes and a
good complexion" and a rather stately manner. He was
twenty-eight when he started for India.

An imperial edict forbade leaving the country but he
went ahead, fortified by a dream. At the beginning of the
Gobi Desert his companions turned back so he continued
alone, without a map or a guide, following the caravan
route by bones and camel droppings.

Presently he saw a vast mirage—thousands of fur-clad
soldiers with glittering lances and shining banners. They
were mounted on richly caparisoned horses, sometimes at
an immense distance, then close at hand, changing, dis-
solving. At first he thought they were robbers, but because
they vanished whenever they approached he knew they
must be hallucinations, so he rode on.

At the first watchtower he was showered with arrows,
palpable arrows, from suspicious soldiers guarding the
frontier. Such a brusque greeting, though, did not distress
Hsüan-tsang; it merely convinced him that he should
make friends with the garrison, which he did.

Supplied with fresh water, food, and introductions to
officers at other forts, he continued his journey.

However, things did not go well. Having been warned
about the soldiers at one particular fort, he left the caravan route in order to avoid them and attempted to proceed by observing his shadow. He got lost, dropped the
water bag, and rode around in circles for five days.
Both he and his horse were almost dead when the horse
scented a pool of water. Greatly refreshed after a pause at
this oasis, Hsüan-tsang climbed into the saddle once more
and made it to Turfan where he encountered a new
problem. The king of Turfan asked him to remain as head
of the Buddhist Church. Hsüan-tsang declined, explaining

that he must visit the West "to seek interpretations of the
Scriptures not yet known outside India so that the sweet
dew of the expanded Law might also water the regions of
the East."

Then the king said: "The Ts'ung Ling Mountains may
fall down, but not my purpose."

Hsüan-tsang again declined. The king insisted. Hsüan-
tsang replied that if he were not allowed to leave Turfan
he would starve himself to death, and to prove he meant
it he stopped eating.

So, after a while, equipped with a new water bag, food,
money for expenses, various gifts, an escort of soldiers,
and a letter introducing him to Yeh-hu, khan of the western Turks, Hsüan-tsang rode on.

Yeh-hu, wearing a green silk robe, greeted him respectfully. The khan's loose hair was bound with a silk ribbon
ten feet long that trailed behind him, and he was surrounded by 200 officers in brocaded robes. On either side
were his troops armed with lances and bows, mounted on
camels and horses, so many that nobody could tell where
they ended. He advised Hsüan-tsang not to go to India,
saying it was very hot and the people had no manners,
but the monk could not be dissuaded.

On to Samarkand, then south to Balkh where he saw a
washbasin used by Buddha, one of Buddha's teeth—yellow-
ish white, pure, and shining—and the Enlightened One's
sweeping brush, its handle set with gems.

Over the snowy Hindu Kush to Bamiyan with its ten
monasteries. By way of the Khyber Pass to Gandhara.
Across the Indus gorges. The roads were dangerous, he
said, the valleys gloomy. "Sometimes one had to cross on
rope bridges, sometimes by clinging to chains." But there
were memorable places to visit, such as a stupa marking
the spot where Buddha pierced his body with a bamboo

splinter in order to nourish an exhausted tiger with his blood. The plants around this stupa are blood red, said Hsüan-tsang, and the earth is full of prickly spikes. "Without asking whether we believe the tale or not, it is a piteous one."

On to Kashmir, whose citizens he found "light and frivolous, weak and pusillanimous."

While sailing down the Ganges he was captured by river pirates who decided to sacrifice him to Durga. Hsüan-tsang requested a period of meditation before being sacrificed in order that he might enter Nirvana with a calm and joyous mind. The pirates did not find this unreasonable, but while they sat around waiting for him to conclude his meditations a storm blew up, smashing trees and sinking boats. The terrified pirates fell at his feet begging forgiveness.

Hsüan-tsang forgave them and moved on to Benares where he met a saintly instructor. He spent a year in this city, visiting holy sites and studying the philosophy of Idealism.

Next he traveled to Bengal—"a low and humid land with plentiful grain." Then it occurred to him that perhaps he should visit Ceylon; but upon reaching southern India he heard reports of famine and civil war, so he turned around. Having come down the east coast, he went up the west coast through the Gujerat peninsula where he admired the imported Persian carpets and heard of a country to the west called Fo-lin—probably Babylon.

He now began to think of going home, although there was no great hurry.

He accepted an invitation to visit King Kumara of Assam, and while he was there his presence was requested by the omnipotent lord of northern India, King Harsha. Kumara responded that he would sooner send his own head to Harsha's court than his revered guest; but then, horrified by what he had said, Kumara tried to apologize by escorting the monk to Harsha's court in extravagant style. Twenty thousand elephants were mobilized and thirty thousand boats sailed up the Ganges.

King Harsha flung himself to the ground in front of Hsüan-tsang, scattered flowers at his feet, and recited poems in his honor.

What happened next is a bit confused, but Harsha seems to have arranged a public debate lasting eighteen days, featuring the wisdom of Hsüan-tsang against all comers. Hsüan-tsang won, perhaps because Harsha did not permit any serious rebuttals. This did not go over so well with some of the contestants and it is said they plotted to kill the wandering scholar.

It was now the year 643. Rejecting all gifts, except a coat of pressed buffalo down which would protect him from the rain, Hsüan-tsang set off for the Punjab.

In 644 he again crossed the Hindu Kush and spent a month visiting the governor of Badakshan. The governor provided an escort to the high Pamir plains. "The cold is glacial," said Hsüan-tsang, "the wind is furious. Snow falls throughout spring and summer. Fruit will not grow here. Trees are few. There is a lake filled with frogs in this desolate valley; it is situated at the center of the world on a plateau of stupendous height."

Descending from the Pamir, he was attacked by thieves in the Tangitar Gorge but managed to escape with most of the manuscripts, statuary, and Buddhist relics he had collected. After that he seems to have made good time.

At Khotan he dispatched a letter to the emperor, describing his travels and much of what he had learned and asking permission to enter China. Seven months later the emperor replied: "When I heard that you who had gone to distant lands to study Buddhism and to seek for religious texts was now returning, I was delighted. I pray you come quickly . . ."

Hsüan-tsang was given a magnificent official reception and then settled down at the Monastery of Extensive Happiness, to which he bequeathed twenty pony-loads of treasure including 150 tiny particles of Buddha's flesh, a variety of icons, and 657 volumes of Scripture. It is believed that he lived peacefully ever after, on close terms with the emperor, who sometimes consulted him about the strange countries he had visited and the rulers he had met. Only one thing grieved him: while fording the Indus he had lost some manuscripts and his collection of flower seeds.

Abu Abdullah Mohammed, better known as Ibn Batuta, that relentless explorer of the Arab world, left home on the fourteenth of June, 1325. Unlike Hsüan-tsang, Ibn Batuta knew precisely where he was going: "I left Tangier, my birthplace, one Thursday, the second day of the month of God, Rajab the Unparalleled . . . with the intention of making a pilgrimage to the Holy House and to the Tomb of the Prophet, on Whom be God's richest blessing and peace. I departed alone, with no companion to delight me, nor with any caravan, my inspiration arising from a limitless desire . . ."

Across North Africa from Tangier to Mecca is approximately 3,000 miles, but Ibn Batuta was young—twenty-one or so. Time hardly mattered.

In Cairo he took a boat up the Nile, expecting to be ferried over the Red Sea at Aidhab, but a war was in progress so he returned to Cairo, spent a while touring Syria, and then approached the holy cities from the north.

After seeing Medina—where he touched a fragment of the palm tree under which Mohammed stood while preaching—he joined a caravan to Mecca. There he walked seven times around the cubical temple as prescribed and kissed the sacred meteorite—a ruby fallen from Heaven that had turned black because of human sin. These obligations performed, Ibn Batuta decided to take a trip. He crossed Arabia to the mouth of the Euphrates, paralleled the Tigris upstream past Baghdad into Turkey, and returned to Mecca where he spent the next three years studying the Koran.

In 1330, anxious to have a look at East Africa, he went sailing down the Red Sea. Somehow—possibly by trading —he had acquired money enough to travel a la mode, with a clutch of wives, servants, and slaves, as well as several children of his own. The party stopped at Aden, crossed the equator and continued south to Mombasa and Kilwa, turned around and sailed through the Indian Ocean to Oman and up the Persian Gulf. Then, hungry for spiritual nourishment, Ibn Batuta made a third pilgrimage to Mecca.

Having steeped himself further in Holy Writ he was off again: slaves, wives, children and baggage. He thought it might be worthwhile to visit Sultan Mohammed ibn Tughlaq who lived in India and who was renowned for his hospitality to learned travelers.

Apparently he tried to get a ship for India but could not find anything suitable, so he set off by land in the opposite direction—first to Egypt, then up the eastern littoral of the Mediterranean, pausing at Ephesus where he bought an attractive Greek slave girl for twenty dinars.

Across the Black Sea to the Ukraine, southwest to Constantinople—a rather lengthy side excursion—and then, having remembered that India was the other way, he continued east as far as the Volga. Here, instead of angling south, he went several hundred miles up the ice-bound river, evidently planning some sort of business with the fur traders, but whatever he had in mind did not work out.

Around the top of the Caspian and Aral seas, down to Samarkand, and so to the Indus, bordering the promised land. That was in September 1333.

Having received an invitation from Sultan Tughlaq, whom he describes as "very fond of bestowing gifts and shedding blood," Batuta led his merry band to Delhi. At this time Delhi was the largest Moslem city in the East, though sparsely populated when he arrived because the sultan had taken a dislike to the citizens and ordered most of them to move out. Those who objected, or tried to hide, were killed. Among these was a cripple who was hurled from a mangonel—a military device ordinarily used for catapulting stones—and a blind man whom the sultan ordered to be dragged from Delhi to Dawlatabad. The blind man fell apart on the road and only one leg reached his new home.

Tughlaq liked Ibn Batuta, appointing him guardian of the mausoleum of Sultan Qutb-ad-Din at a salary of 12,000 dinars per annum, with another 12,000 for immediate expenses, an estate with an income of about the same amount, and a splendid horse.

Batuta took the job seriously. He spent eight years at Tughlaq's court, although his career and his life very nearly were cut short when he was suspected of participating in a conspiracy. Four slaves were sent to watch him, which customarily meant that the watchee was doomed. "The first day I was watched like this was a Friday," Batuta writes. "It pleased God on High to allow me to speak these words: 'God is our help and Sovereign Lord!' On that Friday I pronounced these words 33,000 times."

Miraculously restored to grace, Batuta was told by his capricious employer to lead an embassy to the emperor of China. In the summer of 1342 they started out: fifteen diplomats accompanied by women and servants, Ibn Batuta with his personal entourage—all protected by 1,000 cavalrymen and a stout company of foot soldiers. But they met some rebels, there was a fight, Batuta was captured, and once again he came very near to closing the Koran permanently.

This fight disrupted the expedition so much that historians do not agree on what happened. Some say it continued on its way, others think the cavalcade retreated to Delhi where Tughlaq overhauled it and started his ambassadors off a second time with Batuta still in command. How Batuta escaped from the rebels is not clear. At any rate, Tughlaq's diplomats planned to reach China by sea, because we next hear of them in the Gulf of Cambay, then at Goa and Calicut.

What happened at Calicut also is disputed. If we believe one account, which sounds too neat, a storm blew up, sinking the boats and drowning everybody except our hero who chanced to be ashore praying in a mosque. Another account also mentions drowning, so probably there was a disastrous storm, but in addition there seems to have been a massive desertion which left Batuta by himself on the Calicut beach.

He next turns up in the Maldive Islands, again doing very nicely. Now he is a kazi, a judge, and has married four new wives including a daughter of the vizier. You can't keep a good man down. Batuta, though, disclaims credit. Says he: "It is not difficult to get married in these islands." And here, as at Delhi, he is conscientious about his work, attempting to drive the agnostic islanders to the mosque with a whip, trying to get the Maldive ladies to wear some clothes. At last the vizier began looking at him suspiciously so he decided the time had come to resume traveling.

He booked passage for himself and one wife to the Indian mainland, but the ship was blown off course and they landed in Ceylon. There he saw on the forehead of a white elephant "seven rubies larger than hen's eggs. And at the palace of Sultan Airi Sakarvati I saw a spoon made of precious stone as large as the palm of a hand and filled with oil of aloes. At this I marveled . . ." He marveled further at Mount Sarandib, which he thought must be one of the highest peaks in the world, and said he had been able to see it nine days before the ship reached port. On a black rock of this mountain, he said, one could see the footprint of our venerable father Adam, eleven spans in length, which had been there since time immemorial.

When he left Ceylon the sultan gave him a string of jewels, but no sooner had he waved good-bye from the deck of a ship taking him to the Coromandel Coast than he was seized by pirates who took everything he owned, stripped him, and dumped him on the opposite side of the Indian peninsula without a rupee. If his adventures had not been documented, making allowances for gaps here and there, nobody would believe the story; reading what happened to him is like reading about Sinbad.

Well, off he went again to the Maldives, ingratiated himself as usual, and presently set out for Bengal to visit a notable saint. Then to Sumatra—or perhaps Java—where an old friend from Delhi introduced him at court and where he was astonished to see dancing horses. When he left this island, whichever it was, he had been presented with a fully equipped junk. After a boring sea voyage he landed in southern China and journeyed north to Peking. The Chinese concern for travelers impressed him; he found the country safe and well regulated. But the idolatry troubled him.

He started home to the land of true believers and endured his customary afflictions—getting lost at sea, storms, etc. Safe at last in the Moslem world he could not bypass Mecca, lodestone of his existence, and for the fourth time he paid his respects to the Prophet's birthplace.

From Alexandria he got a ship to Sardinia. From there he sailed to Algeria and continued overland to Morocco, arriving in November of 1349. He had been away twenty-four years.

After a few months he became restless. There was a war going on in Spain and he thought he would like to participate, or at least see it, so he crossed the Straits of Gibraltar, barely escaped being caught by Christian soldiers, and spent a while wandering around Andalusia.

Two years later the sultan of Morocco, who wished to know more about the empires in the south, instructed him to visit the kingdom of Mali. This trip took him as far into Africa as the Niger. He was in Timbuktu for seven months, in Gao for another month. He disliked that part of Africa, partly because the blacks were infidels, but also because they did not give him suitable presents. From the ruler of Mali he got "three cakes of bread, some beef fried in oil, and a calabash of sour curds." He had been expecting money, luxurious robes, and a title. But of course there were wondrous sights. Hippos bathing in the Niger dumfounded him; he had never seen such beasts and thought they must be elephants.

At Tagadda he received a message from his employer asking him to return to the sublime capital of Morocco. He seems reluctant to leave because of the extraordinary Tuareg women: "most perfect in beauty, most shapely in figure, of a pure white color and very stout." However, the sultan's wish was Ibn Batuta's command; obediently he joined a caravan that included 600 female slaves, and upon arriving at Fez he kissed the sultan's hand and "settled beneath the wing of his bounty." It was here that he dictated his book, modestly titled *Travels in Asia and Africa*, to Ibn Juzayy, the court secretary.

Altogether he must have gone at least 75,000 miles, most of it by land, which makes the journey of Marco Polo look like a stroll around the block. Nobody else, with the single exception of Magellan—who was aboard ship —traveled such a distance until the nineteenth century.

Africa has perhaps never welcomed two more disparate personalities than Ibn Batuta and Mary Kingsley. Everything imaginable separates them—religion, nationality, sex, race, cultural tradition, five centuries—yet you cannot help feeling that if their caravans had met they would have become great friends.

Kingsley, Bishop, Taylor, Marsden, North, and those other Victorian ladies—there is something improbable about them all. They are the most unlikely travelers the world has ever known. Halliburton astonishes us, yet he is not surprising; we can be amazed at his recklessness while admitting that reckless young men are nothing new. And although we cannot be sure of much about faraway individuals such as Pytheas, we are able to accept them. Or Hsüan-tsang—at least as remote to a twentieth-century Westerner—we cannot comprehend a medieval Chinese mystic riding through the Gobi and over the Himalayas, and we visualize him only approximately as he was in life, transfixed on the fanciful ocher and yellow background of an ancient Chinese painting in his sandals and silk robe and bamboo backpack. We cannot understand him, nevertheless we believe in him. He may be extraordinary, but he is not unreal. Or that most preposterous and indefatigable wanderer Ibn Batuta, charming one potentate after another, surviving typhoons, psychotic employers, wars and pirates, acquiring so many wives and concubines that you would think he was eating popcorn. He, too, is a storybook personality that we accept.

But the mind just cannot absorb Isabella Bird Bishop at the apex of her fame—shaped like a penguin, holding court in gold-embroidered slippers and a petticoat decorated with gold and silver Japanese wheels, with a royal ribbon and order across her shoulders which had been presented to her by the king of the Sandwich Islands. No, we say. No, no, I'll go along with Ibn Batuta or that Chinese whose name I can't remember, but this woman is too much.

Then there is May French Sheldon on the way to Kilimanjaro in a blonde wig, carrying a ceremonial sword, wearing a rhinestone-studded gown and a dozen Cleopatra bracelets. No. No, she must be the creation of a mad playwright.

They give the impression of being mildly batty, these upright, energetic, innocent, valorous, polite, intelligent, prim, and condescending British females in long skirts, carrying parasols, being conveyed across some of the roughest terrain on earth in wooden carts, stagecoaches, elephant howdahs, coal boats, dugouts, and not infrequently clinging like a huge black moth to the back of a coolie who must have thought he had been engaged by a creature from a different universe. "I am something like the famous Doge at the Court of Louis XIV," wrote Mary Crawford, "and may declare that I see no wonder in this shrubbery equal to seeing myself in it."

So we come upon Mary Kingsley: naturalist, ethnologist, sailor, scholar, guest of cannibals and champion of lost causes. Or, as she refers to herself: "the voyager."

She was born in 1862 and for thirty years lived in a state of suffocating restriction, tight even by Victorian norms. Then both of her parents died and all at once her life made no sense; suddenly she had nobody to care for. Her father had been an anthropologist who traveled quite a bit, but he had never gone to Africa; therefore, in accordance with the Byzantine laws of human behavior, Mary realized that she must go to Africa. At least that's how it appears underneath the green rust of time. But what seems mildly comic from a distance is very often not so at all, particularly to the people involved. Mary herself could hardly have been more despondent: "Dead tired and feeling no one had need of me any more," she wrote to a friend, ". . . I went down to West Africa to die."

However morbid her condition at this point, Mary Kingsley was much too energetic to expire like the pale heroine of a novel. She resolved to study the Africans, to collect zoological specimens, and come home to enlighten her countrymen about the Dark Continent.

Having decided it would be best to represent herself as a trader, she laid in a supply of tobacco, fishhooks, cloth, and such other British produce as might appeal to the locals, after which she embarked for the Congo on a Liverpool cargo boat.

Being unusually bright and observant, she quickly learned about navigation, about stowing cargo and how to manage a crew. Later, after more experience aboard other boats, she would be ready to argue seamanship with grizzled old mariners: "I say you can go across Forcados Bar drawing eighteen feet . . . I have taken vessels of 2,000 tons across that Bar and up the Forcados creeks . . ."

She landed at Saint Paul de Loana, visited the Fjort tribe along the Congo, then marched and paddled in a northerly direction until she emerged at the old city of Calabar. In order to reassure everybody when she materialized from the brush at some remote factory or trading post on the river she would call out: "It's only me!"

She returned to England with several crates of specimens, an ability to speak the traders' lingua franca, and
enough anthropological knowledge to address the London
Society of Medicine for Women. Her lecture was titled
"Therapeutics from the point of view of an African witch
doctor."

In December of 1894 she was off again, this time to
southern Nigeria where she spent five months studying
fish, plants, beasts, the native Bubis, and the immigrant
Spaniards and Portuguese.

She liked mangrove swamps. She would paddle around
for hours examining everything, stung by flies and threatened by crocodiles: "On one occasion a mighty Silurian,
as the *Daily Telegraph* would call him, chose to get his
front paws over the stern of my canoe and endeavoured to
improve our acquaintance. I had to retire to the bows to
keep the balance upright, and fetch him a clip on the
snout with a paddle . . ."

In the spring of 1895 she set out for the Ogowé River in
the French Congo. The forest enchanted her. "It is as full
of life and beauty and passion as any symphony Beetho-
ven ever wrote: the parts are changing, interweaving,
and returning . . . you hardly see anything but the vast
column-like grey tree stems in their countless thousands
around you, and the sparsely vegetated ground beneath.
But day by day, as you get trained to your surroundings,
you see more and more, and a whole world grows up
gradually out of the gloom before your eyes."

To the north lay a belt of forest inhabited by the Fans,
a tribe known to eat human flesh not merely on special
occasions but rather often. She had met some of them,
she admired their virility and thought she should know
more about them. So, in July, accompanied by an Igalwa
interpreter and four nervous Ajumba armed with flint-
locks, she started upriver to say hello to the cannibals.

They met the Fans on an island in Lake Ncovi: "I must say that never—even in a picture-book—have I seen such a set of wild wicked-looking savages as those we faced this night, and with whom it was touch-and-go for twenty of the longest minutes I have ever lived."

For whatever reason, Mary and her edible friends were invited to stay overnight at the village; and there, in a filthy hut, with a crude wooden bench for a bed, dressed in a long black English skirt, high-necked blouse, cummerbund, and closely fitted hat, surrounded by cannibals—having no doubt reassured them by exclaiming "It's only me!"—there she made herself at home and insisted on a cup of tea. Apparently she did not consider this unusual. Quite the opposite. "We each recognized we belonged to that same section of the human race with whom it is better to drink than to fight. We knew we would each have killed the other, if sufficient inducement were offered, and so we took a certain amount of care that the inducement should not arise."

The next afternoon while marching through the jungle she dropped into a game pit, the bottom of which had been furnished with sharpened stakes. "It is at these times," she observes, "you realize the blessing of a good thick skirt. Had I paid heed to the advice of many people in England, who ought to have known better, and did not do it themselves, and adopted masculine garments, I should have been spiked to the bone and done for."

After being hoisted out of the pit by her crew she continued along the trail. Suddenly one of the Ajumba dropped from view with a despairing shriek. He, in turn, was liberated and his wounds bound up with green leaves —"for he, not having a skirt, had got a good deal frayed at the edges on those spikes."

At the village of Efoua they were again welcomed and invited to stay over. During the night she awoke because of an odd stench and discovered a bag of curiosities: a shriveled human hand, a few toes, some eyes and some ears, all of which she emptied into her hat so as to lose none of them, and registered in her notebook the fact that these particular Fans kept mementos of their victims.

Approaching another village, she learned that the inhabitants were killing strangers immediately and inquiring about them afterward. For the first time she may have felt unequal to dealing with Africa. She led her men off the trail, intending to avoid the village, which she did, but ended up in a mangrove swamp. Just in time she realized that the swamp was tidal—a long arm of the Gaboon estuary—and the tide was rising. They all turned and scrambled frantically through the muck for more than an hour before escaping to a hillside.

After that things got easier. Oh, there were little inconveniences. Other swamps, for instance, through which they waded up to their chins in the reeking water: "we got horribly infested with leeches, having a frill of them round our necks like astrakhan collars, and our hands covered with them when we came out." But these were nothing compared to the rewards of travel.

She sailed down the Rembwé River in a canoe with a sail made from an old bed quilt—the canoe being the property of a trader named Obanjo who preferred to be called "Captain Johnson"—and she would later commemorate this trip: "Much as I have enjoyed life in Africa, I do not think I ever enjoyed it to the full as I did on those nights dropping down the Rembwé. The great, black, winding river with a pathway in its midst of frosted silver where the moonlight struck it; on each side the ink-black mangrove walls, and above them the band of star and moonlit heavens that the walls of mangrove allowed us to see. Forward rose the form of our sail, idealized from bed-sheetdom to glory; and the little red glow of our cooking fire gave a single note of warm colour to the cold light of the moon . . ."

Once more in civilization, sailing across Corisco Bay on a missionary's boat named the *Lafayette*, she sounds discontented by so much propriety: "I find I am expected to sit surrounded by a rim of alligator pears and bananas, as though I were some kind of joint garnished for table."

Homeward bound, she stopped in the Cameroons to climb West Africa's highest peak, Mungo Mah Lobeh, by its most difficult side. The rain was like a waterfall, there were rivers to ford, and always the mud and flies and thorns and more genuine threats; but Mary was determined to climb the mountain, although just as determined to do nothing unbefitting an English lady. With mud-caked skirts, scratched and bitten until her face and hands were bloody, she approached a trading station operated by a German; but instead of hurrying toward it she stopped to wash. After all, one should not appear untidy in front of a strange man. Even so, the German was appalled by what came marching out of the brush. He offered her a bath—an offer she declined because, as she asks rhetorically, how could she be expected to bathe in a house with inadequate shutters? Men! she laments. Men can be so trying!

And in London she refused to ride on a bus because it seemed improper. And she disapproved of the bicycle.

Her book, *Travels in West Africa*, was published in 1896, but it did not begin to tell the full story of her passionate affair with the Dark Continent. She omitted some of her most implausible adventures because she did not think anybody would believe what had happened, such as the time she found herself on a tight little island with a hippopotamus and finally persuaded the monster to leave by poking it with her umbrella. Or the time she traded several of her blouses to a naked Fan who wore "*nothing else but red paint and a bunch of leopard tails.*" Or was saved from a gorilla's embrace by a lucky shot. And she almost neglected to tell about the leopard which she released from a trap because the animal was beating itself to death against the bars—and the creature, when it had been freed, stood looking at her in bewilderment until she stamped her foot and shouted, "Go home, you fool!"

And this same woman perceived, when British officialdom could not, that African society was as meticulously structured as European society; and that missionaries were doing more harm than good; and that traders were not villainous swindlers taking advantage of childlike natives; and that taxing a man's property, such as his hut, outraged the African's sense of justice. And being the woman she was, she let it be known what she thought. And the British government, being the government it then was, and is now—which is to say, a government not much different from others of that era, or of this—the British government debated her ideas and then, of course, did nothing. After all, a government is less easy to bestir than a hippopotamus.

The British Museum, though, welcomed her and studied the specimens she had collected and named three varieties of fish after her.

She was eager to return to Africa. There were so many swamps to be investigated, so many insects, lizards, turtles, crocodiles, and leopards to examine, so many cannibals to whom she had not yet introduced herself. You can almost see her emerging cheerfully from the bush. "Hello there! Hello? I say, is no one at home?"

She wanted very much to visit the river country near Lake Chad, but England had stumbled into the Boer War so she volunteered for nursing service. The government sent her to a place called Simonstown where there was an epidemic. Two months later she died of enteric fever. She was thirty-eight. The year was 1900, the year Richard Halliburton was born. And, like Halliburton, Mary Kingsley was buried at sea.

2

The Aztec
Treasure House

Near the end of the nineteenth century a certain William Niven is known to have traveled through the Middle Balsas River region of Mexico, not far from the Pacific coast; and a diary he kept, dated 1896, now belongs to the American Museum of Natural History in New York. But more interesting than the diary is a baked clay figure somewhat less than six inches tall which Niven claimed to have bought in the vicinity of Zumpango del Rio and which, in 1903, he sold to the Peabody Museum of Harvard. This figure represents a seated personage—possibly a man, although it's hard to tell—wearing a skirt and a cape. At that time the figure did not seem to be related to any other ceramics discovered in the area, or to anything found anyplace else in Mexico. Because of this, or in spite of it, Mr. Niven's irregular artifact did not get much attention.

Seventy years later a few stone and ceramic items with similar characteristics, reputedly from the same area, were shown to an expert on pre-Columbian art, Carlo Gay, who concluded that they belonged to the Olmec tradition and that quite probably they were older than any previously known Olmec objects.

Now it should be explained that these people, whatever they may have called themselves, who have been labeled Olmecs—a term derived from an Aztec word *olméca*, meaning those from the land of rubber, from the southern Gulf coast where chico zapate trees provide the material for chewing gum—these Olmec people created the first high civilization of Mexico, dating so far back that the sixteenth-century Mayans encountered by Cortés seem almost as close to us in time as the Vietnam War. The Mayans, as just about everybody knows, developed one of the most sophisticated societies of the New World: they were accomplished architects, they studied the motions of the planets, they knew how to communicate ideas through picture writing, their calendar was quite accurate, and so forth. But what is not commonly known is that the Mayans inherited much of their culture from the Olmecs.

And what is utterly unknown at present, even to professional anthropologists, is where these people came from; because the great Olmec centers of La Venta, San Lorenzo, Cerro de las Mesas, and Tres Zapotes where the huge helmeted basalt heads were discovered, and the jade carvings, and the famous "wrestler" or "pelota player" which is now in the Mexico City museum—not one of these centers shows any sign of evolution. It is as though the Olmec culture arrived completely formed in the land of the chewing-gum tree, as though it had been magically transported from another country. Indeed there is speculation that it may have originated in the Orient and that these people crossed the Pacific several thousand years ago. There are reasons for thinking so.

The early Chinese, for example, painted their funerary

jades red; so did some early Mexicans. Both observed the custom of placing a small object, frequently a jade bead, in the mouth of the corpse. Parcheesi, which originated in Asia, is almost identical to the Mexican game of patolli. Tripod bowls unearthed at Teotihuacán near Mexico City, although made of clay, can hardly be distinguished stylistically from ancient Chinese bronze vessels. The lotus motif, occurring throughout Asia and Indochina, was used by the Mayans; furthermore, in both Asia and America the underground rootlike stem of the lotus, the rhizome, formed the basic element of this motif. The volador game—in which a man at the end of a long rope goes flying around a pole—this mad spectacle occurs on both sides of the Pacific. Then there are very similar conceptions of Hell and the punishments that await us. Alfresco mural painting. Lacquer. Identical musical instruments. Pineapple-shaped mace heads. The list of similarities goes on. How much can be attributed to coincidence?

Still, there are persuasive arguments against this theory, which is why the matter has not yet been decided.

As for myself, I once saw a Mexican woman who, if she had lived centuries earlier, might have been the model for one of those gigantic basalt Olmec heads. She must have been a descendant of those people, she could not have been anything else, and there was nothing Chinese about her. She looked like what she was, a Mexican Indian woman of Jalapa. So, as far as I am concerned, that woman by herself refutes the theory of Asiatic migrants disembarking on the Pacific coast of Mexico. Only now and then, usually while comparing ancient pottery or jade carvings, do I have doubts.

Most authorities, I am pleased to say, agree with me. That is, although they do not yet know where the Olmecs originated they reject the idea of a Pacific crossing. They suspect that the culture developed in one of two places, either in the swampy miasmic Gulf coast where it flourished and degenerated and disappeared, or 500 miles west among the ravines of Oaxaca and on the rocky Guerrero slopes.

Carlo Gay, accompanied by the curator of primitive art at Princeton, visited Guerrero in 1970. They went back twice the following year. As a result of their investigation it became known that several burial sites near the village of Xochipala had yielded a variety of stone and clay vessels and figurines which undoubtedly belong to the Olmec formative period. Ritual implements. Incised bowls. A frog. Ceramic rodents. The head of a serpent. A pyrite mirror. Earspools and other ornamental accessories. And, of course, representations of people. So far the Xochipala graves have given up more than 100 small baked clay figures of men, women, and children.

Tentatively, because these statuettes are unique and therefore disputable, they have been classified as Early, Middle, and Late Xochipala. The stylistic sequence moves from vivid naturalization to rigid formalism—a record of the course of their civilization. Of theirs, to be sure, just as it is a record of all civilizations.

The piece brought back by William Niven, the first example of Xochipala Olmec art to be identified, belongs to the earliest period—which probably is coincidence. At any event it reveals most of the characteristics: an assured portraitlike quality, perfect body rhythm, acute comprehension of anatomy, and a delicate heavy fleshiness which has not been vulgarized by exaggeration. The eyeballs are fully modeled, the pupils picked out. The hair has been parted in the center and carried over the ears. The hands and feet are finely worked. There can be no doubt that this was a person—not a god or goddess whose function and power we will never understand—not a symbol of humanity but a representative of it who lived in the area at that time, who sat cross-legged in the shade of a tree or in some thatched-roof hut while one of his neighbors manipulated the dark clay with a little stick, paused to stare, and tried again and then again in order to get the mouth just right, and the thrust of the nose, and the contour of the cheek, all for the sake of true expression.

Gradually, because the transition was not abrupt, nor even marked—indeed a "transition" exists merely because we say it does—Early gave way to Middle. Less attention is paid to anatomy. Symbolism begins to replace naturalism. The naked or almost naked people of a previous century now are fashionably clothed in ankle-length garments adorned with leaves; they wear kilts, necklaces, and meaningful discs; and sometimes a ritualistic uniform consisting of boots, loincloth, and helmet, which anthropologists think may have been the prescribed outfit for ballplayers. Then there are dancers, and grotesque two-faced people who must have been senators, and a variety of others. But none are individuals; they appear to be only the embodiment of a particular condition or activity.

Toward the end, like the late Etruscans, as if somehow they could sense the future, the Xochipala artists lose the creative impulse that carried their predecessors to such a high plateau. They resort to stereotypes. They do not dare to invent, they do not imagine. They produce coarse figures with few details, with conventionalized features: an oval welt instead of a mouth, flaplike ears, clumsily defined hair, the tool marks showing—as though they were exhausted or discouraged, and scrupulous craftsmanship was not worth the effort. Significantly, the hands quite often are closed, no longer receptive to the stimulus of life.

One of these Xochipala figurines, an early one, the careful portrait of an adolescent who looks rather Slavic, with a sensual mouth and meticulously combed hair ending in a queue, wearing a necklace and a loincloth, sits on top of my bookcase. Whether the figure is male or female, I don't know. At times the Olmecs ignored sexual features. Considered objectively—considering the resolute, authoritative pose—this calm determined personage suggests masculinity and therefore should be referred to as "he." But out of my own predilection, and because the model just might have been a girl, I think of it as female.

She has been atop my bookcase for three or four years, seated cross-legged in a dignified Olmec pose, her solid little hands balanced on her plump knees and her fine Tartar head slightly lifted, almost in the lotus position—reminding me once again that in spite of all objections there is something pervasively Oriental about the Olmecs. I look at her every now and then.

Once upon a time her hair must have been orange; the elaborate clay coiffure has a definite tint, and through a magnifying glass the color becomes obvious. Her body, too, could have been painted. I suspect it was. There seems to be a faint bluish white residue. Her right foot is missing, along with both thumbs and several fingertips. Her lower lip has been chipped, and her torso is afflicted with microscopic growths, stains, spidery cracks, and scratches. Then there are the calcium deposits, which Carlo Gay describes as typical of prehistoric ceramic sculpture found in this area. The figure must have been underground quite a while, judging by the condition of the surface, the calcium, and the root traces wandering like uncertain white worm trails in all directions.

Roots, provided they are large enough, given time enough, will crush whatever they grasp—which partly explains why most of the classic Greek statues are damaged. If roots can decapitate marble gods and pry temples apart, what they can do to a delicate clay bowl or a lady is not hard to imagine.

Innumerable root traces coil around the body of my Xochipala. Some are as thick as a string, which might not sound threatening, but the dealer from whom I bought the figure told me he was surprised that it had not been totally destroyed. Even so, the head and limbs were broken off. Now everything has been glued together in the original position; and all that's missing, except for a few flakes and chips, are the parts mentioned—thumbs, fingertips, and the right foot. Thumbs and fingertips would be easy to overlook, but I'm puzzled about the foot. How could it have been overlooked when the fragments were collected?

Anyway, that's how she appears these days with her coppery orange hair and absent foot—an undeniable presence with her slim, breastless torso on which two clearly raised little nipples cast tiny shadows, and her half-open hands resting on extraordinarily full thighs, sensuously round and thick, and her head just perceptibly lifted as though something or somebody, possibly myself, might be obstructing the view. She hasn't moved for quite a while, unless you count the infinitely slow dislocation caused by roots.

She must have been buried for at least a century, maybe two, when Queen Nefertiti was born. She had been buried more than a thousand years when Pericles ruled Athens. She was seated majestically in the rocky Guerrero soil, perhaps still upright, for 2,000 years when Charlemagne crossed the Pyrenees. Grasped by the tendrils of shrubs and trees that sprouted and grew and ultimately died and decayed and vanished, leaving no proof of their existence except lime white squiggles on the dark burnt clay, she had been there another eight centuries when Cortés led his clanking sweating glittering horsemen over the causeway into the shrill feathered pageantry of Tenochtitlán. And it is for this reason, I think, that whenever I pause at the bookcase to study her for a few moments I never say anything.

I described this little Xochipala figure to a sculptor. I mentioned the clay pellets that make up the necklace, I talked about the precise treatment of the eyes, the subtly raised brows, and the delineation of the coiffure. I thought he would be impressed by such a passion for detail and would want to look at the figure, but he seemed disinterested. He was not anxious to come look at it because exactitude is out of style—except as department-store art for the bourgeoisie. But I insisted, so he did, and was promptly seduced.

He marveled at things I had not even noticed. The breadth of the shoulders, for instance. He said she was like those Asiatic Indian dancers and courtesans on the twelfth-century temples of Khajuraho, men and women both, with unnaturally wide shoulders and a narrow tubular body, conceived by the artist with such harmony that one easily accepts their impossible proportions.

As for the detail—the striations of the hair and so on—having seen the figure for himself, he no longer objected. After all, what matters is not an artist's technique but his vision.

A neighborhood housewife also looked at the Xochipala figure. She asked what I had named it. Ramona? Jennifer? Gladys?

Then she asked why I had bought it.

Now, in order to understand this curious question it should be pointed out that I have a few Greek terra-

cottas—Tanagras, so called for the site where these grace-
ful dainty pre-Christian statuettes were first uncovered—
but the woman who asked why I bought the Xochipala
has never asked why I bought the Tanagras. The explanation is that, while Olmec art is unfamiliar, Tanagra statuary belongs to our Greco-Roman artistic heritage. We
have seen Greek art as long as we can remember; museums are crammed with it, and the history books we read
in school had pictures of Greek and Roman masterpieces.
So, my neighbor reasoned, it would make sense to buy
a Tanagra, but why would anyone want a prehistoric
Mexican statue?

If, on the other hand, we knew nothing about Greek
art but were familiar with Olmec concepts, then she would
have asked why I bought the Tanagras. That is to say,
how we react to something may depend less on what we
perceive than on what we know, or think we know. Arthur
Koestler tells a story about this. He noticed a Picasso drawing in the home of a friend named Brenda. The drawing
had been a birthday present and she assumed it was a
print so she hung it rather out of sight, beside the staircase. When Koestler visited her home the next time he saw
Picasso hanging conspicuously in the front room. Brenda
had learned it was not a print but an original.

Still, the longer I thought about my neighbor's question
the more I wondered why I had in fact bought the Olmec.
That it was supremely successful as a work of art, I had
no doubt—which should be reason enough. But in addition to this Olmec piece I had bought quite a few other
examples of ancient Mexican pottery: Jalisco, Michoacán,
Colima, Maya, Chupícuaro, Nayarit, and so forth. Now
this may not be as strange as collecting old dog collars or
potato mashers or eighteenth-century epaulets, nevertheless I could see why people might regard it as peculiar.

Well then, why had I been acquiring such things? The Tanagras were explicable. But why these Mexican artifacts?

Unfamiliarity with an artistic tradition could not be the answer; if that were the case I might just as easily have picked up Eskimo or Tibetan antiquities. There must be a reason I had collected the work of these long-gone Mexican Indians—because our passions are never accidental. We do not by chance marry somebody with a particular way of walking or a certain kind of nose, or decide to specialize in epaulets.

For example, the scholar Henry Hart spent years researching and writing about fifteenth-century Portuguese explorers. It might not occur to us to ask why; after all, scholars do that sort of thing. But there was a reason. There always is. When Hart was a boy somebody gave him a book about those audacious men who opened up the world—among them da Gama. "I remember," he writes, "the picture of the ghost of Vasco da Gama fleeing in full armor through the air, pursued by his victims in full cry for vengeance—scantily clad men without hands, without arms, with gaping wounds and torture-stricken features, seeking to grasp and punish their mortal enemy.

"Still vivid are the gaudy double-page lithographs of his destruction of the Arab ship, his appearance before the Lord of Calicut, and all the other startling pictures illustrating his career."

Years after that book vanished—"in some unknown manner long ago in those far-off childhood days"—Hart found another copy of it. "Alas," he remarks,

the disillusionment! Its pages are a crowded procession of inaccuracies and misstatements. Those beloved illustrations were stock cuts brought together from various sources and used in the subscription volume. Dom Vasco, discussing the chart of his projected voyage with Dom Manuel, is shown as a wild-eyed old man with a white spade beard. A few pages further on he is depicted as an Elizabethan gallant with an imperial beard, receiving the envoy of the King of Calicut; and in truth he was hardly thirty when he set out on his memorable voyage.

But, though wiser and sadder for this seeing of the book after more than half a century, none the less I cherish it, for it first fired my imagination and interest in history and travel; and though I have visited and sojourned in many of the scenes in its pages, none of what my eyes have beheld in the flesh is as thrilling as those which I visited on its magic carpet, which annihilated time and space, and gilded all with the aura of the golden age of childhood.

And now, alas, after almost as many years, I have had that same experience. In a San Francisco flea market I came across a book with a brilliant tangerine binding— a book I recognized immediately and from a distance, long before I could make out the title. It was *The Aztec Treasure House* by Thomas Janvier, an adventure novel for boys. I recognized it because I had checked it out of the high school library at least four times.

In those days I was a heavy reader of Albert Payson Terhune's dog stories, and I could not get enough of Will James's noble horse Smoky galloping across the western landscape. And I had gone through most of the Hardy Boys thrillers despite the obvious ineptitude of their detective father, Fenton Hardy, who, so it seemed, had usually to be rescued by his teen-age sons. And I had read some Tom Swift. And there was a series about somebody who went to Yale. And, of course, *The Call of the Wild*. But as far as I was concerned, *The Aztec Treasure House* beat them all. I do not specifically remember telling my friends it was the best book in the world, but probably I said so. I do know that I recommended it. I was so impressed, in fact, that I memorized the name of the author.

And now after all these years here it was—the same edition—on a card table in a flea market.

After staring at the book for a while as though it were alive and conscious of me, perhaps the very copy I used to read—at last I picked it up and opened it, and saw penciled on the flyleaf the word *scarce,* followed by the price, $4.00, subsequently crossed out and reduced to $1.49.

My first thought was to buy it. Then I thought, No, I don't want to read it again, it's a boys' book. Besides, there are plenty of things I should read and haven't, and probably won't; it would be silly to waste two or three hours going through this again. It belongs to the past.

Then I thought, Well, if I don't buy it I'll never see it again.

So now I have the book, and just as I suspected I can't read it. The story is told in the first person by a young American archaeologist called "Don Tomas" by his fellow adventurers, these being a Franciscan monk, two Otomi Indians, a member of some gringo "engineering corps," two soldiers of fortune, and a barefoot Mexican boy named, inevitably, Pablo.

Don Tomas, by a great stroke of luck, comes upon a mortally wounded cacique who gives him a hieroglyphic map on a sheet of maguey paper. This map, as all good maps should, points the way to something fabulous—in this case the fabulous "walled city of Culhuacan."

Hurrah! Off we go to search for the walled city and the treasure of the last unconquered Aztecs. And a desperate tale it is, provided you are no older than twelve.

If you happen to be more than that you cannot help noticing a number of implausibilities and inconsistencies floating past like ducks in a shooting gallery, so that reading what I once considered to be the world's greatest novel becomes a fearful chore.

I have tried several times to read it, but I cannot get very far. After a few pages I start to skip. Here is how it begins:

My heart was light within me as I stood on the steamer's deck in the cool gray of an October morning, and saw out across the dark green sea and the dusky, brownish stretch of coast country the snow-crowned peak of Orizaba glinting in the first rays of the rising sun. And presently, as the sun rose higher, all the tropic region of the coast and the brown walls of Vera Cruz and of its outpost fort of San Juan de Ulua were flooded with brilliant light.

And still lighter was my heart, a week later, when I found myself established in the beautiful city of Morelia, and ready to begin actively the work for which I had been preparing myself almost all my life long.

Morelia, I had decided, was the best base for the operations that I was about to undertake. My main purpose was to search for the remnants of primitive civilization . . .

Skipping across half-remembered pages I come to these lines:

" 'Hello, Professor!' Young called out, as he caught sight of me, 'have you given up antiquities . . . ?' "

No. No indeed, Mr. Young! I shout across the years, answering not for Don Tomas but for myself, surrounded as I am by cracked old Mexican pots and mutilated statuettes.

3

Aristokles' Atlantis

"**I** propose a curious excursion," said Captain Nemo to Monsieur Aronnax.

And with that the intrepid submariners, having first put on their diving dresses, set foot on the bottom of the Atlantic at a depth of 150 fathoms. The waters were profoundly dark but Captain Nemo pointed out a reddish spot—a light shining with great brillance—perhaps two miles distant from the *Nautilus*. What this fire might be, what it could feed, why and how it illuminated the ocean depths, M. Aronnax could not say. Was it some electric effulgence? Could it be a natural phenomenon unknown to savants of the earth?

After half an hour's walk the floor of the ocean became stony, lit only by the phosphorescent gleam of medusae, microscopic crustacea, and pennatules. Captain Nemo advanced without hesitation; doubtless he had traveled this road before. M. Aronnax followed with unshaken confidence. But not until one in the morning did they approach a mountain from which the mysterious light seemed to emanate.

Before ascending the slope they were obliged to pass through a thicket of dead trees—yes, a copse of dead trees, all without leaves, without sap—trees petrified by the action of the water. Picture to yourself a forest in the Harz, M. Aronnax advises us, a forest encumbered with seaweed and fucus.

Fishes flew from branch to branch as the explorers pushed onward. Massive rocks were rent with impenetrable fractures, deep grottoes, and unfathomable caverns at the bottom of which formidable creatures could be heard moving. Millions of luminous dots glowed amidst the blackness; these were the eyes of giant crustacea crouched in their holes—monstrous crabs and lobsters setting themselves up like halberdiers, moving their claws with a clicking sound, and frightful poulps whose tentacles interwove like living nests of serpents. M. Aronnax felt his blood curdle.

Beyond this eerie copse lay vast ruins which betrayed not the hand of the Creator but that of man—the vague and shadowy forms of temples and castles over which had grown a thick mantle of vegetation. What was this ghostly portion of the globe which long ago had been swallowed by cataclysms? Who had placed these monumental stones like cromlechs of prehistoric times? Arronax would fain have inquired.

But Captain Nemo pressed forward.

Then, from the peak of the mountain, what a sight did the travelers behold! Under their eyes—ruined, destroyed, lay a city with its roofs open, its dwellings fallen, its arches dislocated, massive columns strewn about. Farther away, the remnants of a lengthy aqueduct. Still farther, an expanse of mossy sunken walls and broad deserted thoroughfares—a perfect Pompeii beneath the waters. And all was reddishly lit by a violent fulguration, for the mountain upon which the submariners stood was, in fact, a volcano. Yes, a volcano, from the crater of which vomited forth a rain of stones and scoriae, while fiery lava cascaded down the slope, illuminating the immense plain like a gigantic torch.

Aronnax could keep still no longer. Where they were, to what point Nemo had brought them, he must know at any cost.

With a gesture Captain Nemo bade him be still. And picking up a piece of chalky stone he advanced to a rock of black basalt upon which he traced the single word:

ATLANTIS

Atlantis! mused Aronnax. The ancient Meropis of Theopompus. The Atlantis of Plato. That continent denied by Origen, Jamblichus, D'Anville . . .

Monsieur Jules Verne quite obviously was not the first to write about the place. The first was a Greek wrestler, Aristokles, better known as Plato—the broad-shouldered one—and it seems likely that he named the doomed continent after the small island of Atalantë which was devastated by an earthquake and tidal wave in 426 B.C. Several quadrillion books and articles about Atlantis have risen and sunk since Plato's day, and a group of journalists, being asked to list the most significant stories they could imagine, put the reemergence of the lost continent fourth, well ahead of the Second Coming of Christ—which testifies to a ferocious grip on the psyche. That is to say, Atlantis ranks with buried treasure, monsters, ghosts, derelict ships, inexplicable footprints, and luminous objects streaking through the sky as topics that never fail to excite us.

The founding father described Atlantis in two of his philosophic dialogues, *Timaois* and *Kritias*. Beyond that we have absolutely no information.

The capital, he said, was a circular city such as we might expect—temples, parks, docks, bridges, racetracks, various public facilities, et cetera—enriched with gold, silver, ivory, and presumably whatever else the heart desires. Atlanteans lived the good life for a long time, but at last they succumbed to moral rot and the bottom dropped out. More specifically, although *Kritias* ends in midsentence, it appears that Zeus just got fed up with everybody and pulled the plug. Why Plato drowned his children instead of frying them forever in Hell is not known, except possibly to psychoanalysts, but it hardly matters. As for the location of Atlantis, he was indefinite, saying only that it lay outside the Pillars of Hercules.

Now, we always have coveted riches—silver and gold and sparkling stones—so you would think Plato's account might have inspired at least a few treasure hunters; but there seems to be no evidence that his fellow Athenians paid much attention to the story, perhaps because he was more adept at wrestling and philosophy than at fiction.

For whatever reason, Atlantis gave up no more than occasional bubbles until the first century B.C. when a certain Poseidonius, meditating upon the effects of earthquake and erosion, wrote that Plato's submerged continent might not have been altogether imaginary.

Another hundred years went by while the Greeks contemplated this, then Gaius Plinius Secundus—Pliny the Elder—very cautiously agreed. And, most cautiously, not eager to sound foolish, so did Plutarch. And then, in a less critical age, less sophisticated men began to argue for the continent's reality.

At this point the Age of Faith closed down like a fog,

obliterating everything concerned with temporal matters, so that nobody thought much about Atlantis until the Renaissance. Even then, as though it were a distant reef, nobody considered Atlantis seriously. But when the New World had been discovered Plato's fable came floating up from the depths. The Spanish historian Gómara suggested that he could have heard rumors of these lands and founded an allegory upon them. The English wizard John Dee drew a map of the new continents and named one of them Atlantis. Sir Francis Bacon wrote *The New Atlantis*. A gentleman with the mellifluous name of John Swann carried it further in *Speculum Mundi*:

". . . this I may think may be supposed, that *America* was sometimes part of that great land which *Plato* calleth the Atlantick island, and that the Kings of that island had some intercourse between the people of *Europe* and *Africa* . . ."

The celebrated naturalist Georges Leclerc, Comte de Buffon, did not find this idea unreasonable in the eighteenth century, nor did the explorer von Humboldt in the nineteenth. However, scraps of evidence had been piling up against such a theory, so that most advocates prudently demoted North and South America to the status of colonies, leaving the capital city on the ocean bed where only Captain Nemo could find it.

About this time along came The Honorable Ignatius T. T. Donnelly, who was not a fabrication of Gilbert and Sullivan but an erudite Philadelphia lawyer. He is now remembered as the author of the most wildly successful book on Atlantis ever written—leaving Plato far behind —a book that has been reprinted fifty or sixty times since it was published in 1882. But even before that *succès fou* Donnelly had made a name for himself. When he was very young he moved to Minnesota and with the help of a few other believers in the tremendous potential of that state he bought a tract of land near Saint Paul. They founded a city, which they named Nininger, and set about promoting it as the new metropolis of the Midwest. They formed a literary society and a musical society, and they opened a restaurant called Handyside House which developed quite a nice reputation, yet for some inexplicable reason Nininger refused to grow. Saint Paul grew and grew and grew. Nininger did not.

Donnelly turned to politics. At the age of twenty-eight he became lieutenant governor of Minnesota. Then he was elected to the U.S. House of Representatives, where he spent most of his time reading in the congressional library. He may have been the most educated man ever to serve in Washington.

In 1870 he retired to his Nininger mansion and there he commenced to write. His first book, *Atlantis: The Antediluvian World*, made him famous on both sides of the ocean.

He argued that civilization originated on a continent that had once existed in the Atlantic outside the mouth of the Mediterranean, and all other civilizations were its descendants. Egypt, for example, was an Atlantean colony. All of our myths and traditions are memories of Atlantis, he said. All gods and goddesses and their magical deeds are nothing but confused memories of historical events. Here lay the Garden of Eden, Olympus, the Elysian Fields, and so forth.

Now you might think these extravagant claims would be impossible to prove, but any book that is reissued fifty times has struck with overwhelming force. In other words, millions of people were convinced, among them Prime Minister Gladstone who asked the British cabinet to send out a ship in search of the sunken motherland.

Donnelly was long on facts, if short on logic; but whether he had the facts screwed on straight, and whether his deductions followed in a seemly fashion, is irrelevant. The point is that Ignatius T. T. Donnelly did more for Atlantis than Plato, Pliny the Elder, Plutarch, Sir Francis Bacon, Alexander von Humboldt, and several other preeminent gentlemen combined. It is possible that nobody else in history ever upstaged so many distinguished intellects.

His successor was Lewis Spence, a relatively moderate Scotsman who edited the *Atlantis Quarterly* and who offered his own version of the calamity in half a dozen books of steadily subsiding interest. Spence did not claim as much for the lost continent. He argued only that there had been a land mass where now there is none, which gradually evolved into two immense islands—Atlantis and Antillia. Atlantis lay outside Gibraltar, just where Plato said it was, and the West Indies are what remains of Antillia. These two vast islands did not disappear overnight; they sank slowly because of geological disturbances. Emigrants from Atlantis influenced later civilizations throughout the Mediterranean while emigrants from Antillia influenced the New World.

Spence is so much more plausible than Donnelly that it is easy to understand why he was never as popular, which might account for the crochety title of his last warning: *Will Europe Follow Atlantis?*

In any case, his theory appears to be substantiated by the existence of a submarine ridge running from Iceland to the South Atlantic. Along this ridge the average depth of the ocean is about one mile, compared to an average depth of three miles on either side, and occasionally—at Ascension island, the Azores, Tristan de Cunha—this ridge breaks the surface. But specialists in the deep-water business are of the opinion that Spence got it backward. The ridge is not what remains of a sunken land mass; instead, it was lifted from the ocean floor, probably by volcanic activity.

However, on the chance that Plato might have been correct, some oceanographers investigated the bed of the eastern Atlantic where the continent was supposed to be. They found an immensely thick deposit of pelagic red clay, consisting mostly of the shells of animal plankton. Now, it is known that this kind of sediment accumulates at the rate of three-tenths of an inch per millennium, and after various calculations it was learned that 500 million years must have been required to deposit all that clay on the supposed site of Atlantis—which is a bit much even for racial memories.

Well, then, where was Atlantis?

The moon has been proposed. Long ago Atlantis was sucked out of the ocean to become the moon. But professionals insist that if such a thing had occurred the Atlantic bed would be violently disturbed, which it is not.

Other candidates include Ceylon, Malta, Iceland, Palestine, the Canary Islands, Spitzbergen, and at least a dozen more.

In 1675 a Swedish scholar, having bent the facts into suitable shape, demonstrated that Plato's continent, fountainhead of civilization, could only have been Sweden, with its capital city located very near Upsala.

In 1952 a German pastor announced that the Atlantean capital lay six miles east of Heligoland on the floor of the North Sea—not far from the pastor's home.

More recently a British investigator suggested Bronze-Age Wessex.

So it goes. At first this predilection for situating Atlantis in one's own neighborhood seems strange, just as it seems strange that devout Christians always expect the Second Coming to take place somewhere nearby—perhaps in the backyard between the birdbath and the azaleas. But of course there's a reason. We like to be associated with significant events, past, present, or future. After all, one must listen respectfully to the person who shook Babe Ruth's hand, or heard the shot fired at Sarajevo, or whose progenitors raised the walls and battlements of the earliest civilization.

Consequently, Atlantis will be found near Upsala or Heligoland or Reykjavík, or in Britain or Jerusalem, or perhaps beneath the mud of the Guadalquivir between Cádiz and Seville—a site favored by Spanish partisans.

The Spanish have a good claim. Many researchers now think that Tartessus—the Biblical city of Tarshish, that storehouse of gold, silver, ivory, apes, and peacocks—settled majestically into the Guadalquivir mud; and if Plato should turn out to be not just a pamphleteer but a historian describing an actual city, this may be the one he had in mind.

There seems to be no doubt that an important city-state once existed in this area, visited often by Greek and Phoenician trading ships. Aristophanes speaks of the delectable eels of Tartessus—which is odd because Tartessus must have disappeared by his time—and various old chronicles mention the city. Silver was reputed to be so plentiful in Tartessus that hogs ate from silver troughs; and Phoenician businessmen, eager to carry away as much as possible, ordered the wood and lead anchors of their ships replaced with silver anchor stones.

What happened to the city has not been determined, but about the sixth century B.C. it was either destroyed or abandoned, perhaps as a result of the Carthaginian blockade, and the place where it stood has become Las

Marismas, a vast marsh inhabited by herds of half-wild longhorned cattle. Archaeologists probing the marsh and other suspected sites in this region have found fragments of unique pottery, and copper and gold jewelry decorated with curious hemispherical knobs and rosettes. The most puzzling find was a ring with an unreadable inscription which appeared to be related to Etruscan and to Greek, and perhaps to the unclassifiable Basque language. Now this sort of thing naturally agitates archaeologists, but Las Marismas' high water table has prevented much digging, so that until now the legacy of Tartessus—if it was Tartessus—consists of these few perplexing items.

Despite the fact that the city has not been precisely located, and therefore a cloud of questions hangs overhead, the resemblances between it and Atlantis are significant. Both lay beyond the Pillars of Hercules at the mouth of a great river adjacent to an irrigated plain. Both were renowned for their wealth and trade, and both vanished.

Apart from Tartessus, the primary candidate seems to be not a city but a happening. That is, Plato's city may have been fictional, or derived from what he had heard of Carthage or Babylon or Syracuse, while the cataclysm he described was factual—the eruption of the volcanic island of Thera in the fifteenth century B.C., an explosion so violent that quite a few scientists believe it destroyed the Minoan Empire.

Sixty-six miles south of Thera on the island of Crete stood the palace of Knossos, omphalos of Minoan civilization. It is still there, ponderously reconstructed by Sir Arthur Evans in accordance with nineteenth-century taste, and if you visit Knossos you need not be an archaeologist to see that something terrible happened. Smoke stains on the walls tell you which way the wind was blowing on that unbelievable day 3,500 years ago.

The most thunderous explosion we know anything about was that of the volcano Krakatoa in the Sunda Strait between Java and Sumatra.

Krakatoa began to spout vapor and pumice during the summer of 1883, and dust from these eruptions was noticed as far away as Singapore. Then on August 26, about 2:00 P.M., the crew of a ship eighty miles distant saw a black cloud billowing upward to an estimated height of fifteen miles. Crewmen aboard another ship much closer to the volcano described this cloud as a huge pine tree with branches of lightning. White-hot lava was observed streaming down the southwest slope and a sinister rumbling could be heard all over Java.

By late afternoon, according to crew members of the ship *Charles Bal,* which at that time was twelve miles from Krakatoa, the air had become choking and sulfurous.

Booming eruptions continued all night and early next morning Krakatoa annihilated itself with four stupendous explosions. The loudest was heard not only throughout the East Indies but in Vietnam, Ceylon, the Philippines, halfway across Australia, and on the island of Rodriguez 3,000 miles to the southwest. Atmospheric shock waves traveled around the earth three and a half times.

By noon it was over. Five cubic miles of volcanic material had been expelled from Krakatoa. The Sunda Strait was choked with floating pumice, the city of Batavia lay in smoky darkness, and a series of tidal waves had swept across hundreds of coastal villages drowning almost 40,000 people. The height of the largest tidal wave is not known exactly, but it is thought to have reached fifty feet. Ripples from these waves were measured at Cape Horn and probably accounted for a slight rise on tidal gauges in the English Channel.

The remnants of Thera and Krakatoa are in several respects very similar. Volcanic calderas are not always formed in the same way, but these two were. For this reason and for other reasons—the details of which excite nobody except geologists—a comparison can be made. The cauldron of Thera is about four times larger than that of Krakatoa. In other words, Thera threw up something like twenty cubic miles of stone and lava. And instead of Krakatoa's fifty-foot tidal wave the Aegean island of Anaphe shows evidence of a wave—unquestionably from Thera—that reached above two hundred feet. The wave might not have been much less than that when it struck the northern coast of Crete at a speed of perhaps 100 miles an hour.

How many people were washed away cannot even be estimated, because no records of that day have survived. But there are Egyptian references to some sort of catastrophe in the sea to the north, and it is believed that Solon heard about this when he visited Egypt in the sixth century B.C. And from Solon's report Plato may have gotten the idea for his cataclysmic deluge.

Whatever his sources—the end of Minoan civilization, the disappearance of Tartessus, the submergence of little Atalantë, some tale of Carthage—wherever he found his touchstone, Plato no doubt intended to write a meaningful allegory. Being dissatisfied with the behavior of his fellow citizens, he resolved to instruct them.

He tells us in *Kritias* that for many generations the Atlanteans obeyed the laws, revered the gods, and so on:

> . . . for they possessed true and in every way great spirits, uniting gentleness with wisdom in the various chances of life, and in their intercourse with one another. They despised everything but virtue, caring little for their present state of life, and thinking lightly of the

possession of gold and other property, which seemed only a burden to them; neither were they intoxicated by luxury; nor did wealth deprive them of their self-control; but they were sober, and saw clearly that all these goods are increased by virtue and friendship with one another, whereas by too great regard and respect for them they are lost, and virtue with them. By such reflections and by the continuance in them of a divine nature, the qualities which we have described grew and increased among them; but when the divine portion began to fade slowly, and become diluted too often and too much with the mortal admixture, and the human nature got the upper hand, they then, being unable to bear their fortune, behaved unseemly, and to him who had an eye to see grew visibly debased, for they were losing the fairest of their precious gifts; but to those who had no eye to see the true happiness, they appeared glorious and blessed at the very time when they were becoming tainted with unrighteous ambition and power.

Zeus therefore pointed a finger and that was that.

Plato's allegory did not make much of an impression, so far as we know. Allegories seldom do. The Athenians did not feel especially rebuked by such criticism; it must have seemed as irrelevant to them as it does to us. Consequently, what endured was not Plato's didactic message but his lovely and terrible image of a drowned city, a city beneath the sea. We cannot stop looking for it.

The old wrestler would have been bitterly surprised.

4

The Innocents' Crusade

Early in the seventh century on Saint Mark's Day, April 25, while the bubonic plague boiled across Europe, Pope Gregory ordered the church altars draped in black and instructed priests to carry shrouded crosses through the streets. And because this ceremony would be repeated year after year Saint Mark's Day eventually came to be known as "Black Crosses." By the thirteenth century, however, it commemorated not only victims of the plague but all who had died in the struggle for Jerusalem and those who still were held captive by the Moslems.

Among the spectators when this grim procession wound through the streets of Chartres in the year 1212 was a shepherd boy named Stephen from the village of Cloyes. The unending prayers, the melancholy litanies, the parade of eerily nodding crosses, the frantic appeals to God for mercy, the screams and groans and seizures of penitents—

all of this evidently excited the boy so much that he began talking wildly about his desire to see the Moslems expelled from the Holy Land.

A few days later some adult approached Stephen in the fields near Cloyes. Whoever he was, this man represented himself as a pilgrim returning from Jerusalem. Stephen offered him food and the stranger told stories of what he had seen and done. At last he revealed to the boy that in actuality he was not a simple pilgrim but Jesus Christ. He then commanded Stephen to lead the children of France on a new crusade, and gave him a letter addressed to King Philip Augustus.

Here the mysterious pilgrim vanishes, and nothing has been learned of him beyond what Stephen said. He might have been imaginary except that the illiterate shepherd boy did possess such a letter in the summer of 1212. Whether or not Stephen managed to deliver it to the king is disputed by historians. Steven Runciman thinks he did. Henry Treece agrees. George Zabriskie Gray, an earlier researcher, was unconvinced: "Whether he [King Philip] had received the letter which Stephen showed, we are not told."

Nor is the pilgrim's motive clear. According to one theory, a villager who had noticed the boy's excitement during Black Crosses decided to play a cruel joke. But most scholars believe it is more complex, perhaps related to the Albigensian heresy.

In the French town of Albi some Christians too wise for their own health had begun objecting to ecclesiastic corruption. They also spread the absurd idea that life is a struggle between the armies of Light and Darkness, and which force will prevail is altogether in doubt. Now, as we know, in the orthodox view Satan has no chance of defeating God. The Albigensian argument therefore was

suicidal. Rigorous Christians could not permit such blas-
phemy to exist. Nor did they. Pope Innocent III butchered
the Albigensians in one of the most sanguine spectacles
you will come across anywhere.

"Slay them all," Innocent responded when asked how
the heretics could be identified. "Slay them all. The Lord
will recognize His own."

At least that is the hideous response attributed to Innocent. He may or may not have said it. One chronicle
hints a vicious German monk contrived the story. The
massacre of the Albigensians, though, cannot be doubted.

This slaughter was under way when Stephen met the
pilgrim, but the Albigensians were not easy to extermi-
nate. A few survivors would cling to their faith and per-
petuate it until it outlasted Innocent himself; and papal
curiosity about these repugnant ideas would finally beget
that Un-Christian Activities Committee known as the In-
quisition. However, the point is that an Albigensian priest
may have decided to use the emotional young shepherd as
a conduit to King Philip. Albigensian arguments could
not reach the king directly, but deluded children sometimes work marvels.

Thus, historians theorize, the mysterious stranger may
have been a Christian heretic. Not that his identity matters; what matters is the result.

Stephen, with the letter in his wallet, set out to visit
the king—which sounds so improbable that it might be
the opening of a fairy tale.

King Philip was spending the summer just north of
Paris at Saint-Denis, burial place of Dionysius the martyr,
one of seven apostles whose efforts converted Gaul to
Christianity. Legend says that Dionysius' head was
chopped off and his corpse thrown into the Seine, whereupon he emerged from the river with his head in his

hands and walked to the place where he wished to be buried. Early in the eighteenth century when Ninon de l'Enclos was asked whether she thought the saint had carried his head such a great distance she replied that the distance wasn't important; what counted was the first step—which has nothing to do with Stephen but does add an ornamental detail.

At Saint-Denis, too, the kings of France had been buried ever since the time of Dagobert, last of the Merovingian rulers, and here the red flag of the Church and holy standard of the realm—the oriflamme—was kept. Because of these attractions Saint-Denis drew a good many pilgrims and tourists.

Stephen preached the crusade as he walked from Cloyes. It seems odd that anybody would listen to the exhortations of a twelve-year-old peasant displaying a letter of authorization from Christ, but then one remembers Jeanne d'Arc two centuries later who was just sixteen when she went to work. And in our own century people have knelt to be blessed and married by a four-year-old minister. So it should be no surprise that Stephen collected an audience wherever he stopped, and it is probable that by the time he reached Saint-Denis he already had picked up some followers.

Here, preaching day and night beside the martyr's shrine as well as in the public market, repeating familiar accounts of Christian suffering in the Holy Land, he became a noticeable figure. He emphasized the difference between the sepulcher of Dionysius, which was a scene of constant devotion, and that of Christ in Jerusalem, surrounded and scorned by Moslems. He asked his audience how they could tolerate this. He likened Jesus to a king banished from his heritage, Jerusalem to a captive queen. He is said to have cried out: "For the last time we have known defeat! Hereafter shall proud barons and mailed knights testify to the power of children commissioned by God!"

These words sound false because we cannot imagine a farm boy today, nor any boy—nor an adult—calling up such regal syntax. Yet what Stephen actually said might not have been very different from the speech attributed to him. As George Orwell points out, in ancient ballads the lord and the peasant speak the same language— which no doubt was poetic convention. Still, all of us who have grown up using English do sense that a long time ago we spoke with eloquence and strength. Maybe the people of every nation feel this. And it could be true: we might all have spoken a superior language in the past.

Stephen referred often to a dream he had in which the Mediterranean divided, allowing him and those who followed him to walk to Jerusalem—just as the Red Sea had opened for another shepherd.

And it is said by medieval historians that while at Saint-Denis he performed miracles.

To those who questioned his authority he showed the letter, telling again of his encounter with Jesus in the fields near Cloyes. He also told a curiously naïve story that has the cast of the Middle Ages on it. When he returned from Chartres, he said, after witnessing the procession of Black Crosses, his sheep had wandered into a field of grain. He was angered and began to beat them, whereupon they dropped to their knees and repented. By this sign, among others, he knew that he was destined for greatness.

People going home from Saint-Denis carried news of Stephen of Cloyes, and very soon the idea of a children's crusade spread throughout France and into Germany— although on this point modern historians disagree. Friedrich Heer states: "There is no discoverable connection between the two Children's Crusades, which started in the same year, 1212, one in the Rhineland, the other in the Loire valley." Runciman, speaking for a majority, says that when reports of Stephen's preaching reached the Rhineland: "The children of Germany were not to be outdone. A few weeks after Stephen had started on his mission, a boy called Nicholas . . . began to preach the same message."

What is certain, though, is that news of Stephen's crusade did seep through France in an astonishingly short time.

Clerics were appalled, considering it sacrilege that the boy should liken himself to Moses, and denounced the crusade as an inspiration of Satan. However, Pope Innocent reputedly said: "The very children put us to shame."

They gathered like thistledown in a breeze, floating toward the place of assembly, Vendôme, justifying their cause with this passage: "Out of the mouth of babes and sucklings hast thou ordained strength because of thine enemies, that thou mightest still the enemy and the avenger."

They referred to Stephen as The Prophet and to themselves—some of them eight or nine years old—as minor prophets. Columns of boys and girls converged on Vendôme, following replicas of the oriflamme. Some of the children swung perfumed censers, others held crosses and burning candles. They sang hymns which they composed as they walked. They prayed and wept and appealed to God and beckoned ecstatically for other children to join them.

"Lord, restore Christendom!" they shouted. "Lord, restore to us the true and holy Cross!"

King Philip, when he realized that the shepherd boy

actually was mustering an army, seems to have become confused. After all these centuries, and with such fragmentary documentation, it is hard to establish the truth; but at first he probably approved the idea. The pope had spoken in favor of it and Philip was not anxious to offend His Holiness.

But then the king's counselors advised him to suppress the movement. A horde of children would cause immense disorder. Many of them would die before reaching Palestine, others just as certainly would be killed there, and France could not afford the loss of these young people. Still, it might be awkward to suppress the crusade. Not only children but a number of adults were beginning to idolize Stephen. Then, too, there was a possibility that God did in fact wish it.

Philip turned for advice to the University of Paris, whose doors had recently opened. Those most learned men, the doctors of the university, should know how to resolve the problem.

According to Strayer and Munro: "They told him that the movement was unwise and he commanded the children to return home. They did so, and the children's crusade in France came to an end." But only the first half of this judgment can be supported. The university savants did advise against it, and King Philip did issue an edict ordering the children to go home. That much can be verified. What happened next is a different story.

The king's edict apparently was ignored. The children paid no attention and the adults charged with enforcing it did not do so with any vigor. Philip himself, rather strangely, seems to have stepped aside. Possibly he felt that by the issuance of a decree he had identified his position to the pope, which was the important thing.

Thus, with slight opposition, the children continued assembling at Vendôme. A few of them must have had permission to join the crusade; others simply disregarded their parents and ran away.

In Germany the crusade preached by Nicholas was similar, but not identical. Most of what we know about it comes from the account of a monk named Godfrey who was writing in Cologne between the years 1162 and 1237.

Nicholas must have been approximately the same age as Stephen, perhaps younger. And, like the French boy, he believed himself supernaturally ordained: a blazing cross appeared in the sky and he heard a voice. He may have been persuaded of these things by his father, described as a wicked man, who hoped to profit by his son's celebrity.

Nicholas copied Stephen's technique and established himself near a shrine. Cologne was the religious center of Germany and attracted thousands of pilgrims because the bones of the Magi were laid out in the old Byzantine cathedral, thanks to Archbishop Raynuldus who had accompanied Frederick Barbarossa to Italy and brought back three skeletons as part of his loot. During the nineteenth century, we are told by Gray, somebody discovered that one of the skulls was that of a child with milk teeth. But again, this should be considered an ornamental detail.

In Nicholas's day there they were, side by side, the undoubted bones of the wise men, adorned with jewels and gold trinkets, surrounded by votive offerings. He had only to point to them, just as Stephen could point to the sepulcher of Dionysius. Would true Christians permit the Savior's tomb to remain in the filthy grasp of Moslems while embellishing that of the Magi with precious gifts?

Appeals for the liberation of Palestine were familiar enough to adults who had heard it all their lives—the First Crusade having been launched more than a century earlier—but to children it sounded like an original idea. And there was, in fact, one singular difference. Nicholas, more so than Stephen, emphasized that this crusade would accomplish its purpose not by warfare but through conversion. Moslems, as soon as they had listened to the children of Germany, would gladly and without hesitation discard their faith like a worn-out cloak in order to put on the cross of Christianity. Therefore it would not be necessary to slaughter them.

Nicholas may or may not have considered meeting the French procession somewhere along the way, but his army was ready to march by the end of June and he understood that it must get moving. There was no alternative. His crusaders had almost no money and very little food. Traveling through the countryside they might forage enough to keep themselves alive, but they could not camp day after day in the streets of Cologne.

So, one fine morning about the first of July, he led 20,000 adolescents out of the city, leaving perhaps an equal number behind. Some authorities believe this exodus may be the origin of the Pied Piper legend, although how the rats got into the story is puzzling. Unless, of course, they represent the army of hungry children.

Nicholas's young crusaders wore a uniform—those who could afford it—the long gray cloak of a pilgrim with a cross sewn on the breast, and a broad-brimmed hat. Many of them carried a palmer's staff, symbolizing a visit to Palestine. Their average age, according to the Sicardi chronicle, was about twelve—slightly older than the children who gathered around Stephen. And for some reason the German crusade attracted more girls. A few adults went along: youthful priests, calculating merchants, stargazers, fanatics, whores, and idlers. In other words, a fair slice of humanity.

The chronicles do not explain why the Germans did not all march together, nor when the second army left Cologne, nor who its leader was.

Very little is known about this second army, which might possibly have started a few days earlier than Nicholas. It moved through central Switzerland, crossed the Alps at Saint Gotthard Pass, and like a swarm of dying locusts surged down the Italian coast through Ancona as far as Brindisi in the heel of the boot. Militant German emperors such as Barbarossa had not left the Italians with a great love for their blue-eyed northern neighbors, and the sins of the fathers fell heavily on these unfortunates. Those that survived the Alps, disease, starvation, wild animals, and human predators at last met their destiny in brothels, or, if they were lucky, as servants. According to the *Chronicon Rhythmicum*, which is thought to be the work of a contemporary, perhaps Benedictus Gentilotus: "Illi de Brundusio virgines stuprantur. Et in arcum pessimum passim venumdantur." At Brindisi the young girls were raped, sold to whoever wanted them.

The fortunes of Nicholas's army are better documented. He chose a course up the Rhine to Basle, through western Switzerland to Geneva, and crossed the Alps by the Mont Cenis Pass. At this point half of his army was gone. Some of the children deserted and tried to get home, but most of the absent troops were dead. Many of them starved. Others froze, or were murdered, or drowned while attempting to wade through mountain streams. Some were devoured by wolves.

Another 3,000 died before Nicholas arrived at the gates of Genoa on August 25.

He petitioned the Genoese senate, asking that his regiment be allowed to stay within the walls overnight, saying that next morning when the sea divided he would march on to Jerusalem.

The senators granted permission to remain a week. They assumed that the children would go back to Germany once they realized how foolish they had been, but after the long trip and the disappointment they would need a few days of rest. It is said that Nicholas and his captains accepted this offer derisively, they were so sure the Mediterranean would roll apart.

Within hours, though, after thousands of fanatical half-crazed children had pushed into Genoa, the senators rescinded this invitation. The army could stay overnight, but no longer.

From Genoa the crusaders marched to Pisa: it might be here, after all, that the sea was meant to divide. We have no record of how many died on the road to Pisa.

The Senones chronicle states that two shiploads of German children sailed from Pisa to the Holy Land. They never returned.

Nicholas's failing army turned inland. Small tattered sickly companies are known to have reached Florence, Arezzo, Perugia, and Siena, like the unraveling end of a rope. A few children walked to Rome, where Innocent granted the leaders an audience. "Moved by their piety but embarrassed by their folly," the pope told them to go home.

Nicholas himself may not have been invited to this audience. His prophecies had not turned out too well and he might have been deposed. He might possibly have been murdered. A thirteenth-century chronicle reports that later he fought bravely at Acre and at the siege of Damietta, returning unharmed; but this last seems very questionable because it is on record that when the people of Cologne learned what had happened to their children they hanged his father.

Stephen's army continued assembling at Vendôme for several weeks after the departure of the Germans and when he gave the order to march sometime in midsummer approximately 30,000 children followed him. Although they were not dressed as uniformly as their Teutonic cousins, each had a woolen cross sewn on the right shoulder.

Animals, birds, and butterflies are said to have joined the French crusade. Butterflies, bearers of the soul, were especially significant. Much later Jeanne d'Arc would be asked during her examination: "Is it true that you and your banner go into battle among a cloud of butterflies?"

Stephen chose a path southward through the rich heart of France, across the Loire to the Rhône at Lyons, through Valence and Avignon to Marseilles. It was a more hospitable route than that chosen by the Germans and Stephen traveled more comfortably than Nicholas, who had walked. He was looked upon as a saint so he traveled in a chariot padded with carpets, with a decorated canopy to protect him from the August sun. Around his chariot rode the honor guard—a dozen boys from aristocratic families, armed with lances, mounted on the best horses available.

He often addressed the multitude, standing up in his cart, and it is said that many children were trampled to death during his speeches. Except for the lances it is probable that he, too, would have been buried by the reverent mob, so anxious were they to pluck a splinter from his vehicle, or a thread from his cloak, or a hair from the mane of one of the horses. Any of these items would almost sanctify the owner and could be sold or exchanged for food.

Whether Stephen was satisfied merely to address his disciples while trundling through the countryside in regal solitude, or whether he now and then helped himself to a few delirious bodies will never be determined; but Roger of Wendover, writing soon after the event, says that

Stephen was "a child in years but accomplished in vice." So, lascivious or continent, reclining beneath a brightly painted canopy, he bumped along on wooden wheels toward Marseilles.

Both in France and Germany that summer was unusually hot and dry, which seemed to foretell the evaporation of the Mediterranean, but at the same time it resulted in a shortage of food. Stealing became the order of the day, fights erupted, corpses decayed beside the road, and because they had no idea where Jerusalem was they would ask, whenever a castle was sighted on a hill—ignoring the fact that they had not yet crossed the sea—if that could be the Holy City. And inevitably, when they found just another castle, the children grew more disenchanted and listened with less excitement to Stephen's exhortations.

About the end of August they reached the Mediterranean coast. Some had died or dropped out, but they had not been forced to cross the Alps, which decimated the Germans, and along the way they had picked up fresh recruits, so that almost as many children reached Marseilles as had left Vendôme.

The city elders responded very much as the Genoese had. They sympathized and wished to help, because they wished to see Palestine liberated; however, the sight of such a host was alarming. Stephen assured them that his army would remain only one night. In the morning when the waters parted they would be on their way.

It is gratifying to think that whenever a body of people has fallen upon hard times there always have been other people anxious to help them out. So it happened here. Two merchants of Marseilles appeared. The chronicles do not give their names in the French form; they are spoken of as Hugo Ferreus and William Porcus, which translates readily into Hugh the Iron and Will the Pig.

Seeing the children gathered disconsolately on the shore, these merchants volunteered to charter as many ships as necessary—*causa Dei, absque pretio*—for the sake of God, without price.

The waters of the Mediterranean, therefore, would indeed roll back, and all those who wished to continue would walk to Jerusalem as Stephen had prophesied.

Seven ships were chartered. The number of children who went aboard can only be estimated, but there must have been at least 5,000. We do not know the exact date the fleet sailed, nor much else about it. Almost certainly the departure was accompanied by the traditional hymn: "Veni Creator Spiritus."

A month or so later, when they should have had time to reach the Holy Land and news of their arrival should be spreading, those who came back from that part of the world—pilgrims, adult crusaders, merchants—were questioned. But the answer was always the same: no such fleet had dropped anchor at any port.

In 1215, three years after the children left Marseilles, John of England with very little grace drew his X on the Magna Carta. A year after that Pope Innocent died, Honorius became pontiff and immediately preached the Fifth Crusade. In 1222 the Mongols invaded eastern Europe. Philip Augustus died the following year. Saint Francis of Assisi died in 1226. Genghis Khan died a year later.

In 1230 a priest returned to Europe from Egypt and said that he had sailed with the children. At least four medieval chroniclers—Albericus, Belgicum, Roger Bacon, and Thomas de Champré—have preserved this priest's account of what happened.

Not many leagues southwest of Sardinia lay a bleak, deserted island called Accipitrum, which refers to the falcons that nest among the cliffs. On the third day out of

Marseilles the fleet was close to Accipitrum when a storm drove two ships against it. They broke up and everyone aboard was drowned. The five ships that survived the storm did not sail around Sardinia and enter the straits of Sicily as had been expected, but veered south toward Africa and then followed the coast westward to the Moslem city of Bujeiah. Here the children were taken ashore and sold. Some remained in Bujeiah. Others were sent to Alexandria where the governor, Maschemuth, bought many of them for use in the fields. Some were taken to the Holy Land—past the city they had intended to liberate—to Damascus and Baghdad, where a number of them were decapitated, drowned, or shot by archers because they would not renounce the Christian faith. All the rest, about 700, including the priest who told this story, were bought by the sultan of Egypt, Malek Kamel, who took them to Cairo. Eighteen years later the priest was freed, although the chronicles do not say why. And by these accounts nobody else aboard the ships that left Marseilles ever returned to Europe.

Hugo Ferreus and William Porcus, after turning a nice profit, apparently skipped town. They had been in the business of selling Christians for a long time, although never on such a scale, and they might have become uneasy. News that they had sold 5,000 children could get back to France.

We hear of them only once more. The emir of Sicily, Mirabel, employed them to kidnap or assassinate the German emperor, Frederick II, but things did not quite work out. Mirabel, his two sons, and the flesh merchants were caught. All five were hanged on the same gallows.

As for Stephen, medieval historians do not mention him after his army reached Marseilles. Consequently we have no idea if he drowned in the surf at Accipitrum, or was beheaded at Damascus, or spent his life in the fields near Alexandria, or whether he declined to go aboard the Judas ships and started walking back to Cloyes.

In any case, when Pope Gregory IX heard the priest's story he decreed that a monument should be built to honor the children. Of the sites accessible to Christians it was felt that the most appropriate would be that island where two ships of the fleet had been wrecked. Many bodies had washed ashore during the storm and though most of them decayed a few were buried by fishermen. These remains were exhumed and placed inside a church which was built at the pope's direction. It was called the Church of the New Innocents, Ecclesia Novorum Innocentium, a reference to the murdered children of Bethlehem, and the pope endowed it so that twelve prebends could live on the tiny island and pray unendingly, day after day, year after year.

Accipitrum became a shrine. Boatloads of pilgrims arrived to worship the drowned children whose bodies—miraculously whole and uncorrupted, says Albericus—were on display.

But at last, during the sixteenth century, the church was abandoned and then forgotten.

In 1737 several Christians who had been held captive at Tabarca on the African coast managed to escape and sailed to the island. They settled there and founded the village of Carlo Forte. But when they landed they discovered the ruins of the Church of the New Innocents, which surprised them because they thought that except for an occasional fisherman they were the first people to have arrived. They could not imagine who was responsible for this structure, so they looked upon it as a mysterious and perhaps sinister place.

The ruins are on a gentle rise behind the village.

Nearby are two deep wells which probably were dug at the time the church was built, and there are some catacombs not far away. The church was quadrangular with a peaked roof. If there was a tower it has fallen. The altar was at the eastern end, beneath a window. The front has collapsed and the other walls are crumbling. Grass grows inside. The site overlooks much of the island, which now is called San Pietro, and across the strait you can see the rocky outline of Sardinia.

5

Prester John

He lived in Asia, later in Africa, but first in the land of Pentexoria in a city called Susa, with the Great Khan's daughter as his wife. Twelve archbishops attended him, who themselves were mighty lords. His chamberlain was a king. His cupbearer was a king. His steward was a primate and king. His marshal was a king and archimandrite. His cook was an abbot and king. Beneath his banner lay seventy-two kingdoms whose monarchs, each utterly subservient, ruled several lesser kings —which ought to give you an idea of his importance. Nevertheless, as we know from his famous letter to Emperor Manuel Comnenus, he chose to be addressed simply as Presbyter Johannes.

Manuel Comnenus, a Greek, in that year of 1165 the most powerful Christian on earth, forwarded copies of Prester John's letter to Pope Alexander III and to the Holy Roman emperor, Frederick Barbarossa; and news of it roared like fire across Europe because the three ac-

knowledged leaders of the Western world had been told
they were insignificant.

This is what the letter said:

I, Johannes the Presbyter, Lord of Lords, am superior
in virtue, riches and might to all who walk under
Heaven. Seventy-two kings pay tribute to Us. Our
might prevails in the Three Indies. Our lands extend to
the Farthest Indies where the body of St. Thomas the
Apostle rests ... Our country is the home and dwelling-
place of elephants, dromedaries, camels, metacol-
linarum, cametennus, panthers, tinserete, white bears,
white merles, cicadas, mute gryphons, tigers, hyenas,
wild horses, wild oxen and wild men, horned men, one-
eyed men, centaurs, fauns, satyrs, pygmies, giants ...
Thirty thousand people eat at Our table each day, apart
from guests, and all receive gifts from Our stores. Our
table is of emerald supported by four pillars of ame-
thyst ... When We ride to war We are preceded by
thirteen lofty crosses of gold ornamented with precious
stones, and each is followed by ten thousand mounted
soldiers and by one hundred thousand men on foot ...
When we go forth on other occasions a plain wooden
cross is borne before Us, that We may recall the passion
of Our Lord Jesus Christ, and also a golden bowl filled
with earth to remind Us that Our flesh must return to
its original substance. But We carry also a silver bowl
filled with gold, that everyone may recognize Us and
render homage. Our magnificence surpasses the wealth
of the world ... If thou canst count the stars of the sky
and the sands of the sea, then shalt thou know how to
judge the vastness of Our realm and Our power.

With these imperious words, and more, Prester John
informed Europe of his existence, although for a long time

there had been rumors of a Christian kingdom somewhere in the east beyond the Moslem empire.

In 1122 a Bishop John of India—by some accounts he was an archbishop—arrived to visit Pope Calixtus II. He stayed twelve months, delighting everybody with wonderful stories of Saint Thomas who had traveled to India after Christ's crucifixion to preach the gospel. Saint Thomas was well remembered throughout India, the bishop said, for he had converted many, and his martyrdom had not been forgotten. In fact, the saint's body still could be seen, unchanged and uncorrupted, on the day of the feast of Saint Thomas. The corpse stood erect within a precious silver shell: "The face shines like a star, having red hair hanging down almost to the shoulders, and a red beard, curly but not long, the entire appearance being beautiful to behold. The clothes are as firm and complete as when they were first put on."

In 1145 another high ecclesiastic emerged from the shadowy East. Hugh, Bishop of Antioch, came to the pope for help because Moslems were threatening the Christian enclaves in Syria. Hugh's visit was meticulously recorded by Otto of Freising, one of the most famous and reliable historians of the Middle Ages. According to Otto, the Syrian bishop told the pope about a certain priest-king in the Orient whose name was John, who was a Christian, and whose army had defeated the Medes and Persians after a three-day battle and occupied their capital city. Then the priest-king had marched to the aid of Jerusalem, but was stopped by the river Tigris. Unable to cross the river, King John led his army north because he had been told that sometimes the Tigris froze. He waited several years for this to happen; but finally, when it did not, he was obliged to return to the Orient.

Europe had no further news of this redoubtable Christian leader, nor of any Christian settlement in Asia, until the letter arrived.

Twelve years elapsed before the letter was answered. The probable explanation for this is that the letter was a fake, and the pope and both emperors realized it. The original copy has long since disappeared, but scholars have more or less reconstructed it by working backward from later versions. They suspect that the original did not include either a date or a place, which would be unlikely if it were authentic, and the bombastic tone rings untrue. Nor would any monarch announce himself to another with such conceit, not unless his object was war. Then too, the prose reeks more of literary craft than diplomatic craft. But the most convincing evidence of fraud is that many details in the letter can be found in books available to an educated European of the twelfth century. The writer borrowed from Marbod of Rennes, Isidore of Seville, from at least two books about Alexander the Great, and almost certainly paraphrased other medieval writers.

As to who wrote it—unquestionably somebody who had visited the East, perhaps a Crusader or a monk, or a European living in the Near East. He mentions Samarkand, which had been for centuries a trading center on the silk road to China. The Greeks and Romans knew about Samarkand, but Europeans of the Middle Ages did not, and there is no reference to Samarkand in any Latin document earlier than Prester John's letter—which suggests that the author had at least traveled through the fringes of the Orient. And he seems to be familiar with a ninth-century tale then unknown in Europe, *The Thousand and One Nights*.

As to why he wrote that letter, we can only speculate.

It was translated into Anglo-Norman by an English knight, Roau d'Arundel, who accompanied King Richard the Lion-Hearted on the Third Crusade. Roau picked up a copy of the Latin text in Constantinople, and prefaced his translation by saying that the letter offered an instructive view of Eastern miracles which one could either accept as truth or read for entertainment.

Modern analysts think it is more substantial than that. The letter may have been written to encourage the Crusaders by telling them about an invincible ally in the Orient; or it could have been a parable meant to embarrass the two emperors and the pope, because Prester John points out that in spite of immeasurable wealth and power he remains a humble priest in whose domain everything belongs to everyone—as opposed to Europe where leaders consider themselves divine, where the rich get richer while the poor get poorer, and justice is a foreign word.

In any case, on September 27, 1177, Pope Alexander III wrote to Prester John: *"Magnificus Rex Indorum, Sacerdotum sanctissimus . . ."*

The pope went on to say that he had heard from various sources about John's good works and piety, but at the same time the Roman Catholic doctrine of papal authority over all Christians should be understood. In other words, there could be only one successor to the first pontiff, Saint Peter—namely himself, Alexander, in Rome. And because he had heard that Prester John was anxious for guidance he was sending his personal physician, Magister Philippus, to offer instruction.

Having pontifically signed and sealed this response, Alexander told Magister Philippus to deliver it.

Just why the pope answered a letter that he knew to be fictitious—especially a letter addressed not to himself but to Emperor Comnenus—is unclear. It is thought that the remarkable circulation of Prester John's letter throughout Europe at last compelled the pope to restate the guiding principles of Christianity. If so, the letter must have been intended as a social or moral tract.

Concerning Magister Philippus, he obediently marched off in the direction of Asia and right off the pages of history.

On Easter Sunday, 1245, a Franciscan monk named John de Piano Carpini climbed on a donkey and set out from Lyons, directed by Pope Innocent IV to assess the situation in windswept Asia and, if possible, to convert the king of the Tartars—whoever he was, and whatever he might be called. Brother Carpini was also told to keep an eye out for the spectral Christian monarch. Any information would be appreciated.

Innocent gave him some letters which might be useful along the way, and included a stern reproof to the Tartar king: "We find ourselves greatly surprised that you, as We have learned, have attacked and destroyed many countries belonging not only to Christian peoples but to others . . . We wish all to live in peace and in fear of God, according to the Prince of Peace. Therefore We pray and earnestly beseech you to relinquish such undertakings, above all your persecution of Christians, and by suitable penance to appease the wrath of God which you surely have brought upon yourselves by reason of your many deeds of outrage."

Carpini, a former pupil of Saint Francis of Assisi, was sixty-two years old when he rode away from Lyons. It took him almost a year to reach Kiev, which had been practically obliterated by the Mongols. Here he got an escort. His Mongol guides did not waste time. They followed the imperial highway—extending from Kiev to Canton—and changed horses several times a day at relay stations. Carpini's journal reports that he was in the saddle from early morning until night, sometimes late at night. He had nothing to drink except melted snow, and his meals during the forty days of Lent while he was trotting across Asia consisted of boiled millet. On July 22, Mary Magdalene's Day, Brother Carpini was delivered to the court of Kuyuk—a grandson of Genghis Khan—just in time for Kuyuk's coronation festivities.

It must have been quite a show. The Russian Prince Yaroslav was there, along with various princes of the Kitai and the Solangs, and two sons of the king of Georgia. A sultan was there to represent the caliph of Baghdad, and Carpini was told by the imperial recorder that a number of other sultans were present. More than 4,000 ambassadors came to witness and to celebrate the ascension of Kuyuk.

In November the indestructible Franciscan started home. He traveled all winter, sometimes sleeping out: "When we awoke we often found ourselves covered with snow which the wind had blown over us . . ."

A year later he entered Lyons and gave the pope a message from Kuyuk:

You must come yourself at the head of all your kings and prove to Us your fealty and allegiance. If you disregard this Divine Commandment and fail to obey Us, thenceforth We must look upon you as Our enemy. Whoever recognizes and submits to the Son of God and Lord of the World, the Great Khan, will be saved. Whoever refuses will be annihilated . . .

Kuyuk then asked:

How do you know who is worthy in the sight of God to partake of His grace? We pray to God, and by His power we shall lay waste to the earth from east to west.

If a man did not possess the strength of God how could he have done such things? When you say: "I am a Christian, I praise God and despise all others," how do you know whom God considers righteous and to whom He will show His mercy?

Just what effect this menacing soliloquy had on the pope, we can only guess, but he must have felt some disappointment because the Mongol's reply seemed to indicate that he did not, at least for the present, care to be baptized.

Nor did Brother Carpini have much news of Prester John, mentioning him only once. Carpini describes him as an Indian king, a black Saracen, who had once defeated a Mongol army.

William of Ruysbroek, a Flemish Franciscan, set out from Constantinople in May of 1253. His instructions were pretty much the same, to see what he could see, because bad news kept trickling out of Asia and it would be helpful to get in touch with Prester John—if there was a Prester John—or with his successor—if there happened to be any such. William, "a fat and sturdy man," was accompanied by another monk, Bartholomew of Cremona, about whom we know very little. Also in the party was an interpreter named Homo Dei, a slave boy named Nicolaus whom the monks bought in Constantinople, and somebody called Gosset.

They sailed across the Black Sea and landed at a Venetian trading post in the Crimea where quite possibly they met Niccolo and Maffeo Polo. This would have been just about the year Marco was born.

By oxcart and horse they rode into Mongol territory, encouraged by rumors of Christians somewhere ahead. At the court of Batu—another of Genghis Khan's grandsons—Nicolaus and Gosset were detained, although we aren't told why. So the two Franciscans and Homo Dei continued eastward, almost paralleling Carpini's route, until they were brought to the camp of Mangu Khan—who had been elected chairman after the death of Kuyuk.

On January 3, 1254, they were escorted to Mangu's house. And there at the end of the world, on the Great Khan's doorstep, wearing sandals and ragged brown cloaks, Brothers William and Bartholomew folded their hands and started to sing, because it was Christmastide in Asia as surely as it was in Europe:

> *A solis ortus cardine*
> *et usque terrae limitem*
> *Christum canamus principem*
> *natum Maria virgine.*

After they finished singing they were searched for knives. Then they were allowed into the presence of the khan. They saw a middle-aged, middle-sized, flat-nosed man lolling on a fur-covered bed beside his young wife. He had a daughter named Cirina by a Christian woman who was now dead. Cirina was seated on another bed with some babies, and to William's eyes she appeared "horribly ugly." The room, hung with gold cloth, was heated by a fire of wormwood, thorns, and cow dung.

"Fear not," said the khan.

"Had I been afraid," said William, "I would not have come."

Mangu invited them to drink: wine, mare's milk, rice wine, or mead. William declined with thanks, and presumably Bartholomew did the same; although out of respect William tasted the rice wine, which he found clear and aromatic. Homo Dei, the interpreter, accepted a cup without hesitation. Homo Dei then had another and another, so that before long the Franciscans could not understand what he was saying. The khan also got drunk. In fact, reports Brother William, during the four months they stayed at Mangu Khan's court this happened very often.

In April, at a final audience, the Mongol ruler told them:

"We believe there is only one God. By Him we live and by Him we die. Before Him we are righteous of heart. But just as God has given the hand a variety of fingers, so has He given mankind a variety of ways. To you He has given the Scriptures, yet you do not abide by them. . . . To us He has given soothsayers. We do what they say and we live in peace."

William and Homo Dei then started back, carrying a jeweled belt as a talisman against thunder and lightning. Brother Bartholomew remained at Karakorum, not because he wanted to but because he was sick, and that was the last anybody ever heard of him.

A year later William and Homo Dei reached the fortress of Acre, in what is now Israel. There William stopped to preach and to write a long account of his trip. His senses were acute, his memory exceptional, and unlike many servants of the Lord he did not restrict himself to ecclesiastic observations. He noted, for example, that the Caspian was an inland sea, not an arm of the ocean as geographers of the time maintained. He had watched the Tartars building and coloring their gigantic tents, which were transported on carts, twenty-two oxen drawing each cart. The oxen were yoked in two ranks, eleven abreast. And the shaft of the vehicle, he said, was as long as the mast of a ship.

He remembered that Orengai tribesmen were in the

habit of fastening polished slats of bone to their feet so that they could glide across frozen snow and ice.

He described Mongolian money—bits of cotton paper, a handsbreadth square, "on which they print lines like those on Mangu's seal. They write with a brush such as artists use, and in one sign they combine letters to form a complete word."

He did not think the Asiatics could be converted. They appeared sympathetic to every religion, he said, but would submit to none. They were beyond understanding.

As for Christianity in that part of the world, he confirmed its existence, saying that on the thirtieth of November, Saint Andrew's Day, he and Brother Bartholomew entered a Nestorian church in the village of Cailac and "sang joyously, as loud as we could, *Salve regina*, it having been a long time since we last saw a church."

Nestorius, the fifth-century patriarch of Constantinople, had sent missionaries into Asia. Just how far they traveled will never be known, but they may have gone all the way through China, perhaps to the Pacific coast, because in the seventeenth century some undeniably hard evidence turned up. At Singanfu, capital of the province of Shen-si, laborers accidentally unearthed a stone tablet surmounted by a Nestorian cross embellished with flowers. This tablet, which measures eight feet by three feet, is covered with nearly 2,000 Chinese characters, followed by an inscription in Syriac. It repeats part of the Old and New Testament, and tells of a Bishop Adam, or A-lo-pen, who brought the Scriptures to Emperor Tai Tsung in the city of Singanfu. Tai Tsung, second emperor of the Tang dynasty, reigned from A.D. 627 to 649. According to the tablet, he approved of Christ's message and ordered it to be preached.

However, during religious persecutions of the late Tang

era Christianity was prohibited and Christian churches were torn down. The huge tablet probably was buried at that time, at the direction of Nestorian priests, in order to save it from destruction. No other trace of Christianity has been found in this part of China, yet it is conceivable that a remote memory of Bishop A-lo-pen and his Chinese followers lasted until the Middle Ages. If so, he may have been the original Prester John.

In any event, Brother William had little use for Nestorians. Their polygamy troubled him, the amount of wine they drank, the beating of drums during Mass, and various other things:

"They say their offices, and have sacred books in Syriac, but they do not know the language, so they chant like those monks among us who do not know grammar, and they are absolutely depraved. . . . When they enter church they wash their lower parts like Saracens. They eat meat on Friday and have their feasts on that day in the Saracen fashion. A bishop rarely visits this place, hardly once in fifty years."

Concerning the elusive priest-king, he summarized what the Mongols had told him, but his account is a spider web of tales. Scholars say that he must have become confused by their half-truths, flights of memory, and luxurious fabrication. Still, fantasy is more persuasive than reality, and Brother William's rich narrative played dreamily upon the imagination of Europe:

Somewhere in Asia a powerful Christian monarch . . .

Marco Polo, like the Franciscans, listened for news of him.

After twenty-five years of travel Marco returned to Venice and reported that there had been a great Christian lord called Uang Khan, or King John, but he was killed in battle a long time ago.

Still the idea refused to wither. If Prester John could be found and his armies allied with those of Europe—as soon as that could be accomplished the Turks would be overwhelmed and Jerusalem set free.

During the fourteenth century Prester John moved to Africa.

He was now 200 years old, but very possibly he had access to that marvelous fountain "which hath within itself every kind of taste, for it changeth taste every hour by day and night, and is scarce three days' journey from Paradise." Whoever drank from this fountain three times, while fasting, would never again get sick and would remain thirty-two years old forever.

His first manifestation in Africa was vague—an Ethiopian patriarch who governed a vast number of archbishoprics, each of which contained many bishops. But then a peripatetic Dominican named Jordanus de Sévérac produced a book titled *Mirabilia Descripta*, regarding a number of countries he had visited and some he had not. About Ethiopia he wrote: "The lord of that land I believe to be more potent than any in the world. He is said to have under him fifty-two kings . . ." and so forth. Sévérac also announced that the people were Christian, which was partly true because there had been a Christian sect in Ethiopia ever since the fourth century.

A few years later an unknown Spanish friar wrote a book which unequivocally located the priest-king in Africa. Not only had he himself traveled through John's domain, said the friar, he had visited its capital city, Malsa. "From the time I came to Malsa, I saw and heard marvelous things every day. I inquired what the terrestrial paradise was like . . ."

In Madrid are three manuscript versions of this friar's fabulous narrative. One of them has a drawing of John's imperial banner: a Latin cross between two shepherds' crooks.

Confronted by visible evidence, supported by personal testimony, who could doubt that the omnipotent monarch now reigned on the opposite bank of the Nile —for it was agreed during the Middle Ages that this river separated the two continents.

King João of Portugal, meditating upon Islamic power in Africa, ordered Affonso de Paiva and Pedro da Covilhão to find Prester John. João's command was not a death sentence, but it is probable that the emissaries told everybody good-bye with unusual affection.

Go find Prester John, said the king, so that we may combine our forces. And I would like to know more about India—what sort of goods we might buy and sell there. Also, find out whether the Indian Sea is surrounded by land, as Ptolemy taught, or whether it connects with the Ocean Sea. Let me know where Africa ends.

In May of 1487, with 400 golden cruzados and a briefcase full of credentials that might or might not provide insurance, Pedro and Affonso set out from Lisbon on horseback, charged by their sovereign "to discover and learn where Prete Janni dwelt, and whether his territories reached unto the sea; and where the pepper and cinnamon grow . . ."

At Barcelona they got a ship to Naples, and after a bit of difficulty sailed along to Rhodes. Here they were advised to continue the trip disguised as merchants, so they bought some honey to serve as merchandise and then proceeded to Alexandria, where they fell sick. While they were hors de combat their supply of honey disappeared. One scholar believes the thief must have been the sultan's chamberlain. Another says the governor of Alexandria confiscated the honey because he thought the

Portuguese were about to die. No matter. They surprised the Egyptians by recovering and then managed to get paid for the stolen merchandise—which sounds incredible.

On to Cairo, where they joined a party of Moorish traders going to Aden in a dhow. And here they decided to carry out the king's orders by traveling in different directions. Affonso would look for Prester John in Africa while Pedro would continue to India. They would rendezvous at Cairo.

Covilhão sailed across the Arabian Sea to the Malabar Coast where he observed how business was influenced by the monsoon: ships from the west arrived in August or September and departed a few months later on the northeast monsoon—loaded with silk, porcelain, emeralds, rhubarb, ginger, frankincense, musk, cinnamon, amber, cloves, sandalwood, and other such exotic items.

Silks and jewels and intricate ivory carvings still are valuable, of course, but herbs and spices have become so common that we cannot imagine paying much for them. Five centuries ago things were different. Toast sprinkled with sugar and pepper was a rare delicacy, the delight of wealthy Portuguese. And enough pepper would kill the taste of spoiled meat. And bathing was not fashionable, so that anything—perfumes, aromatic herbs—anything that masked the odor of reeking flesh was bought eagerly. A citizen would often breathe through a perfume-drenched handkerchief when chatting with a neighbor who had not bathed for a couple of years. Covilhão's observation, therefore, was not that of an idle tourist. The king would be much interested in the kinds and quantities of Indian spices and knowing when the traders sailed.

He went next to Ormuz at the mouth of the Persian Gulf, and from there he caught a ship to the golden city of Sofala far down the coast of East Africa. Here he picked up information suggesting that Africa did come to an end somewhere below, which meant that King João's sea captains should be able to make it all the way. And with this important news Covilhão decided to start back. It was now the year 1490, about time to meet Affonso de Paiva in Cairo.

Affonso was not there.

Covilhão eventually learned that his associate had returned in very poor health and died without telling anybody where he had been.

For a while Covilhão seems to have hesitated, uncertain whether he should report to the king or continue the search for Prester John. He was about to start for Portugal when the king's secret service—a rabbi and a shoemaker—intercepted him. They said the king was most anxious to hear about Prester John. Covilhão obediently wrote an account of his trip for the shoemaker to take to Portugal; then he and the rabbi booked passage to Ormuz, because the rabbi had some sort of business there and did not like the idea of traveling alone.

At last, with the rabbi off his hands, Covilhão was free to resume the search. But instead—and nobody can quite explain this—he sailed past Ethiopia and disembarked at Jidda on the east bank of the Red Sea. From here he traveled to Mecca disguised as a Moslem pilgrim, dressed all in white, his head shaved. Apparently he wanted to take a look at the holiest of Moslem relics, the sacred meteorite. Very few unbelievers have been reckless enough to attempt this. Covilhão not only saw the stone, he got away without being discovered and decapitated.

Still he did not carry out the king's orders. He continued north to Sinai where he visited the monastery of Saint Catherine and heard Mass for the first time since leaving the Christian world four years earlier.

Only then did he sail down the Red Sea once more.

It was known that he got off at the port of Zeila, but there King João's secret agents lost track of him.

Five years later Vasco da Gama, en route to India, put in at Mozambique and inquired about Prester John: "We were told that Prester John resided not far from this place, that he held many cities along the coast ..."

But da Gama was told also that the domain of the great ruler could be reached only after a difficult journey on the backs of camels. It was beginning to sound familiar. Prester John was always just around the bend. Besides, if there should be a Christian king somewhere in this country, no matter what he might be called, he could not be the legendary monarch of the past. So, probably without much reflection, da Gama declined a camel ride and sailed off to India. Scholars think he may have picked up rumors of the ancient Zimbabwe Empire.

In 1520 a group of Portuguese reached the court of Lebna Dengel, the Christian ruler of Ethiopia, and it seemed that the priest-king had at last been found. That his name happened to be Lebna Dengel was unimportant. By the inscrutable laws of European logic he must be Prester John. Europe had heard about a Christian king of Ethiopia named Prester John. Here was a Christian king of Ethiopia. Ergo: Lebna Dengel must be Prester John.

His limitless realm, though, was terribly disappointing —a kingdom of mud huts.

As for his subjects: "They are a poor civil people with miserable clothes, and they come into the water uncovered, a black tall people with thick matted locks, which from their birth they neither cut nor comb, so that they wear their hair like a lump of wool, and they carry pointed oiled sticks with which they scratch the vermin which crawl beneath, because they cannot reach their scalps with their fingers, and scratching their heads is their sole occupation."

Lebna Dengel did not mind being called Prester John. He had a good many other titles and if the visitors were pleased to call him this—so be it. What did interest him about the Portuguese was their version of Christianity. The wafers used in Holy Communion, what were they like?—because in Ethiopia an ordinary roll served the purpose. Lebna Dengel was fascinated to learn that the Portuguese had an iron with which they imprinted a crucifix on each wafer.

What sort of garments did European priests wear?

Father Francisco Alvares, the expedition's chaplain, was obliged to get dressed up for Mass, meanwhile explaining the symbolism of each garment. Lebna Dengel was not satisfied; Father Alvares had to go through it a second time. "I brought to him the full vestments, the chalice, corporals, altar stone, and cruets. He saw all, piece by piece, and ordered me to take it and unsew the altar stone, which was sewn up in a clean cloth, and I unsewed half of it, and had it again covered up . . ."

Lebna Dengel said that he understood there were two Churches in the Western World, one under the authority of Rome, the other of Constantinople. How could there be two?

Father Alvares explained the Roman Catholic position: although spiritual leadership of the Church had at one time emanated from Constantinople, this no longer was true. Lebna Dengel, whose Christianity derived from the Coptic Church of Egypt, did not argue with Alvares; he merely listened.

On Christmas Day the Portuguese assembled a little choir. Lebna Dengel did not attend the service, he remained out of sight; but each time they began anew he sent a messenger to ask what was being sung.

Ethiopian services were not favorably reviewed by

Father Alvares. Ethiopian priests did nothing but dance and sing and jump, he said, and while jumping they touched their feet with their hands. Lebna Dengel asked if Portuguese priests danced like that. No, replied Father Alvares, they did not. "Upon this he sent to ask whether, as that was not our custom, we thought theirs bad. We sent word that the service of God, in whatever manner it was done, seemed to us good."

Another topic of mutual interest was the possibility of smashing Islam. Lebna Dengel thought the Portuguese should build a number of forts, for which he would gladly supply provisions and laborers. And Zeila should be captured in order to assure control of the Red Sea. After that, through the combined strength of Ethiopia and Portugal, the Moslem armies could be defeated and Mecca itself would fall.

"This seemed good to the Prester," Alvares wrote, "and he again said he would give the provisions, gold, and men, and all that was necessary."

During these discussions the interpreter was Pedro da Covilhão—now an old man but in good health, with a native wife and quite a few children. In Portugal it was thought that he had died many years ago, because there had been no word of him since he landed at Zeila. Alvares says nothing about the first encounter with Covilhão, which is strange, because they must have heard about his mission. Even if they had not known anything about him they must have been astonished to find a countryman at the court of the Ethiopian king.

Covilhão had not spoken Portuguese for such a long time that he had trouble telling his story. He had reached the Ethiopian court during the reign of Eskender, who was delighted to receive an envoy from a distant Christian monarch. Eskender promised to send Covilhão back to Portugal with a message of appreciation to King João, and with all sorts of gifts. Unfortunately he died and his brother, Na'od, inherited the throne. Na'od told Covilhão that foreigners were not permitted to leave the country.

Fourteen years later Na'od died and the crown passed to his son, Lebna Dengel. Covilhão tried again. Lebna Dengel said no.

According to Father Alvares, Covilhão was generally esteemed and had great influence over Prester John. His only problem was that he could not leave Ethiopia. When the other Portuguese left in 1521 he was still there.

Prester John would be heard from again. And again, and again, his majesty augmented by the invention of movable type. He began to reign over a kingdom of chapbooks—cheaply printed pamphlets illustrated with crude woodcuts and sold by street peddlers. Not many of these chapbooks have survived, for which we may be grateful; it is always embarrassing to come upon a hero in the marketplace.

In 1590 a forgotten traveler published *The Rare and Most Wonderful Thinges which Edward Webbe, an Englishman Borne, Hath Seen and Passed in His Troublesome Travailles in the Citties of Jerusalem, Damasko, Bathelem, and Gallely; and in the lands of Jewrie, Egipt, Grecia, Russia, and in the land of Prester John.* Webbe tells us that the Prester "keepeth very beautiful court" and "hath every day to serve him at his table, sixty kinges wearing leaden crowns on their heads, and those serve in the meat unto Prester John's table: and continually the first dish of meat set upon his table is a dead man's scull, cleane picked, and laid in black earth; putting him in mind that he is but earth, and that he must die, and shall become earth again."

Another Englishman borne, not a traveler but a poet

of some repute, by name Wm. Shakespeare—or Shak-
speare, or Shekespere, however you like it—this poet wrote
his epitaph:

"I will go on the slightest errand now to the Antipodes
that you can devise to send me on; I will fetch you a
toothpicker now from the furthest inch of Asia; bring you
the length of Prester John's foot; fetch you a hair off the
Great Cham's beard . . ."

After that we don't hear much of him. When we do it is
always faintly, and more faintly, like the distant tinkle
of a camel's bell.

6

To the Indies

Enea Silvio Piccolomini, whom you may know better as Pius II, declared in 1461 that just about everybody agreed on the spherical shape of the earth: *Mundi formam omnes fere consentiunt rotundam esse.* This conflicts with popular wisdom, which holds that nobody until Columbus truly understood the situation.

All the same, scholars insist that pre-Christian Greeks knew the earth was a globe, and they tell us that this knowledge was not lost during the Middle Ages—which sounds logical; consequently I am willing to go along with Enea Piccolomini.

What's curious, though, given this knowledge, is that until the fifteenth century there was no organized effort to find out what might be happening among the antipodes. Only a few people had crossed the horizon, and most of them went not because they were inquisitive but for some commonplace reason. The monks, naturally, to meditate and proselyte; the others to make money. There were very few pure tourists in the old days. Those who traveled merely for the satisfaction of wandering seem to have been oddities.

The one whose name is synonymous with visits to far-away places, Marco Polo, accompanied his father and uncle on business, and the fact that we know where he went and what he experienced is simply a result of Marco's bad luck. Some time after their return, probably about 1296, during the war between Genoa and Venice, he was captured and spent a while counting his toes in a Genoese prison. There he met a professional storyteller named Rustichello and dictated to him that *sui generis* account of Eastern marvels. If he had not been imprisoned he might sooner or later have employed a scribe to record this unique trip, or he might not.

Anyway, Rustichello preserved Marco Polo's flamboyant narrative, which seeped gradually into the consciousness of Europe and crystallized, along with who knows how many other molecules of thought, until the Infante, Dom Henrique of Portugal—whom we call Prince Henry the Navigator—moved from Lisbon to Sagres and the earth we recognize yet never comprehend began to be unveiled.

Marco Polo's contribution to this can only be estimated, but it can be estimated more closely than you might suspect. For one thing, Henry's elder brother Pedro spent a while in Venice and was presented by the Signoria with a copy of Marco's travels. Henry must have examined this valuable gift and surely it affected the course of his explorations—though we will never know just how much because so many documents from those days were destroyed in the Lisbon earthquake of 1755.

We do know, however, that Columbus was influenced by Marco Polo because he took aboard the *Santa María* a Latin edition of this famous book. His personal copy now belongs to the Columbian Library in Seville and shows much use, its margins studded with notes in the admiral's handwriting. Especially significant is the fact that Marco located Japan far to the east of its actual position, thus bringing it much closer to the West, and his good student Columbus therefore underestimated the distance he would have to sail.

Still, unless you are mad you do not set off across an unknown ocean with no more than a book for guidance; and Columbus, however obsessed he may have been, was not mad. He had studied not only Marco Polo but everything else available—certainly the reports of Portuguese captains who went sailing uneasily down the African coast.

In 1412 the first attempt had been made to round Cape Bojador. It failed. So did the next attempt, and the next, and eleven more. If you look at a map you will see a minuscule extrusion of Africa just a fraction of an inch below the Canary Islands. It does not look in the least fearsome, but early mariners were terrified by the prospect of this cape which, in Arabic legend, marked the entrance to the Green Sea of Darkness. There a ship would stick fast in gelatinous slime, loathsome monsters hovered in the depths, and men turned black beneath a scorching sun.

Gil Eanes, one of the bravest men who ever lived, finally rounded this cape in a barca—a tiny ship with square sails—and to the amazement of everybody aboard, including himself, they saw open water to the south. As proof that he had succeeded, Gil Eanes brought home to his prince a flowering plant from Guinea.

In 1435 he again rounded the cape and went a little farther south, accompanied by Henry's "royal cupbearer," Affonso Baldaia. They rowed ashore to look around and saw footprints and camel tracks.

On the next trip Baldaia put two mounted knights ashore to reconnoiter. They rode into the desert until they were confronted by a group of citizens armed with assegais, at which point the knights wisely went galloping back to their ship.

A few years later Antão Goncalves returned with ten captured Africans, some gold dust, an oxhide shield, and several ostrich eggs which were cooked and served to Dom Henrique. "And we may well presume," writes the royal chronicler Azurara, "that there was no other Christian prince in this part of Christendom who had such eggs upon his table." No doubt this was true. Henry must have enjoyed his eggs, which sounds like an innocent pleasure, but you may be sure there were those who bitterly objected. People might be out of work, yet there sat the prince scooping up an ostrich omelet.

Things began to change, though, because Captain Nuño Tristão brought back twenty-nine Africans. Then more captives arrived. People stopped criticizing Henry's expeditions.

"Their covetousness," writes Azurara, speaking of the Portuguese, "now began to wax greater. And, as they saw the houses of others full to overflowing of male and female slaves, and their property increasing, they thought about the whole matter and began to talk among themselves."

One of Henry's retainers, who called himself Lancarote —Lancelot—was awarded the first slave-hunting license. His caravels anchored at an island off the Guinea coast and raided a village: "And at last our Lord God, who rewards every noble act, willed that for the toil they had undergone in His service . . . they took captive of these Moors, what with men, women and children, 165, besides those that perished or were killed."

Lancarote eventually came home with 235 captives.

Henry, as sponsor, was entitled to a royal fifth, but he gave his share of the slaves to friends and courtiers. The successful voyage pleased him more than any profit, we are told, and he reflected "with great pleasure" upon the salvation of those souls which before were lost.

How remote it sounds—this medieval morality in which lives and bodies lay at the disposition of Christians. Azurara observes that the lot of Moorish slaves "was now quite the contrary of what it had been, since before they had lived in perdition of soul and body . . . And now consider what a reward should be that of the Infante at the hands of the Lord God, for having thus given them the chance of salvation, and not only them, but many others whom he afterward acquired . . . And so forthwith he made Lancarote a knight."

About this time Henry's endeavor received papal attention. In 1452 the bull *Dum Diversas* authorized Portugal to attack Saracens, pagans, and unbelievers, to capture and keep all their goods, and reduce the owners to slavery.

It sounds unreal and most un-Christian; but of course only the visage of morality changes. You recall the United States ambassador to Laos during the Vietnam War who explained that while we regretted the terrible suffering of the Laotian people it was better for them to die in the ruins of their country than for America to permit the advance of atheistic Communism. And the army officer who explained that in order to save a certain village it had to be destroyed. Plus ça change, plus c'est la même chose, say the French, who seldom deceive themselves about human nature.

The slave trade grew quickly, along with Portuguese knowledge of the African coast, and Henry seems always to have valued knowledge above profit. He demanded full reports from his captains.

Goncalo Pacheco went raiding, but his landing party was ambushed. Seven Portuguese were killed and reportedly were eaten. Azurara, that faithful scribe, says the rumor was untrue; only their livers were eaten.

Nuño Tristão pushed on south with twenty-two men. He and nineteen of his crew were killed by poisoned arrows. The survivors were desperately wounded. Five ship's boys—all that remained of the company—managed to get the ship back to Portugal.

An Italian in Henry's service, Alvise da Ca' da Mosto—Cadamosto—explored as far as the Gambia, returning with news of palm wine, elephants, marriage customs, snake charmers, exotic foods, and so on. Everything interested him. He saw and described the hippopotamus, which he called the horse-fish, and he discussed the artificial elongation of women's breasts. The Renaissance was opening; life should be investigated.

He reported that while ashore in Gambia the natives would come to stare at him: "They were amazed no less at my clothing than at my white color . . . some touched my hands and arms, and rubbed me with saliva, to see if my whiteness was a dye or really flesh, and seeing that it was flesh, stood agape with wonder."

When some natives were aboard ship he told a sailor to play the bagpipe. The Gambians thought it must be a living animal until the sailor showed them how it worked; then they decided "God had made it with His own hands, that it sounded so sweetly, with so many different voices."

Cadamosto taught them to make candles, and they were delighted.

He traveled inland to visit a petty king named Budomel who had more wives than he could count. There were nine in the first village, each of whom kept five or six servant girls subject to the king's desire. All the same, Budomel was not happy and demanded of Cadamosto, "having been given to understand that Christians knew how to do many things, whether by chance I could give him the means to satisfy numerous women, for which he promised me a fine reward."

Farther south, Cadamosto's expedition was attacked by a fleet of fifteen canoes: "In each were eight to ten warriors, imposing figures in white cotton robes and white headdresses decorated with a wing on each side and a feather in the middle . . . They all lifted their paddles up in the air and stared at us as if we were ghosts. Suddenly, without provocation, they took up their bows and shot a cluster of arrows at us." About this time the Portuguese sailors decided they had seen enough of Africa, so Cadamosto was obliged to turn around.

Prince Henry died in 1460, still dreaming of a route to the Indies.

A French scholar, Gilbert Renault, reflecting on this abstemious visionary—this devout ascetic who, in actual fact, slept on a bed of gravel and wore a hair shirt—wrote that twice a day the tides came sweeping toward the Sagres promontory as they had done for thousands of years, and to Henrique the waves seemed to beat, or sigh, or thunder, according to the humor of the ocean, these words: "Portugal! Portugal! Your destiny lies not among the mountains of the east, for all your glorious victories, but on my flowing plains whose infinite spaces I shall reveal to you . . . Portugal! Portugal!"

The prince himself wrote nothing; or, if he did, whatever he wrote has disappeared. We have no personal statement of what passed through his mind. And after death, for some inexplicable reason, he failed to decay; one Diogo Gomes, having been ordered to examine his body before it was reinterred at Batalha, found his corpse dry and intact—except the tip of the nose.

He was just the patron Columbus needed, but they missed each other by thirty years. It seems unfair, as though a cog slipped and the machinery of the world did not quite mesh.

Dom Henrique's insistent probe of the African coast may have seemed a trifle moonstruck to his contemporaries, but he had his reasons, only the first of which might be called impractical. He had a wish to know what lay beyond Cape Bojador, says Azurara, yet when his defeated captains returned again and again he listened courteously to their accounts and rewarded them as well as if they had fully executed his wishes.

Such tolerance might be attributed to a man's natural grace, but under the circumstances there has been speculation. For one thing, he never married and his captains all were surprisingly young. At the same time Portugal was exploring the Atlantic, yet the more experienced Atlantic captains do not seem to have been treated with any lenience. As one historian delicately puts it, Henry's graciousness when confronted with failure after failure by his youthful Sea of Darkness adventurers is difficult to understand "except in terms of special relationships."

Apart from this he sounds pragmatic. He wanted commerce with other lands. He wanted to learn the extent of Moslem power. He was anxious to convert pagans. He hoped to find and join forces with that legendary Christian king of Asia, Prester John. So his young captains moved farther and farther south, uncertainly, but with rising confidence.

It's odd that nobody knew the shape of Africa. Egypto-Phoenician explorers during the reign of Necho II, about 600 B.C., had sailed completely around the continent:

they went down the Red Sea, doubled the Cape of Good Hope, and entered the Mediterranean at Gibraltar. Herodotus summarized this voyage, so it's curious that the outline of Africa could be forgotten. Indeed, Necho's expedition may not have been the first; although evidence is meager, Egyptian mariners during the reign of Queen Hatshepsut—nine centuries before the Phoenicians—may have done the same thing.

One gets a feeling that some echo of these voyages survived until the time of Prince Henry, causing him to order his captains out again and again, as though he sensed that the hideous Green Sea of Darkness on Arabic charts already had been crossed.

In 1469 "a respected citizen of Lisbon" named Fernão Gomes was granted a five-year monopoly on the Guinea trade, provided he would explore 500 leagues to the south. His coat of arms was a silver shield with the heads of three Negroes, each wearing gold earrings, a gold nose ring, and a gold collar—which nicely illustrates what the Portuguese had in mind. His pilots reached the equator and were dismayed to find that the coast, which had been trending almost due east—as though they must be near the continent's end—now turned south again. Possibly it went south forever.

Diogo Cão sailed in 1482. He discovered a broad river which the natives called Nzadi, which the Portuguese corrupted to Zaire, which we call the Congo. He traveled some distance upstream before edging farther south, and when he returned to Portugal he was knighted by King João II.

A couple of years later he sailed again, venturing farther—almost four-fifths of the way to the bottom of the continent—but as far as he could tell it had no end.

Nothing else is heard of Diogo Cão, not even where

and how he died; and because his name is written small in the logbook of explorers he is easy to forget. But he took with him on both trips some marble *padroes* which were set up at significant points—a *padrão* being a stone pillar surmounted by a cross. Until then each stage of a route had been marked with a wooden cross, or by carving on trees; but King João felt that the route to the Indies should be immortalized with something permanent. Cão set up four of these columns. All have been recovered, either in fragments or complete. On two of them the inscriptions still are legible. The last *padrão*, erected twenty-two degrees below the equator on Cape Cross, was found in 1893 and is now in Germany. It gives this information:

> 6685 YEARS HAD PASSED SINCE THE CREATION
> OF THE WORLD, 1485 SINCE THE BIRTH OF CHRIST,
> WHEN HIS MOST ILLUSTRIOUS AND SERENE
> HIGHNESS KING JOÃO OF PORTUGAL ORDERED THIS
> PILLAR TO BE ERECTED BY HIS KNIGHT DIOGO CÃO.

How many of us will bequeath to posterity such a dignified monument?

Bartolomeu Dias, being a larger name, was one you were expected to memorize in school, together with what he did; yet all that lingers is the melodic name. His tremendous accomplishment is meaningless now. He turned the corner of Africa, and did so without knowing it.

In August of 1487 two caravels and a supply ship started out, not on another coasting voyage but with the definite intention of rounding the southernmost cape—if there was a cape. Foul weather enveloped them; they ran before it with close-reefed sails day after day, and the sea grew cold. Out of the storm at last, far off course, Dias gave orders to steer eastward in search of land. Nothing appeared, so he altered course to the north. Mountains came over the horizon and in February of 1488 they dropped anchor at a pleasant bay. They went ashore to refill the water casks and then continued along the coast, wondering where they were. But the land bore steadily east, which told them what had happened, so Dias set up a *padrão*.

He was anxious to look further but supplies were short, the storm had been fearful, and his men wanted to go home. He wheedled three more days out of them, that was all. At the threshold of the Indian Ocean, just where the coast began curling north, they forced him to stop.

As they sailed back in the direction of Portugal, past the *padrão*, Dias acknowledged it "with as much sorrow and feeling as though he were taking his last leave of a son condemned to exile."

Again they doubled the cape, which he named Tormentoso because it was so stormy. King João renamed it the Cape of Good Hope, according to a sixteenth-century historian, "for that it promised the discovery of India that was so much wished for, and sought over so many years."

Dias would approach this cape one more time, in 1500, on his way to India with the fleet of Pedro Álvares Cabral. Almost within sight of the *padrão* a hurricane struck. Four ships were lost, one of them captained by Dias. The chronicler Galvão had this to say about him: "Q se pode dizer qvia terra da India, mas ña entrou nella, como Mouses nã terra de promissam." Even if you are not adept at sixteenth-century Portuguese the meaning is moderately clear; he saw India, but, like Moses and the Promised Land, he did not enter in.

However, that's looking ahead. His arrival at Lisbon after doubling the cape must have been very fine. What is more interesting, though, is that the ubiquitous and persistent Columbus somehow contrived to be present when Dias knelt before the king. On the margin of his copy of *Imago Mundi* Columbus wrote: "December of this year 1488 Bartholomaeus Didacus, commandant of three caravels which the King of Portugal had sent to Guinea to seek out the land, arrived in Lisbon. He reported that he had reached a promontory which he called Cabo de Boã Esperança . . ."

Who actually named the cape Boã Esperança—Dias or King João—we do not know. It's unimportant, of course; but still, such details should be preserved.

Cortés, Pizarro, Balboa, de Soto, Coronado, Ponce de León—however unique they may have been in life, as most assuredly each man was unique, they slant down the centuries in a group. So do those fabulous Elizabethans: Drake, Raleigh, Frobisher, Hawkins, and the rest. And the Portuguese: Magellan, da Gama, Eanes, Dias, Cão. But we never associate anybody with that blue-eyed red-haired mystic from the golden age of discovery: Columbus.

His mother was Susanna Fontanarossa. She must have been lovely, with such a name. His father, Domenico, was a weaver, a fact which embarrassed Columbus. His parents are not mentioned in any of his writings. Late in life, when he had become famous and could associate with kings, he would boast that he was not the first admiral of his family. And according to his son Ferdinand he declared: "Let them call me by what name they will. After all, David first tended sheep before becoming King of Jerusalem." And, like Shakespeare, he wangled a coat of arms. A coat of arms! The most celebrated explorer of all time and the most renowned dramatist. Surely it must be true, as somebody said, within the forehead of every man lies a world of streaming shadows.

He died at the age of fifty-five or so in Valladolid, half

a day's travel northwest of Madrid. The old house is gone, except for part of one wall scarred by centuries of weather and overgrown with vines in which some officious sparrows have nested. Bolted to the wall is a blunt proclamation on a metal tablet:

AQUI MURIO COLON

Where the house once stood there is now a gloomy little museum which nobody visits. Valladolid is and has long been a cultural center, a university town, but it does not have much appeal for tourists. A few come to visit the College of San Gregorio where there is a large and important collection of sixteenth-century painted wood sculpture—flamboyant, gilded, intensely religious works by Hernandez, Berruguete, Juan de Juni, and many others; but compared to the glamorous cities of Valencia and Seville and Granada and Toledo, Valladolid remains unknown. Architecturally it has developed like most cities, adding lifeless appendages of concrete and brick, while its heart beats on and on at the university—generation after generation. Now you see the dark-bearded dark-eyed boys in turtleneck sweaters jiggling pinball machines at their smoky hangouts, the girls with notebooks and lipstick and fashionable boots and jeans and long hair flowing. On the new walls, spray-painted here or there, today's graffiti: APALA LIBERTAD. F.E.I. LEGALIZACION. AMNISTIA TOTAL, Y AHORA! Demands that briefly mean so much.

Even the Casa de Colón, as the little museum is called, appears impatient with the past; it displays a TV antenna on the roof, perhaps because the elderly caretaker has not enough to do. Perhaps he is thinking about his favorite program, wondering who stole the diamonds or which team will win the soccer match, while he follows you around and gravely turns on a strand of weak yellow lightbulbs in one room after another.

Maps. Maps. All the maps you could possibly care about.

A nameless conquistador's sword and dented helmet. Did somebody drop the helmet or was it dented by an Aztec mace? One is tempted to ask, but that's not the sort of question the caretaker is prepared to answer.

Fragments of prehistoric clay sculpture from the New World—a disorganized offering of broken masks and pots.

Fourteen gold-framed representations of Columbus by various artists. All except two show the strong nose, the soft oval face, the incipient baldness. Those two exceptions present a lean, sinewy individual related to Don Quixote.

Then there is an eighteenth-century painting of the admiral on his deathbed, as white and calm as a saint. Diego kneels beside his father. Américo Vespucio, Judas-like, stands thoughtfully watching us. And a covey of brown-robed, hooded, candle-carrying Franciscans, obviously expectant, wait to ensure the Admiral's soul.

Thus you proceed through the solemn exhibit while the caretaker follows at a courteous distance, turning off the lights. There are no other visitors to the museum; there might be no more today, nor any tomorrow.

So much for all that. Maps and artifacts and etchings do not interpret what happened during the late fifteenth century, during those few years that affected the world more than anything else since the birth of Christ. Look at it this way: on a pedestal in front of the museum, a few steps from that ancient weather-pitted sparrow-infested wall, sits a black iron replica of the *Santa María* sailing firmly nowhere.

You might feel closer to him at one of Valladolid's sumptuous restaurants with leaded glass windows, heavy crimson drapes, and those ponderous hand-carved Spanish thrones called chairs. After enough brandy, seated like Ferdinand on one of those immovable chairs, you could

imagine the admiral across the black oak table from you
—except for the traffic noise outside. These days it's almost
impossible to dream.

Well, in Valladolid on the twentieth of May, 1506, he
died. This fact is useless, of course, unless you are preparing to take an examination; yet when we know a man's
beginning we should know at least something about his
end.

He was born and grew up in Genoa, as practically
everybody agrees; but how he got from Genoa to Lisbon
has been disputed. Probably as a seaman aboard an
armed merchant ship that was attacked and sunk near
Lagos. By some accounts he swam to shore while clutch-
ing a piece of wood from the ship.

Whatever happened, he reached Lisbon in 1476 and a
year later he sailed to the British Isles. Near Galway he
saw two corpses with bloated faces washed up on the
beach. He described them as "men from Cathay." Presumably they were Lapps; if they were Chinese their
bodies would have decomposed long before the boat
drifted to Ireland. But their nationality isn't important; he
thought they were Oriental, and nobody can even guess
how much that misapprehension shaped the future of the
world.

After several years in Lisbon he married the daughter
of the first governor of Porto Santo, which is an island
near Madeira. This, too, sounds unimportant, but one
result of the marriage was that he inherited the old man's
marine charts and documents. Bartolomé de las Casas
tells us that this acquisition "pleased him much, and made
his desire to study cosmography the more ardent. He
thought more and more of this each day, and his imagination was set aflame."

In addition to bringing him all those maps and charts,
his bride Felipa was related to the Portuguese royal fam-

ily. Columbus seems to have been one of those men who are at the same time preoccupied and icily pragmatic. It seldom hurts to be related, however distantly, to a king. They went to live on Porto Santo where he continued to nourish his fantastic idea. Here again, as though the gods had met and decided, corpses with Oriental features washed up on the beach. And branches of unfamiliar trees. And a plank carved with a strange design.

In 1484 he got an audience with the king. João de Barros, court historian, speaks of Columbus as

. . . an eloquent man, a good Latin scholar, but much inflated with pride . . . Full of the dreams that came to him from his continual travels and the conversations he had had with men of our land well-known for past discoveries, he came to ask Dom João for ships to sail to Cypango through the Ocean Sea . . . The King, seeing his stubbornness, sent him to Dom Diogo Ortiz, the bishop of Ceuta, to Master Rorigo and to Master Jozé, whose authority he customarily accepted in matters of geography and discovery, and they all considered Columbus' words to be vain, for all that he said was founded on imagination or on fictions such as the isle of Cypango in Marco Polo.

Then Felipa died. Las Casas writes with majestic ecclesiastic indifference: "It pleased God to take his wife from him, for it was proper that for his great enterprise he be freed of all cares."

After Felipa's death he left Portugal furtively, perhaps to escape some debts, and showed up at the Spanish court.

Ferdinand and Isabella listened to his wild proposal "with gracious countenance, and decided to submit the matter to a commission of learned men . . ." Now, anybody who has been obliged to deal with a commission of learned men knows what to expect.

Columbus waited two years. Two years! What took so long? You would think a group of men could study the situation and report within a few days, or a couple of weeks. Two years! And still—after two years—they couldn't make a recommendation.

So he went back to Lisbon for another try at King João. And that was when Bartolomeu Dias arrived—home from Cabo de Boã Esperança with banners flying. King João of course was delighted. Columbus, we should assume, would be sick with dismay. Yet, judging from the marginal note on *Imago Mundi,* he seems to have been interested rather than depressed—as though he did not see how Dias's accomplishment might conflict with, or subvert, what he himself had in mind.

It's hard to imagine why Columbus did not quit when Dias returned. A sea route to the Indies had been found; that should have ended the matter. Instead, he traveled to Spain once more and renewed his petition.

Their Catholic Majesties could not make up their minds. They disliked the thought of Portugal establishing sea trade with the Indies and if Columbus could find a shorter route, excellent. Asia might be reached by sailing west, the royal cartographers admitted, yet they agreed that such a voyage would take three years. Under the circumstances should one gamble?

In the summer of 1491 Columbus again grew tired of waiting and decided to try his luck with Charles VIII of France, but hardly had he left court when Isabella sent for him. So he returned and waited some more. Then she said no.

He was riding away on a mule when he was overtaken by a captain of the guards. Isabella once again had changed her mind.

Why? An appeal to Spanish pride, according to some scholars. An unexpected offer of financial help, say others. Maybe both.

Personally, I like the story about Ferdinand playing chess. In this version the king busied himself with a game while Isabella gave Columbus the bad news. Hernando del Pulgar, the queen's secretary, was observing the game and noticed that unless the king made a particular move he would lose a rook. Hernando murmured to Isabella, who then whispered to her husband. Now this is dirty chess. And King Ferdinand—one cannot help feeling repelled—Ferdinand listened to the whispered advice and saved his rook. Consequently he won the game, which pleased him so much that he said to Isabella: "Oh, go ahead, give the Genoese whatever he wants!"

For this reason it came about that just before sunrise on the third of August in a year we all know, the *Niña, Pinta,* and *Santa María* slipped out of Palos harbor.

According to authorities who have studied this trip, and his later trips, Columbus was a superb dead-reckoning navigator. He was also dishonest. Like many a businessman today, he kept duplicate books: one for the facts, one for the public. His men were uneasy about this adventure, so the public log registered fewer leagues than they actually sailed. But in spite of the deception there was much grumbling and muttering while September faded, and by early October the unmistakable smell of mutiny emanated from his fleet.

On the seventh, after an argument with the *Niña's* captain, Columbus altered course to the south. If he had not done this they would have landed in Florida near Cape Kennedy.

Signs of land floated by: green branches, plants, a carved stick. Overhead they saw migratory birds.

About ten o'clock on the night of October eleventh the admiral saw a light which he described as like a candle flame rising and falling. If he did see a light, what was it?

Fireworms spawning on the surface of the water? This is the theory of a British marine biologist. Indians fishing by torchlight? Luminous jellyfish? The Savior beckoning?

None of these, we are told by Samuel Eliot Morison, who explains that the natives of San Salvador often build fires outside their houses on October nights to drive away sand fleas. Morison arranged an experiment in 1959, duplicating as nearly as possible the conditions of 1492. He chose a night when the moon was in the same phase, and he looked toward San Salvador from the deck of a boat several miles offshore. The fire was visible, he said, flaring up each time his associate piled on more wood. So perhaps that was it. But still, crewmen aboard all three ships were gazing ahead, each hoping to claim the 10,000 maravedis offered by Ferdinand and Isabella to the first man who sighted land. The *Pinta*, in fact, was ahead of the *Santa María*, yet not until two in the morning did a sailor named Rodrigo aboard the *Pinta* sing out: "Tierra! Tierra!"

If those fires were occasionally replenished during the night why did nobody except Columbus see them?

All we know is that he claimed for himself, and got, the 10,000 maravedis, leaving the sailor with nothing—a fact one would as soon forget. However, that may be a twentieth-century bias. Las Casas speaks from a more godly age: "It was proper that the reward should go to that one man who had always kept the faith." Symbolically, philosophically, yes, all right, one can't argue. And Rodrigo's sharp eyesight at least guaranteed his corner in the history books: Juan Rodriguez Bermejo, "marinero de la *Pinta*," who was born in the village of Triana.

They anchored at sunrise. Then, very much as we have seen in popular paintings, the three commanders went ashore accompanied by the royal banner of Castile and by the standard of their patrons. They knelt to kiss the land, "thanking God who had requited them after a voyage so long and strange."

Columbus drew his sword, pointed at the sky, and claimed possession of everything in the name of his sovereigns, repeating as many of their titles as he could remember. He thought he had reached an island close to Cypango, the beginning of the Indies.

Morison, that indefatigable navigator, claims to have located the exact strip of beach where this bizarre Shakespearean prologue occurred. The site has been marked with a white cross.

Our heroes next took off for Cuba, stopping frequently, gathering beans, wild cotton, fruit, and other evidence, meanwhile trying to learn where all the gold was and where the Great Khan might be found. So the Arawaks, realizing that something was wanted and eager to be helpful, agreeably pointed ahead.

On Cuba, which he thought must be a Chinese peninsula, Columbus dispatched two ambassadors to the khan—Luis de Torres and Rodrigo de Xerez. They were well qualified. Torres spoke Arabic and Hebrew, therefore he should be able to converse with the Chinese. Xerez had once visited an African chief, so he knew how to approach royalty. The ambassadors started off with a porter, a guide, Latin passports, strings of glass beads, and a letter from Their Catholic Majesties addressed to Magnus Canus. It sounds like Gilbert and Sullivan.

Away they went, up an Indian trail through the Cacoyuguin valley to a settlement near the present town of Holguín. There they met an affable cacique who enter-

tained them for the next four days. They lolled on ceremonial stools called *dujos*—"like some animal with short
arms and legs, the tail lifted up to lean against, and a
head at the other end, with golden eyes and ears"—while
the villagers kissed their hands and feet, and the women
explored their bodies to see if they were made of flesh
like ordinary men.

Columbus wrote in his journal on the sixth of November that his messengers had seen natives carrying
"some sort of cylinder in which sweetly smelling herbs
were glowing. These they supposed were dried herb stalks
covered by an equally dry but broader leaf. The people
sucked the opposite end of the cylinder and, as it were,
drank the smoke. Although this apparently intoxicated
them it also seemed to protect them from fatigue. The
natives called these cylinders *tabacos*."

On Christmas Eve while approaching Haiti the *Santa
María* gently spiked herself on a coral reef and could not
be saved. From her planks they built a little fort, called
Navidad, and Columbus asked for volunteers to man the
garrison until he returned. Most of the ship's crew volunteered, along with several men from the *Niña*. He instructed them to explore the land, to trade for gold, and to
treat the people with respect.

Soon afterward he sailed for Europe aboard the *Niña*,
carrying with him some kidnapped Arawaks.

"Let it not be said," he wrote about the natives, "that
they give freely only that which is of little value, for they
give away gold nuggets as willingly as they do a calabash
of water; and it is easy to recognize when a thing is given
from the heart. . . . These are most loving people, who
do not covet. They love their neighbor as themselves."

Opposite the Azores in mid-February a gale blew up.
He states in his log that the waves were fearsome, and

during the night of the fourteenth he lost sight of the *Pinta*. Lots were drawn three times to see who would represent their ship by making a pilgrimage, assuming *Niña* survived the storm. Some chick-peas were shaken in a sailor's cap, one pea inscribed with a cross. And twice—twice out of three lotteries—Columbus himself drew the marked pea.

He must have been afraid the ship would go down, because he wrote an account of his discovery on a sheet of parchment which he wrapped in a piece of waxed cloth and addressed to the Spanish king and queen. The packet was placed in a small tightly caulked barrel and thrown overboard. It has never been found.

This undelivered message to Ferdinand and Isabella should be mentioned in the flat past tense, instead of implying that tomorrow or the next day somebody wandering across a deserted beach might notice the remnants of a fifteenth-century barrel with a waxed package inside. After all, it's been some time. However, the barrel might yet be recovered—though one should be cautious. In 1892, for instance, a London publisher claimed to have obtained it from a Welsh fisherman. This perhaps is conceivable, but the fact that the manuscript had been written in English would make most buyers suspicious.

And in Germany a facsimile edition entitled *My Secrete Log Boke* appeared on imitation vellum enhanced with authentic barnacles and authentic seaweed.

Well, in early March another storm drove the bedraggled *Niña* northward. Once again, gravely alarmed, they shook up the chick-peas in a sailor's cap and Columbus drew the marked pea. The odds against this are prohibitive.

At last they raised the European coast near Lisbon, and what should be riding at anchor in the Tagus but a

great Portuguese man-of-war whose master was Bartolomeu Dias. The contrast between these two ships—
and the coincidence of Columbus meeting Dias at this
instant—is pure Hollywood.

Dias pulled over in a longboat with an armed escort
and told Columbus to report aboard the warship. The
admiral refused, but showed his credentials, which satisfied Dias who perhaps only wanted a closer look at the
Indians. Then half of Lisbon came aboard to stare at
them.

Columbus dropped anchor at Palos on March 15, having been gone thirty-two weeks. Ferdinand and Isabella
were in Barcelona so he started overland to the peripatetic court. We are told that six Arawaks went with him.
They wore gold nose rings, feathers, and guaycas—belts
studded with gold and polished fishbone—and they carried cages of parrots. Las Casas, at that time a youth in
Seville, remembered seeing this extraordinary procession.

But he had brought back ten Indians, not six. What
happened to the other four?—those that didn't travel to
Barcelona. Were they abandoned in Seville? Were they
sold? Did they become a sideshow? So many flakes of
paint are missing from the mural.

He must have ridden through Barcelona like Alexander through Persepolis. True, his caravels had not returned packed with silks and spices but the next trip
should take care of that. Cypango could not be much
farther.

News of his achievement spread slowly beyond the
Mediterranean countries. In midsummer, months after he
reached Lisbon, the *Nuremberg Chronicle* published
"the events most worthy of notice from the beginning of
the world to the calamity of our time," but failed to mention Columbus. And several days later a Nuremberg scientist urged the Portuguese king to seek a western route to

the Indies. Northern Europe's ignorance seems very strange.

Before leaving on his second voyage Columbus traveled from Barcelona completely across Spain to the shrine of the Holy Virgin of Guadalupe in the mountains of Estremadura, fulfilling the promise he had made during the storm. It is almost certain that he passed through the village of Trujillo where another lad stared at him—an illiterate young swineherd named Francisco Pizarro.

He then returned to Seville by way of Medellín where Cortés, at that time eight years old, undoubtedly saw him.

Why such encounters should be interesting is something I can't explain, any more than it should be interesting that Las Casas watched Columbus pass through Seville. Yet the circumstances remain oddly fixed in the mind. During the Second World War, when I was a navy cadet at Pensacola, I was walking across the base one day and waited at an intersection for a black limousine to go by. Attached to its front fender was an admiral's flag. The limousine stopped at the corner, and because I had never seen an admiral I bent down and looked into the back seat. A gnarled old man with shaggy yellow eyebrows stared out at me. For two or three seconds we looked at each other, then the limousine drove off. I had been staring into the eyes of old "Bull" Halsey, scourge of the Pacific. I was fascinated. Pizarro, on a crooked dusty street in Trujillo, may have felt the same.

On September 25, 1493, Columbus sailed from Cádiz with a fleet of seventeen ships, under order to establish a permanent colony. He took along just about everything you need for settling in an unfamiliar world—sheep, horses, wheat seeds, grapevine cuttings, hundreds of ambitious young men, even a cavalry troop—just about everything except women. Presumably this was not an oversight.

He bore a little south of his previous track and had

an easy crossing to Santo Domingo. Here he turned north and on Guadalupe—named for the Estremadura shrine —his ships frightened some Indians out of their village. The Spaniards went ashore to inspect it. The expedition's doctor wrote in a letter to the municipality of Seville:

> We inquired of the women who were prisoners of the inhabitants what sort of people these islanders were and they said Caribs. . . . They told us that the Carib men use them with such cruelty as would scarcely be believed; and that they eat the children which they bear them, only bringing up those whom they have by their native wives. Such of their male enemies as they can take alive they bring here to their homes to make a feast of them, and those who are killed in battle they eat up after the fighting is over. They declare that the flesh of man is so good to eat that nothing in the world can compare with it; and this is quite evident, for of the human bones we found in the houses, everything that could be gnawed had already been gnawed so that nothing remained but what was hard to eat. In one of the houses we found a man's neck cooking in a pot. . . . When the Caribs take boys as prisoners of war they remove their organs, fatten them until they grow up, and then, when they wish to make a great feast, they kill and eat them, for they say the flesh of women and youngsters is not good to eat. Three boys thus mutilated came running to us . . .

The fact that the fleet did not at once sail for Navidad indicates that Columbus was not worried about a cannibal attack.

When they did arrive they found Navidad destroyed— burned—the bodies of a dozen Spaniards nearby. But it had not been a Carib raid. Almost as soon as they were left alone the members of the garrison had begun to argue. Some went to demand gold from a village chief and then carried off several girls. The Indians retaliated by burning the fort, which was undefended because the hedonistic Spaniards were living separately in little huts—each with five or six women.

Columbus searched for the gold they must have accumulated. He even had the settlement's well dug up, thinking it might be concealed there.

Then the fleet moved on, looking for a more hospitable place.

Isabella was established on the north coast of Haiti a few miles east of Navidad, and like the first colony it soon began to disintegrate: sickness, putrid food, inexperience, a humid climate, hidalgos reluctant to soil their hands—and there stood an administrator who detested administration. "It was inevitable," Las Casas wrote, "that in the face of so many problems to resolve the Admiral should alienate everyone."

After several months at Isabella, bored and irritated and exhausted by his duties, he sailed away from his dissatisfied subjects. He wanted to find out if Cuba was an island or a promontory of China.

Bernáldez mentions something curious which happened on this excursion. A crossbowman who went ashore was surrounded by about thirty Indians, one of whom wore a long white tunic reaching to his feet. The Spaniard at first thought it must be the Trinitarian friar from the ship's company. Then two other light-complexioned Indians appeared in white tunics. The crossbowman was frightened and ran to the edge of the water calling for help.

Columbus, when told about this, must have concluded that he was indeed halfway around the world because three men in white tunics could only be disciples of the Christian king of the Orient, Prester John, whose realm lay close to the Great Wall of China. He tried for the next two days to find these priestly Indians, but scouting parties reported no men in white tunics, nor humans of any sort, only the tracks of some animals which might be griffons or lions.

Early in 1496 he returned to Spain, discouraged because of the problems at Isabella and because he had not located any gold mines. To punish himself, he put on the coarse brown dress of a Franciscan, and except when aboard ship he wore this gown the rest of his life.

Ferdinand and Isabella received him politely. They listened with interest and inspected a few gold nuggets he had brought, along with more Arawaks and various other tropical showpieces. Perhaps they were still enthusiastic, but two years elapsed before he got permission to try again.

This time he went farther south: "I wish to verify what Dom João claims, namely that there is a very large mainland toward the west."

The Portuguese may not have been the first to suspect the existence of South America, nor the first to reach it. Phoenician traders might have landed there, and medieval Africans almost certainly did. Pedro Martir, describing Balboa's trek across Panama, states that the explorers encountered black men whom they believed to have come from Ethiopia on piratical voyages, who were shipwrecked and so established themselves in the mountains of Panama: "The inhabitants of Caruaca have internal fights full of hatred with these Negroes. They enslave each other . . ."

Columbus himself spoke of having received *guanines* from the Indians on Haiti, or Española as he called it.

They told him that black people from the south had visited the island and their spear points were made of this metal. *Guanin* is an African term referring to an alloy of copper and gold. The specimens acquired by Columbus on Haiti were assayed in Spain and contained the same proportion of copper to gold as specimens from Guinea—which might or might not be coincidence.

A few years ago I was talking to a dealer in pre-Columbian artifacts who mentioned that Venetian glass beads sometimes are found in Sinu tombs. He said he had seen lots of them in Colombia, but he did not buy any because they had no market value. I asked how he could be sure it was Venetian glass, and he replied that he knew those beads when he saw them because he used to live in Venice. Besides, Sinu Indians never made glass beads. All of which means very little, unless you know that Sinu tombs date from about the twelfth century.

How did the beads get there?—assuming, of course, that the dealer was not mistaken and that he was telling the truth. I believed him, mostly because he was not trying to sell me a string of beads. He had none to sell. He mentioned them in reference to something else and seemed bored by my questions. Beads, beads. There's no money in beads. Jade, yes. Ceramics, yes. Gold, yes. Beads, no.

Well, on his third voyage Columbus veered so far south that he sailed into the equatorial doldrums. Wine turned to vinegar, water to vapor, wheat to ashes. Lard and salted meat putrefied. But at last the wind came up and brought him to an island which, because of its three peaks, he named Trinidad. Next day his caravels entered the Gulf of Paria, fed by the many mouths of the Orinoco. Two weeks later, leaving this freshwater sea, he perceived the truth:

"If this river does not flow out from Paradise, it comes from an immense land to the south, whereof, until now, no one has had any knowledge."

Then he turned north to Haiti. And there, in September of 1500, the royal inquisitor Francisco de Bobadilla, who had come to reorganize the dreadful administration of the New World, threw Columbus in jail.

Las Casas writes: "When it came time to put the Admiral in irons none of those who were present dared to do the deed, out of respect for his person. But a lowly cook of his household who happened to be there put them on him, with an air of shameless impudence and as much self-assurance as if he were serving him some savory dish."

Columbus must have thought he was going to be executed, because the following dialogue took place when an equerry came to his cell:

"Vallejo, where are you taking me?"

"Sire, I am taking you to the ship that you are to board."

"Vallejo, is this the truth?"

"I swear it on Your Excellency's life that you are going aboard ship."

These words, according to Las Casas, brought him back to life.

When they were at sea, beyond the reach of Bobadilla, Vallejo offered to take off the chains. Columbus refused, saying he would permit them to be removed only at the command of his sovereigns. And in Spain, when they were taken off, he insisted on keeping them. His son Ferdinand remembered these chains; he said they occupied a place of honor in his father's house, and that his father left orders for the chains to be buried with him.

Aboard ship Columbus wrote a long self-justification. He appealed indirectly to Isabella, who had always favored him:

The world has ever treated men ill. It has attacked me a thousand times; until this moment I have resisted all such attacks. Today it casts me down most cruelly; but the hope in Him who created all things sustains me, for His help has ever been at hand. Once before I was downcast and He said unto me: "Man of little faith, fear not, be comforted. I am with thee." . . . For nine years I have done deeds worthy of memory. They have counted for naught. Today even the lowliest of men revile me; only the virtuous do not consent so to do. If I had taken the Indies as booty and given them unto the Moors, I should not have been shown more hatred than in Spain. . . . If I have erred, it is not through evil intentions, and I believe that Their Majesties will so judge. I hold for certain that they will show me mercy, for my errors were committed unwillingly, as they will soon recognize, and will take account of my services, which will each day prove greater.

The ability to write with eloquence can be a useful art; he was freed and invited to present himself at court.

Las Casas tells us that the sovereigns received him graciously, assuring the admiral that his imprisonment had not been by their command, promising that all would be remedied and his privileges restored. Isabella seemed particularly anxious to console him.

Even so, it was late afternoon. Never again would he be trusted to administer a colony. Their Catholic Majesties might welcome him and listen with a show of attention to his monotonous lyric, but they were not anxious to finance another trip.

Eventually he wore them down: four caravels left Seville in the spring of 1502. It is generally thought that Ferdinand and Isabella authorized this last voyage in order to get rid of him. He might continue exploring, but they charged him to avoid Santo Domingo.

He still believed that Cuba was an extension of China and that below it he would find the Malay Peninsula. Accordingly, somewhere below Cuba there must be a strait leading to the Indian Ocean. Once through that strait he might encounter Vasco da Gama, who just then was en route to India for the second time via the Cabo de Boã Esperança. And should they meet on the underside of the world after having sailed in opposite directions, what a triumph that would be.

Ferdinand and Isabella thought it quite possible; they gave Columbus a letter of introduction to da Gama.

His route after he struck the Central American coast looks like a seismograph. Better than any written account it shows his desperate obsession. From Honduras south to Panama, as far as the Gulf of Darien, he beat against the shore like a bird fluttering at a window.

If only there had been a sea passage to the other side. If only there had been a passage he would have emerged on the Pacific and sailed like a god to the Indies. He seems to have sensed how close he was.

Near the end, when the leaking caravels had been so devoured by worms that they resembled honeycombs, his fleet was almost sunk by a waterspout. As this terrifying phenomenon approached—a twisting column of water "the width of a cask"—Columbus unsheathed his sword. He traced a giant cross upon the sky and drew a protective circle around his ships. Then he opened the Bible and read to his men about the tempest on the Sea of Galilee, concluding: "It is I: be not afraid."

Eleven years later, as everybody except John Keats must know, Vasco Núñez de Balboa stood silent upon a peak in Darien, after which he descended from the mountains and waded into the Pacific. We are told by the chronicler Ovalle that Balboa entered the water with a naked sword in his hand and took possession of it, with all its coasts and bays, for the crowns of Castile and León.

Gil Eanes, Diogo Cão, and others probed the African coast until Dias rounded the cape. Da Gama then sailed on to Calicut, opening an eastern sea route to the Indies.

Balboa saw the western route, though he did not live to exploit it; the governor of Darien ordered his head chopped off, which was very often the way things turned out in those ebullient days.

And it is commonly held that Columbus never reached the Indies. However, this depends on your interpretation. Describing the island of Haiti to his sovereigns, he wrote:

> In it there are many harbors on the coast of the sea, beyond comparison with others that I know in Christendom, and many rivers, good and large, which is marvelous. Its lands are high; and there are in it very many sierras and very lofty mountains, beyond comparison with the island of Teneriffe. All are most beautiful, of a thousand shapes, and all are accessible and filled with trees of a thousand kinds and tall, and they seem to touch the sky. I am told that they never lose their foliage, and this I can believe, for I saw them as green and lovely as they are in Spain in May, and some of them were flowering, some bearing fruit, and some at another stage, according to their nature. And the nightingale was singing, and other birds of a thousand kinds, in the month of November there where I went.

7

The Sea Must
Have an Endynge

To find a northwest passage and sail through it, said Martin Frobisher four centuries ago, was "the only thing of the world that was left yet undone whereby a notable mind might be made famous and fortunate." Nor did he doubt that such a route existed, for it stood to reason that the world was a harmonious place, symmetrically balanced, with sea routes both north and south; and he, Frobisher, would accomplish what Christopher Columbus had not, and be first to drop anchor in the Orient.

Earlier explorers had probed those "icie seas." First came Irish monks. Brendan, who lived from 484 to 578, evidently reached Greenland where he beheld an iceberg or a glacier front and sailed serenely among its monstrous water-sculpted passages: "Run the boat now through an opening," he is reputed to have told the helmsman, "that we may get a closer view of the wonderful works of God."

Not long after Brendan's excursion we find documents by scribes whose names echo dustily down the corridors of forgotten college Lit courses: Adamnan, Dicuil, the Venerable Bede, et al. They write of Cormak seeking islands to the west, and of visitors from Thule where in summer the sun remains visible from one day to the next, so that, although it be midnight elsewhere, "a man may do whatever he wishes, even to picking the lice from his shirt."

Then came the Norse, scouring those upper latitudes, who forced the monks westward: "Iceland first was settled in the days of Harald the Fairhaired, son of Halfdan the Black . . . At that time Iceland was covered with forests between mountains and seashore. And Christians whom the Norsemen call Papes were here; but afterwards they went away because they did not wish to live together with heathen men, and they left behind Irish books, bells, and croziers . . ." Just how far west those touchy monks traveled is not known.

Norse settlers followed them. Eric, or Eirik, a red-bearded murderer expelled from Iceland, led a fleet of colonists to Greenland in 986. Many of them drowned en route, but it is thought that about 400 set up housekeeping along the southwest coast, and perhaps 10,000 Norse lived there during the prosperous years of the settlement. Eventually the colonies were abandoned because Europe did not care what became of them, Eskimos threatened them, and the climate got worse. So the last Vikings in the New World died of starvation and scurvy just about the time Columbus was getting organized; but during those five centuries they explored the northeastern fringe of the American mainland. Undoubtedly they put in at Newfoundland, almost certainly at Nova Scotia and New Brunswick, perhaps at Cape Cod, and how much farther south we can only guess. And it would be curious if these sea people did not investigate the northern waterways—which implies that some of them may have approached Alaska.

Various Bristol merchants also beat Columbus to America: there are records of six voyages to "Markland"—someplace on the east coast of Canada—before 1490. Columbus himself, prior to his famous trip, visited England and probably Iceland and took a careful look beyond, for there is an excerpt from a letter or diary that reads: "In the month of February, 1477, I sailed a hundred leagues beyond the island of Thule . . ." The identity of his Thule has been argued, but most historians think he meant Iceland. And he refers to another island beyond this, which might have been Jan Mayen Island within the Arctic Circle; all of which indicates that Columbus thoroughly researched his project long before the *Santa María* hoisted anchor.

In 1497 a Venetian named Giovanni Caboto got Bristol financing for a voyage of exploration to the northwest. He reached Nova Scotia or Newfoundland—possibly very close to the ruins of Leif Eiriksson's settlement—and returned with news that he had found the Asiatic mainland. The report caused a sensation: "He is called the Great Admiral and vast honour is paid to him and he goes dressed in silk, and these English run after him like mad."

Caboto—John Cabot—thought he had indeed touched a projection of Asia, and that by coasting southwest he could reach Cypango. So certain was he, or so persuasive, that an Italian in London wrote to the Duke of Milan: "Perhaps amidst so many occupations of Your Excellency it will not be unwelcome to learn how His Majesty here has acquired a portion of Asia without a stroke of his sword. . . ." And His Majesty, Henry VII, known to be "wise and not prodigal," rewarded the explorer with ten English pounds.

Cabot set out again the following year as commander

of five merchant ships. Very little is known about this expedition. One ship soon returned to England, the other four vanished. A contemporary account remarks that Cabot had found his new lands "only on the ocean's bottom."

His son, Sebastian, may have accompanied him on the first voyage, and in 1508 Sebastian himself may have led two ships northwest until they were blocked by ice. What Sebastian did after that is even more uncertain. He is said to have discovered the northwest passage and might have sailed through to Cathay, but his crew revolted; he is said to have sailed so far north that his crew froze to death in July; he is said to have explored as far south as Cuba. In other words, Sebastian is not unfamiliar; most of us have met him somewhere along the line. He pops up again in 1521, trying to raise money for a new expedition, whereupon Henry VIII asked some knowledgeable merchants what they thought of him. They answered that it would be a "sore aventour to joperd five shipps . . . uppon the singuler trust of one man, callyd as we understond, Sebastyan, whiche Sebastyan, as we heresay, was never in that land hym self, all if he makes reporte of many thinges as he hath heard his Father and other men speke in tymes past."

However, Sebastian landed on his feet like an acrobat; such charmers customarily do. Before bowing out he became a governor of the Muscovy Company and Grand Pilot of England.

Then for quite a few years almost nobody looked northwest. The excitement that followed Columbus's voyages seems to have faded, and trade with Russia appeared more lucrative than wild-eyed explorations of distant ice-clogged bays that might or might not lead to the Orient. But along came Frobisher—lace ruff, doublet, sword, slippers, Vandyke beard, baggy pantaloons and all, with a horse pistol in his hand to prove that he meant what he said. And a northern route, quoth he, "was as plausible as the English channel."

Even so, it was not easy to raise money; the seas closer to home were alive with floating morsels, galleons wallowing in from the Caribbean glutted with silver and gold. But the Earl of Warwick listened, and a few other moneyed gentlemen, and on June 7, Anno Domini 1576, Captain Martin Frobisher aboard the *Gabriel* set out from Ratcliff. He was followed by the *Michael* and by a seven-ton pinnace. As they sailed down the Thames past Greenwich they saw Elizabeth waving from a palace window.

Before reaching Greenland they encountered such a storm that the pinnace sank, its four-man crew drowned. Then the *Michael,* "mistrusting the matter, privily made its way home," and the crew of the *Gabriel* implored their captain to do likewise. Frobisher said no.

Authorities on shipbuilding agree, contrary to what you might expect, that sixteenth-century English vessels were not as reliable as tenth-century Viking ships, and perhaps not as safe as a Mediterranean bireme of the fourth century B.C. In any event, the storm had sprung the *Gabriel*'s mainmast, her fore-topmast was blown away, and "water issued out of her and withal many things floated over the ship's sides." But Frobisher said no, no, he would not turn back. In fact, he told the dismayed members of his crew, he would "rather make a sacrifice unto God of his life than to return home without the discovery of Cathay." And besides, "the sea at length needs must have an endynge."

So they patched things up with glue and string and continued on their course.

After poking about in various Arctic bays the explorers

anchored beside an island, went ashore, and climbed a hill. From there they could see two headlands with a broad opening between, which—because of the flooding tide—they judged to be the passage they had been looking for. Beyond those headlands must lie the beaches of India and Cathay.

They also noticed three houses covered with sealskin as well as "a number of small things fleeting in the Sea a farre off," which Frobisher at first took to be "Porposes, or Ceales, or some kind of a strange fishe," but which turned out to be Eskimos in kayaks, and it occurred to the English that maybe they should quit sightseeing and get back on their boat.

Presently quite a few Eskimos showed up "making signs of friendship."

Christopher Hall, master of the *Gabriel*, describes them thus: "They bee like Tartars, with long blacke haire, broad faces, and flatte noses, and tawnie in colour, wearing Seale skinnes, and so doe the women, not differing in the fashion, but the women are marked in the face with blewe streekes . . ."

Alas for signs of friendship, or perhaps what occurred was Frobisher's fault. At any rate, when the *Gabriel* started home several days later five crewmen were missing and one kidnapped Eskimo was aboard.

Hall describes the attempt to find them: "We stoode in neere the shoare, and shotte off a fauconet, and sounded our trumpet, but we could heare nothing of our men: this sound we called the five mens sound, and plyed out of it, but ankered againe in thirtie fathome, and oaze: and riding there all night, in the morning, the snow lay a foote thicke upon our hatches."

As to the Eskimo: "Whereupon he found himself in captivity, for very choller and disdain he bit his tong in-twayne within his mouth; notwithstanding, he died not thereof, but lived until he came to Englande, and then he died, of colde which he had taken at Sea."

Along with this miserable captive Frobisher brought back a queer little black rock which he seems to have regarded as a curiosity, because he gave it to the entrepreneur responsible for financing his expedition—Michael Lok. And here the water becomes somewhat muddy. Mrs. Lok was said to have tossed this rock into a fire and then quenched it in vinegar, whereupon it "glistered with a bright marquesset of gold." As a result, the rock was tested by professional assayers, who agreed that it was quite promising.

Michael Lok admitted long afterward that he had contrived the story about his wife throwing the rock into the fire. He also had invented the assayers' verdict. As a matter of fact he did submit it to three assayers, all of whom agreed that it was worthless.

Why did Lok falsify the verdict? Because Frobisher's voyage had not been profitable and therefore Lok, who promoted it, was no longer welcome at the club. If Frobisher had discovered gold, though, every door would open.

Lok sounds like a total charlatan, which he could have been. But he wanted so desperately to believe in the gold-freckled rock that he may have convinced himself as thoroughly as any alchemist.

Whatever his motive, the scheme succeeded and within about fifteen minutes everybody from Dartmouth to Birmingham heard the news: Frobisher has found gold!

Lok then organized the Cathay Company, whose purpose was to scoop up the ore that littered the beaches of the New World. There was no shortage of investors. Elizabeth herself, with a long nose for gold, subscribed 1,000 pounds.

So, next year, Frobisher retraced his route, enjoined to

proceed "onely for the searching of the ore, and to deferre the further discovery of the passage until another time." He now commanded one tall ship of Her Majesty's named the *Ayde*, as well as the much smaller *Gabriel* and *Michael*. They were comfortably provisioned with beer, brandy, wine, cheese, butter, oatmeal, salad oil, almonds, raisins, licorice, and barrels of honey.

It does sound good—almonds, licorice, etc.—but the reality of shipboard life in those merry days may not have been so attractive. The interior of a sixteenth-century English ship was described by one voyager as "right evill and smouldring hote and stynkynge," furnished with rats, lice, roaches, and bilge water. The food and drink, too, no matter how appetizing it might appear on the menu, must have called for a robust stomach. Frobisher's men got seven gallons of beer a week because soon after leaving port the water would be covered with slime and anybody who drank much of it would feel his bowels turning to sludge. As to the weekly food ration—well, your able seaman got four pounds of brined beef known as salt horse, delicately flavored with maggots, and seven pounds of biscuit harder than limestone, called scouse, which was the home of many weevils. Indeed, we are told, sailors customarily began a meal by banging their food against the table in order to dislodge a certain number of bugs. Each man also received four sun-cured cod and a measure of plum duff—a mixture of hardtack, raisins, and drippings.

This bill of fare week after week naturally brought about swollen bleeding gums, loosened teeth, blisters, palpitations, aching joints, shortness of breath, exhaustion and—on long voyages—death.

Apart from that, one had to beware of ship's officers. The reward for profanity could be a marlinspike in the mouth. For more odious conduct, such as failing to attend religious services, a transgressor might be ducked from the yardarm or tied to the mizzen shrouds with iron weights slung around his neck and his hands full of nettles. Talk of mutiny brought out the cat-o'-nine-tails—a stick covered with red baize from which dangled a series of knotted cords. One victim, having lived through fifty lashes, compared his shirt to a butcher's apron.

Those were lusty days at sea or ashore, what with garbage hurled from the window, bubonic plague, witches howling and writhing at the stake, human heads displayed on pikes for public instruction, and convicts let down alive from the gallows so that they might be castrated or disemboweled while still quivering.

Frobisher is said to have been a fierce disciplinarian, which of course made him unpopular, but he was not likely the most malevolent of sixteenth-century captains. No doubt he ruled heavily, but he also was more intrepid and skillful than most. A muscular, vigorous man—who every so often would be arrested for piracy, scolded, and released—he seems also to have been by our standards extremely credulous, looking beyond Greenland's horrendous icebergs toward the silks, jewels, and spicy breezes of Cathay.

Anno Domini 1577 he set forth.

Elizabeth honored this second departure even more highly; she permitted Captain Frobisher to kiss her hand.

His squadron rolled through the usual weather:

"The 4. of July we came within the making of Frisland. From this shoare 10. or 12. leagues, we met great Islands of yce, of halfe a mile, some more, some less in compasse . . . Here, in place of odoriferous and fragrant smels of sweete gums, & pleasant notes of musicall birdes, which other Countreys in more temperate Zones do yeeld, wee tasted the most boisterous Boreal blasts mixt with snow and haile . . ."

And so onward to Eskimo land, where numerous citizens "shewed themselves leaping and dauncing, with strange shrikes and cries."

Master Dionese Settle speaks of other wondrous things: "On this West shore we found a dead fish floating, which had in his nose a horne streight and torquet, of length two yards lacking two ynches, being broken in the top, where we might perceive it hollow, into the which some of our sailors putting spiders they presently died. I saw not the triall hereof, but it was reported unto me of a trueth: by the vertue whereof we supposed it to be the sea Unicorne."

On an island near the mouth of what now is called Frobisher Bay some Eskimos insisted that three of those five Englishmen lost on the previous trip were still alive.

Frobisher wrote them a note: "In the name of God in whom we all believe, and who, I trust, hath preserved your bodyes and souls amongst these Infidels, I commend me unto you. I will be glad to seeke by all meanes you can devise for your deliverance, either with force or with any commodities within my Shippes, which I will not spare for your sakes, or anything else I can do for you. I have aboard of theirs a Man, a Woman, and a Childe, which I am contented to deliver for you . . ." He also sent them a pen, paper, and ink so that they could reply.

Nothing was learned of these missing crewmen for almost three centuries. In 1861 the American explorer Charles Hall visited some Baffin Island Eskimos and was told by an old woman that long ago some white men—Kodlunas—had come there. Five of these white men were captured by her tribe, she said, and while trying to build a boat they froze to death.

Frobisher, after waiting several days, concluded that further delay would be useless. Obedient to his commission, he loaded 200 tons of glistering ore and returned straightaway to England. He lost just two men on this trip: "one in the way by Gods visitation, and the other homeward cast over borde with a surge of the sea."

He brought with him the man, woman, and child. The English seem to have been surprised at the propriety of the adult Eskimos, who were not a couple. Although obliged to share a bunk, nothing happened between them: "The man would never shift himselfe, except he had first caused the woman to depart out of his cabin, and they both were most shamefast, least anye of their privie parts should bee discovered . . ." In England the trio drew great crowds, but they flourished no better than the previous exhibit; despite being fed raw meat all three died within a month.

As for the gold-bearing rock: it might be valuable or it might not. Opinions differed. Elizabeth had the ore locked up and guarded in Bristol Castle and the Tower of London.

Investors scrambled to finance a third voyage.

Early in 1578 he set out again, leading a fleet of fifteen ships. Elizabeth draped a gold chain around the neck of "her loving friend Martin Frobisher," and graciously allowed his captains to kiss her hand.

Approximately forty men died on this trip, which was not a lot, according to one chronicler, not if one considers how many ships there were.

They returned to England with 1,300 tons of ore, only to learn that during their absence the London assayers had concluded it was iron pyrite. Fool's gold. Now, what can you do with 1,300 tons of fool's gold? Frobisher dumped part of it in Dartford harbor, which must have been embarrassing. As to the rest, the stones "when neither gold nor silver nor any other metal could be extracted from them, we have seen cast forth to mend the highways."

That ended Frobisher's visits to the New World. The gold rush had not been his idea, nevertheless he was held responsible. Yet he seems to have been a lucky man, or a man whose quality lifted him like a cork to the surface no matter how far down he had been thrust. He joined the navy and was so quickly promoted that ten years later he was commanding one of Elizabeth's most potent warships when the Spaniards made their colossal mistake. And in 1594 when he died, still battling Spain, his popularity rivaled that of Sir Francis Drake.

"We have taken this fort," he wrote to the Queen's lord high admiral after he had been mortally hurt. "They defended it verie resolutelie. And never asked for mercie. So they were put all to the sword, saving five or six . . . I was shot in with a bullet at the battery alongst the huckle bone . . ."

Until his final breath he thought he had found the Northwest Passage, although in fact what he had seen was the entrance to Hudson Bay.

John Davis, solid and moderate as his name, was the next to go looking. Seven years after Frobisher's last voyage he sailed from Dartmouth aboard the *Sunneshine* accompanied by a four-piece orchestra, which was customary in those ornamental days, and by the *Mooneshine*. He pushed north along the west coast of Greenland, past the Viking ruins, and mentions a grave "with divers buried in it, only covered with seale skinnes, having a cross laid over them"—which must have been either the grave of some medieval Vikings or that of a Christianized Eskimo family.

Unable to find a passage in the north, Davis looked around in the south and then sailed back to England reasonably satisfied. After all, one step at a time. "The northwest passage is a matter nothing doubtfull," he wrote to Sir Francis Walsingham, "but at any tyme almost to be passed, the sea navigable, voyd of yse, the ayre tollerable, and the waters very depe."

Ready again, off he sailed with the *Sunneshine* and *Mooneshine*, followed now by the *Mermayd* and *North Starre*. What an engaging fleet: *Sunneshine, Mooneshine, Mermayd* and *North Starre*. Not only can you see it, you can all but hear the miniature orchestra.

This time he explored a bit farther, studied the climate and topography, did his best to make friends with the Eskimos, and encountered "a flie which is called Muskyto, for they did sting grievously." Frobisher, too, had met the muskyto, because Master Settle mentions "certaine stinging Gnattes, which bite so fiercely, that the place where they bite shortly after swelleth and itcheth very sore."

Once again Davis's backers were satisfied, though not completely. They agreed to finance another voyage with three ships but insisted that the two larger vessels bring home some fish. Davis might use the small boat for sightseeing, gathering ferns, or whatever. And again John Davis came home unscratched, loaded with stockfish. And he wrote a correct, formal letter to his principal sponsor:

"Good M. Sanderson, with Gods great mercy I have made my safe returne in health, with all my company, and have sailed threescore leagues further then my determination at my departure. I have bene in 73 degrees, finding the sea all open, and forty leagues betweene land and land. The passage is most probable, the execution easie, as at my coming you shall fully know."

But Spanish warships soon would dot the English channel and everything else must wait a while.

Only one name fills the twenty-year gap between Davis and Henry Hudson. George Weymouth was commissioned by the East India Company to probe the strait found by Frobisher and confirmed by Davis, to see if indeed this could be a northern route to the Orient. His voyage is nicely documented and it is a pleasure to observe that among various expenses, including the sum of 120 pounds and 3 shillings for beer, a certain Mr. Seger was paid 6 pounds, 13 shillings and 4 pence "for writing her Majestie letters to the Emperor of China and Cathay."

Despite such preparations Weymouth never reached the gigantic bay. Storms, fog, and a fearful noise which they found to be "the noyse of a great quantity of ice, very loathsome to be heard" so frightened his men that they altered course while Weymouth was in his cabin. The leader of this revolt was the preacher, who had packed a new clerical gown in order to impress the Chinese—a detail that almost gives the squalid little affair some elegance. However, Weymouth got partly through the strait and saw no land ahead. The merchants at home were encouraged.

Then out of absolute obscurity stepped that strange figure gripped by a vision of sailing to China, not carefully through subpolar waterways, but right over the top of the world; for in those days it was commonly held that beyond the Arctic ice lay a mild and placid sea in whose center loomed a black rock—the Pole.

Those English businessmen listening to Hudson surely liked the tone of what they heard; here stood somebody who knew what could be done and was not afraid to do it, ice be damned. Of course he might get stuck up there, which meant one's investment would be lost. Still, it should be worth a try.

They gave him the *Hopewell*—a forty-ton relic that had not been new when it accompanied Frobisher twenty-nine years earlier—a crew of ten, and a cabin boy.

So, having been victualed and wished Godspeed, Henry Hudson weighed anchor and drove straight for the Pole. He got within 600 miles of it; nobody knows how, because the ship had been rotten when it left England.

On his way home, passing the Spitzbergen Islands, he noticed quite a few whales.

Next year, ready again, he persuaded the Muscovy Company that with a little help he could sail round Russia. He got to Novaya Zemlaya before ice and a doubtful crew stopped him. On this voyage a marvelous sight was noted: "One of our companie looking over boord saw a Mermaid, and calling up some of the companie to see her, one more came up, and by that time shee was come close to the ships side, looking earnestly on the men: a little after, a Sea came and overturned her: from the Navill upward, her backe and breasts were like a womans, (as they say that saw her) her body as big as one of us; her skin very white; and long haire hanging downe behind, of colour blacke: in her going downe they saw her tayle, which was like the tayle of a Porposse, and speckled like a Macrell."

Home again, deeply disappointed, Henry learned that his sponsors no longer were interested in a new route to the East. No indeed, not when there was a fortune to be made by sending whalers to the Spitzbergen Islands.

At this point most men would have quit the struggle and begun writing their memoirs, or have sued the Muscovy Company for a share of the whaling profits, or settled into a sympathetic pub until time ran out. Not Henry. Off he went to Amsterdam where he wrestled the burghers of the Dutch East India Company and emerged with a contract for one more attempt at Arctic Russia.

The smallest vessel the Dutch merchants could find that would not capsize outside the channel was the *Half*

Moon, and the men they collected seem to have been waterfront dregs. Thus equipped, off went Henry once more, determined to circumnavigate Russia in a cockle-shell. He zigged and zagged his way through the ice to Novaya Zemlaya and was still afloat when his sterling crew again revolted. They had seen enough of the Arctic. After some negotiation, however, they agreed to attempt a southerly route to Cathay, westward via the United States—for most geographers thought the North American continent must be divided by a waterway. So the *Half Moon* came about, laid a course to Newfoundland, and began inspecting the coast.

The passage could not be located—only that river we now call the Hudson, up which they traveled as far as the present site of Albany. No doubt much aggrieved, Henry sailed home a third time.

But instead of proceeding directly to the Netherlands he put in at Dartmouth, which was a mistake. English merchants complained about an English captain serving Dutch rivals and the authorities then announced that he had undertaken a voyage "to the detriment of his country." The ship and the Dutch crew were released. Henry himself was detained.

But he wrestled with this as he had wrestled for his rights before, and when the struggle ended he had been outfitted for his next odyssey by three affluent gentlemen: Smith, Digges, and Lord Wolstenholme. They rented George Weymouth's reliable old bark *Discovery* and hired twenty-two crewmen, including a defrocked priest named Abacuck Prickett. Prickett, who was the sponsors' watchdog, wrote the only surviving account of Hudson's last voyage. It is not a happy story.

They steered for a passage noted by John Davis and got through after a tremendous effort that lasted five weeks.

"Some of our men this day fell sicke," writes Prickett. "I will not say it was for feare, though I saw small signe of other griefe. . . . Our course was as the ice did lye."

Once inside—the first Europeans to enter that huge bay —they bore south, assuming they had reached the North Pacific. But the coast fell away southeast, not southwest as they anticipated, and in early September the *Discovery* sailed into a cul-de-sac. Winter approached, provisions were short, and their captain had led them not to the Spice Islands but into some grim bottle; the crew, most of whom never had liked this voyage, grew increasingly mutinous. There was no escape, though, not until spring. The carpenter built a little house and the men who were not disabled by scurvy went scrounging for food. Some willow ptarmigan were caught, and later "Swannes, Goose, Ducke, and Teal, but hard to come by." They began to eat frogs, moss, tamarack buds—anything that would nourish them "how vile soever."

As soon as the ice broke up they started north.

But Hudson had been suspected of concealing food, and on the morning of June 22, with the ship again stopped by ice, and only fourteen days' rations remaining, he was seized and bound. His son John, six crew members —five of them ill—and the captain himself were forced into the ship's tender. Just before they were abandoned the carpenter chose to join them rather than accompany the mutineers. With an iron pot, a fowling piece, and a handful of meal they were cut adrift. And because they died so miserably and unjustly we might at least preserve their names: Michel But, Sydrack Fenner, John King, Arnold Ladlo, Adam Moore, Philip Staffe, Thomas Woodhouse.

The mutineers sailed a short distance, took in the topsails, and began searching the hold for food. They found some butter and meal, half a bushel of peas, and twenty-seven slices of brined pork. Then the tender came into view, the castaways rowing after them, and in Prickett's words the mutineers "let falle the maine saile and out top sailes, and fly as from an enemy."

How long Hudson and his companions lived, or how they died, has never been determined. Some historians believe they made it to an island in James Bay and subsequently reached the Canadian mainland where they might have survived for several months, possibly years.

The *Discovery* got back to England with eight or nine men aboard, the rest having died en route. Four are said to have been killed by Eskimos and one starved to death. The survivors were arrested and imprisoned, though later freed. The official inquiry reads in part:

"They all charge Master Hudson to have stolen the victuals by means of a scuttle or hatch cut between his cabin and the hold; and it appears that he fed his favourites, such as the surgeon, etc. and kept the others at only ordinary allowance, which led those who were not so favoured to make the attempt and to perform it so violently."

One of the mutineers, Robert Bylot, accompanied the next expedition under Captain Thomas Button, whose purpose was to verify the good news that a northwest passage had been found, for it was still believed that Hudson had reached the Pacific. But the expedition had a second purpose: to attempt his rescue. The mutineers, dancing frantically before the tribunal, had stressed the idea that Hudson just might be living comfortably somewhere around James Bay. However, the farther he got from England and the gallows, the more did Bylot disparage this idea. Consequently they did not retrace Hudson's route; once inside the bay, instead of turning south to look for him, they continued west in the direction of China.

And when Captain Button at last saw land dead ahead he named the region Hopes Check'd. He veered south, but found no great flood tide welling in from the Pacific. He turned north, still optimistic, but finally realized the truth. The fact that he has been almost forgotten is rather unjust because it was he who deduced that Hudson Bay was an impasse; and therefore the Northwest Passage, if such a thing existed, must lie elsewhere. The reason he has been forgotten is that his employers suppressed the details of his survey; they did not want any commercial rivals to make use of it.

Bylot sailed again in 1616 as captain—which sounds odd considering his part in the Hudson debacle. William Baffin was pilot-navigator, and on this voyage they discovered the true passage, Lancaster Sound, although neither guessed what it was. Baffin charted it as an ice-clogged inlet. Having charted it as such, and finding no other passage, they steered for Greenland to collect some scurvy grass because the crew was falling sick. Then they sailed home.

At this point Bylot disappears from history. He died unnoticed. Baffin's exit was spectacular. He got a job with the omnipresent East India Company and in 1622 he took part in an Anglo-Persian assault on the Portuguese fort of Kishm in the Persian Gulf. According to Samuel Purchas: "Master Baffin went on shoare with his Geometricall Instruments, for the taking the height and distance of the castle wall; but as he was about the same, he received a small shot from the Castle into his belly, wherewith he gave three leapes, by report, and died immediately."

Two Danish ships under the command of Jens Munck, the *Unicorn* and *Lamprey*, entered Hudson Bay in 1619. They fetched up on the bleak west coast and the expedition turned into a horror story—though a student of

Gothic drama would not be surprised because there had been numerous omens. First, a sailor jumped overboard. Next, the *Lamprey* sprang a leak off southern Norway and when Munck put in at Karmsund he saw that the carpenters had left three bolt-holes open. Another crew member died before they left Karmsund. So it went. Munck took a shot at some birds: the gun exploded and tore away the brim of his hat. The anchors of the *Lamprey* were crushed by ice. Two days later the rudder head of the *Unicorn* was smashed.

Sickness and starvation picked off the crew. On February 20, says Munck, the priest died. On the eighth of March died Oluf Boye, who had been ill nine weeks. Next day died Anders the cooper, ill since Christmas. On the twenty-first died Povel Pederson and the surgeon, both ill since almost Christmas. "Now, and afterwards, the sickness raged more violently . . . I was then like a wild and lonely bird."

Sixty-four men had left Norway. Munck and two others eventually got back. They had not found the passage.

In 1631 two British expeditions sailed within a few days of each other, both persuaded that it must empty into Hudson Bay. Luke Foxe deftly mapped the northern coast and returned to England before winter. Thomas James had some problems:

October 7th it snowed all day, so that we were fain to clear it off the decks with shovels; and it blew a very storm withal. It continued snowing and very cold weather, and it did so freeze that all the bows of the ship, with her beak-head, was all ice. Afterwards the sun did shine very clear, and we tore the top-sails out of the tops, which were hard frozen in them into a lump, so that there they hung a-sunning in a very lump, the sun not having power to thaw one drop of them

. . . The land was all deep covered with snow, the cold did multiply, and the thick snow water did increase; and what would become of us, our most merciful God and preserver only knew.

James spent the winter on Charlton Island—where Hudson may have died—and probably surprised himself by getting out alive. His trip is said to have inspired "The Rime of the Ancient Mariner."

After Foxe and James the bay was taken over by traders; a quick profit in furs was what excited European merchants. The fugitive passage was ignored—with one exception—until the British Admiralty dispatched Sir John Ross in 1818.

That exception was the attempt by James Knight, a longtime employee of the Company of Gentlemen Adventurers Trading into Hudson's Bay—later known as the Hudson's Bay Company. Knight often had asked permission to explore the northwest, but not until he was almost eighty years old did the adventurous London gentlemen who controlled the purse strings cautiously acquiesce. They let him use the *Albany Frigate* and a sloop called *Discovery*.

Knight left Gravesend in 1719, expecting to return that fall. He did not show up. Nor did he come back the next year.

In 1721 the sloop *Whale-Bone* was ordered to look for him, but as it was a bit late in the season the search did not get under way until 1722. The *Whale-Bone's* master then reported nothing significant, so everybody assumed that Captain Knight had discovered the Northwest Passage and very probably was loitering in China or California.

Forty-five years later a boat passing Marble Island off

the west coast of Hudson Bay noticed the ruins of a house. In five fathoms of water lay what was left of Captain Knight's ships. Some very old Eskimos in the area were questioned. They said that at the beginning of the third winter no English were still alive. The last two, the Eskimos said, lived much longer than the rest and often climbed to the top of a large rock where they spent a long time looking to the east, after which they sat down together and wept.

Sir John Ross sought the passage farther north, in the region where two centuries earlier Baffin had stopped. Ross entered Lancaster Sound and sailed about fifty miles until he saw a chain of mountains ahead, which caused him to turn back. Several of his subordinates, including Edward Parry, were unable to see any mountains and thought he should have continued.

In 1819 Parry led an expedition through the sound as far as Melville Island—halfway to Alaska—before being halted by ice. Yet even then Parry failed to recognize the truth. Twice more he probed the area without trying Lancaster Sound again.

The next assault, led by George Back, was planned as a variation on a familiar theme. Instead of going all the way by sea they would sail up Hudson Strait to the neck of the Melville Peninsula, drag some boats overland, and proceed by the next waterway. So the sturdy ship *Terror* was refurbished and in 1836 they set out.

Very soon they were caught by Hudson Bay ice. Since there was no escape until spring, Back ordered the upper masts dismantled, housing erected, and the decks banked with snow. Stoves were set up and a system of pipes carried off vapors. From a distance the *Terror* resembled a factory. After about a month the ice began drifting eastward. Lashed by gales, compressed and twisted by masses of ice, the *Terror* almost collapsed. The captain's door split, reinforcements thrown up by the carpenter were squeezed out of position, and "beads of turpentine started from every seam." Back preached a sermon to which his crew listened "with the most profound and serious attention."

Ten months later the ship was released somewhat closer to home. That is, farther from their goal. Back was understandably embarrassed about having traveled the wrong direction and might have attacked the Arctic again, but his ship had been ruined. Nobody knew if it would stay afloat until they reached England.

They set a course for Stromness. After one more gale, however, Back drove straight at the Irish coast and deliberately ran aground on the first sandy beach. Next day at low tide they inspected the hull and "there was not one on board who did not express astonishment that we had ever floated across the Atlantic."

The British Admiralty was quite put out by this. One must expect failures but it was now well into the nineteenth century. Four centuries of failure seemed a bit much.

So they decided to launch an elite expedition commanded by the veteran Sir John Franklin. They provided him with a good ship, the *Erebus,* and the reconditioned *Terror.* Both had been meticulously overhauled. The masts were painted white, the superstructures yellow, the hulls black. Sheet iron covered the bows. Twenty-horsepower railway engines were installed along with an apparatus that would lift the propellers if they were threatened by ice. An ingenious hot-water system warmed the cabins.

Twelve months should be sufficient to negotiate the passage—wherever it might be—but *Erebus* and *Terror* were provisioned for three years. Besides vast quantities of fuel and food, each ship carried all sorts of agreeable accessories: solid Victorian silver, handsomely cut glass, decorative China, et cetera. Each carried a hand organ that would play fifty tunes, and each had a library of 1,200 books—everything from Dickens to manuals on steam engines to the latest issues of *Punch*.

The 129 crew members were selected for experience, initiative, and physical condition. None of your Elizabethan wharf rats.

Everyone understood that Franklin would succeed; no question about it. No previous expedition had been so liberally endowed or so thoughtfully planned.

A photograph of him taken for the occasion shows a relaxed, portly gentleman in late middle age, jowls awash. He wears a somewhat rumpled coat with a twin row of brass buttons and fringed epaulets, one of those preposterous commodore hats, and he holds a collapsible telescope.

The Admiralty at first had been dubious. Said the First Lord: "I might find a good excuse for not letting you go, Sir John, in the rumour that tells me you are sixty years of age."

Franklin replied: "No, no, My Lord, I am only fifty-nine."

His two captains, Crozier and Fitzjames, look amiable enough, though not especially forceful. The sort of men you meet in a pub.

All the officers in the group photo have assumed those calcified nineteenth-century poses—gazing beyond the camera or pensively aside, arms folded. Only one man looks alert: Lieutenant Graham Gore. There is something rakish about him in the tilt of his cap and his faint, dark, sardonic smile. He resembles one or two of the cavalrymen in the last photograph of Custer's doomed squadron.

Erebus and *Terror* sailed in May of 1845. On July 26 they were becalmed near a whaling ship in Baffin Bay. Franklin asked the whaler's captain to supper, but during the afternoon a breeze came up and the expedition sailed westward. That was the last time anybody saw them.

Five years later some clues were found: shattered bottles, ropes, a rock cairn, meat canisters, bird bones, a scrap of paper. Then the embankment of a house, washtubs, coal bags, clothing, and the graves of three men.

In 1859 a search party under the command of Leopold McClintock, financed by Lady Franklin, met some Eskimos and bought from them six silver spoons and forks, a medal, a length of gold chain, several buttons, and some knives fashioned out of iron and wood from one of the ships. McClintock's party subsequently came upon a partly clothed skeleton lying face down in the snow and concluded that the man must have been either a steward or an officer's servant because of his blue double-breasted jacket with slashed sleeves and braided edging, and because his neckerchief had been tied with a loose bowknot—a style not used by seamen. Near the skeleton they found a pocket comb and a clothes brush.

Not long after that they saw a boat mounted on a sledge —a total weight of 1,400 pounds. In this boat lay two skeletons. One had been torn apart, perhaps by wolves. The other skeleton was dressed in furs. Beside them lay five pocket watches, two loaded guns, remnants of a pair of handworked slippers, and half a dozen books including *The Vicar of Wakefield* and a devotional manual inscribed by Sir George Back to Graham Gore. Nor was that all. McClintock reported "an amazing quantity of clothing" such as silk handkerchiefs and eight pairs of boots, towels, sponges, soap, toothbrushes, bayonet scabbards, nails, saws, files, two rolls of sheet lead, and twenty-six pieces of silver plate—eight of them bearing Franklin's crest.

On King William Island a cairn was discovered in which there was a rusty tin box containing a note. It told of Franklin's death, the deaths of nine officers and fifteen enlisted men, and of abandoning the ships on April 22, 1848. This information had been scribbled by Fitzjames on the margin of a bureaucratic form that gave precise directions in six languages:

WHOEVER finds this paper is requested to forward it to the Secretary of the Admiralty, London, with a note of the time and place at which it was found: or, if more convenient, to deliver it for that purpose to the British Consul at the nearest Port.

QUINCONQUE trouvera ce papier est prié d'y marquer le tems et lieu ou il l'aura trouvé, et de le faire parvenir au plutot au Secretaire . . .

CUALQUIERA que hallare este Papel, se le suplica de enviarlo al Secretario del Almirantazgo, en Londrés . . .

EEN ieder die dit Papier mogt vinden, wordt hiermede verzogt . . .

FINDEREN af dette Papiir ombedes, naar Leilighed . . .

WER diesen Zettel findet . . .

Lieutenant Frederick Schwatka of the U.S. Army came across more relics and bones in 1879. He also heard from Eskimos that a group of about thirty white men had died in a remote cove and that their bodies, when the Eskimos saw them, had been surrounded by papers. But not until 1923 did anyone visit this cove, at which time the bones were still visible, although no trace of the documents remained.

Schwatka's party discovered a few other things: the graves of two Englishmen, scraps of red and blue cloth, tin cans, blankets, sledge harness, copper kettles, a two-gallon jug, cookstoves, a brush with the name H. Wilks, various iron and brass implements, an empty grave, human bones scattered in the snow, and a silver medal—a prize for mathematics that had been awarded by the Royal Naval College in 1830 to John Irving, third officer of the *Terror*. Schwatka also picked up a fragment of paper on which there was a drawing of a hand with the index finger pointing, but the paper had rotted, so that whatever message might have accompanied the hand had disappeared.

In 1929 a Canadian surveyor talked with two ancient Eskimos who said that when they were young they had come upon several wooden cases on a small island. Inside these cases were containers filled with white powder. They could not imagine what the powder was, so they and their families tossed it up into the air to watch it blow away.

Other commonplace articles, now curiously poignant, have been recovered: wine bottles labeled BRISTOL GLASS WORKS, a barrel-shaped wooden canteen, an ax, part of a backgammon board presented to the *Erebus* by Lady Franklin, a pewter medal commemorating the 1843 launching of the steamer *Great Britain*, a George IV silver half crown dated 1820, and one snowshoe marked MR. STANLEY.

In 1931 several more skeletons were found, and since then other bones, but altogether only about half of Franklin's men have been accounted for.

A footnote in W. H. Markham's *Life of Sir John Franklin* tells us something else. About 700 preserved meat tins "filled with gravel" were found at the expedition's winter quarters on Beechey Island. A great many more of these tins lay nearby. They had been supplied under directions from the Admiralty, and it seems that another consignment which was delivered to the British navy at home had turned out to be putrid. Because such a quantity of meat as these empty tins were calculated to hold could not possibly have been eaten by Franklin's party during that first winter, Markham notes, "it is supposed that the defective condition of the contents of the tins was discovered, and a survey of them ordered. If this surmise be a correct one, the loss of so large a proportion of what would be considered fresh, in contradistinction to salt, provisions would be most serious . . ."

You can almost see the faces of Franklin's men while those tins of putrid meat were being opened. Most serious. Indeed.

What happened, as closely as it can be reconstructed from Eskimo oral history and from the remains, is that Franklin died—probably of heart failure—on June 11, 1847. At just about this time Lord Egerton was writing in the London *Quarterly Review*: "With interest which accumulates by the hour do we watch for the return of these two vessels which are perhaps even now working their way through the Bering Strait into the Pacific. Should the happiness be yet allowed us of witnessing that return, we are of the opinion that *Erebus* and *Terror* should be moored henceforth on either side of the *Victory*, floating monuments of what the Nelsons of discovery can do, at the call of their country in the service of the world."

Several months after Franklin's death one of the ships was crushed by ice and probably sank. The other stayed afloat, although trapped, and the surviving explorers—perhaps 100—built sledges and tried to walk to a Hudson Bay post.

What became of *Erebus* and *Terror* is not altogether certain. Some investigators believe that both ships may have drifted until 1849, or possibly longer, with a few men still aboard.

In mid-April of 1851 an extraordinary spectacle was noted by the crew of the English brig *Renovation* en route from Limerick to Quebec. Just off the Newfoundland banks an officer of the watch, Robert Simpson, observed two ships resting on a large ice floe. Their hulls were painted black and both vessels corresponded in size and appearance to *Erebus* and *Terror*. Simpson reported this apparition to the captain, who,

being very ill at the time, did not notice at first what I said. I again repeated the circumstance, and asked him what he intended to do, but he only groaned out, "Never mind", or something to that effect. . . . I was anxious to get up on deck again, but before I went up called Mr. Lynch (a passenger), who immediately jumped up and looked at the vessels. . . . The largest one was lying on her beam-ends, with her head to the eastward, and nothing standing but her three lower masts and bowsprit; the smaller one, which was sitting nearly upright, with her head to the southward, with her three masts, top-masts on end, and top-sail and lower yards across, and to all appearance having been properly stripped and abandoned.

The ships remained in sight for approximately an hour, at a distance of about three miles, and were studied through a telescope by several members of the *Renovation*'s crew. Her captain, though, did not wish to be bothered.

Later, during an Admiralty investigation, the captain testified that he got out of his sickbed in order to look at the ships. He stated that he considered them to be mere wrecks, and being pressed for time, with bad weather imminent, he concluded that they were not worth examining. The captain's testimony is regarded as suspect. It is thought that he may have lied in order to conceal the fact that he had passed close by *Erebus* and *Terror* without doing anything.

Regardless of what the *Renovation*'s captain did or did not see, there are various eyewitness accounts. J. S. Lynch, the passenger, wrote to his uncle—a Mr. Creilly—in Limerick soon after the brig docked in Quebec:

> We arrived here on yesterday . . . The icebergs we met with were frightful in size, as the basis of some of them would cover three times over the area of Limerick; and I do not at all exaggerate when I say that the steeple of the cathedral would have appeared but a small pinnacle, and a dark one, compared to the lofty and gorgeously-tinted spires that were on some of them; and more to be regretted is that we met, or rather saw at a distance, one with two ships on it, which I am almost sure belonged to Franklin's exploring squadron, as from the latitude and longitude we met them in they were drifting from the direction of Davis's Straits. Was there but a single one, it might have been a deserted whaler, but two so near each other, they must have been consorts . . .

And there is a splendid letter from crew member James Silk to his brother John:

> . . . On the 14th day in the morning wee saw a very large hice Burgh to whindward of ous, and 12 o'clock 14th, wee saw as many as 6 hice Burg . . . Apon one

of the very large burghs in which wee see there was 2 large ships on them, 1 laying Apon her broad broad side, and the other were A laying as comfortable as if she was in the dock fast to her moreings. The wether was very fine and the wather very smouth, but the captain being laid up at the same time it was not reported to him untell 8 o'clock, and we out of sight of them, so, dear friends, I canot tell you whether there was any living sould there are not.

Rupert Gould, an inquisitive and versatile historian who loves such occurrences, sifted just about everything turned up by the Admiralty investigation and concluded that the ships on the floe were, indeed, *Erebus* and *Terror*. Gould adds, however, that his judgment "may be due simply to a subconscious prejudice in favor of the marvellous." He also points out that his friend Mr. R. J. Cyriax, who is perhaps the leading authority on the Franklin disaster, does not share his opinion.

No matter what happened to Franklin's ships, the course of the men on land is clear. Some turned back toward *Erebus* and *Terror*, obviously planning to reboard them. Others who were too sick or weak to travel simply camped and waited. Others continued marching, dragging sleds piled with necessities and with luxuries—dying as they marched. No doubt some of them encountered Eskimos, but the English did not understand, or refused to admit, that their only chance of survival was to emulate the natives. Instead, they went on towing the crested silver plate, the wine goblets, the boxes of nails, the sheet lead, the silk handkerchiefs, the soap, the medals, the backgammon board, the bayonet scabbards, and the cookstoves, and bottles, and brushes, and *The Vicar of Wakefield* until they fell down exhausted in the snow. At this point they were longitudinally just about halfway between Alaska and Greenland, approximately 2,000 miles north of Nebraska.

The saws they had carried did become useful. At the end, collapsing from stupidity, scurvy, and starvation, some of the explorers lopped off the skulls of dead companions in order to get at the brains. This bit of gastronomic news when it reached the British public was most unpalatable. One could not bear to think that men from good families would turn savage, so it was agreed that Eskimos must have been responsible.

The Franklin catastrophe chilled England's perennial search for a northwest passage. Enough was enough.

In 1903 a brash young Norwegian named Roald Amundsen set off in a seventy-foot fishing boat, the *Gjoa*, after having reinforced the hull and installed a thirteen-horsepower engine. Six other young men went with him. They sailed on a foggy night to escape a creditor. After paralleling Baffin's route up the Greenland coast they bore west into Lancaster Sound and followed Franklin's presumed course south toward the Canadian mainland. For almost two years they stayed on King William Island, catching plenty of fish and game, although this was the area in which Franklin's men starved to death.

In August of 1905 they were able to push through the ice, and on the morning of the twenty-sixth Amundsen was awakened by his second-in-command, who told him there was a vessel in sight—the *Charles Hanson*, a Bering Sea whaler out of San Francisco.

They spent that winter locked in by ice and one crew member died of pneumonia. Next summer they were on the Pacific, six presumptuous Scandinavians in a herring boat.

If Amundsen was the first man to sail the Northwest Passage—and as far as anybody knows, he was—his *Gjoa* might not have been the first ship to make it through.

There is a story about the merchantman *Octavius* which is so bizarre that one cannot help feeling suspicious. Yet it may be true. If not, never mind: it's marvelous.

On the morning of August 11, 1775, the *Herald*, a whaler under the command of a Captain Warren, was just west of Greenland when the lookout reported a vessel ahead. At first the hull could not be seen, only her masts protruding above an iceberg, but when she drifted into view Captain Warren looked through his telescope. The vessel glistened with ice. There seemed to be nobody aboard.

Accompanied by four crew members, he pulled over in a longboat. They went aboard and found the entrance to the forecastle blocked by snow, but after this had been cleared away they were able to open the door. A musty stench poured out. In the forecastle twenty-eight dead seamen were lying on their bunks, each man wrapped up as though he had tried to protect himself against the cold.

The same musty odor poured out of the master's cabin. They found the master slumped in a chair with his hands resting on a table. A faint green mold obscured his features and veiled his eyes, but his body had not putrefied. The log was open, a quill pen beside it.

Captain Warren gave the log to one of his men and they entered the adjoining cabin. They discovered a woman lying in a bunk, covered with blankets, her head on her elbow as though she had been watching something when she died. A sailor with a flint in one hand and a piece of steel in the other was sitting cross-legged on the deck. Some wood shavings had been heaped together on the deck in front of him. Nearby lay the sailor's jacket. Under it was the body of a small boy.

Captain Warren inspected the galley, which had no provisions. He wanted to inspect the hold but his men refused and threatened to pull away in the longboat, so they returned to the *Herald* and watched the *Octavius* drift out of sight.

When Captain Warren asked for the logbook the sailor who had been carrying it handed over the binding and four pages. The book had come apart while the sailor was getting into the longboat and most of it had dropped into the water.

This log is now said to be in the archives of the London Registrar of Shipping. The first two pages list the ship's company, including the captain's wife and ten-year-old son, and disclose that the *Octavius* left England bound east on the China trade on September 10, 1761. The next page carries the earliest entries, mentioning fair weather, good headway, and sighting the Canary Islands. The last page contains what must have been the final entry. It is dated November 11, 1762, and obviously was written by a crewman. It gives an approximate position—Longitude 160 W., Latitude 75 N.—and states that the ship has been enclosed by ice for seventeen days. After noting that the master has unsuccessfully attempted to kindle a fire, the entry concludes: "The master's son died this morning and his wife says she no longer feels the terrible cold. The rest of us seem to have no relief from the agony."

Longitude 160 W., Latitude 75 N. is in the Arctic Ocean high above Point Barrow. The log's missing pages might have explained why the *Octavius* was so far north, but without them we can only speculate. On his return voyage, instead of charting a course around the Cape of Good Hope, the ship's captain must have yielded to some desperate urge. He must have thought he could accomplish what Frobisher and so many others had not, and be the first to navigate a northwest passage.

8

El Dorado

If you go to Bogotá and visit the Banco de la República you will see, in the bank's Museo del Oro, nearly 10,000 pre-Columbian gold artifacts: labrets, nose rings, brooches, masks, spoons, pincers, receptacles, representations of birds, snakes, crocodiles, people, animals. You walk down a corridor lined on both sides with display cases, each case packed with these opulent creations. You turn right, walk down another corridor past more of the same. Then more. And more. Finally, instead of going out, you are led into a dark room. After you have been there awhile the lights begin rising so gradually that you expect to hear violins, and you find yourself absolutely surrounded by gold. If all of Tut's gold were added to this accumulation, together with everything Schliemann plucked from Mycenae and Hissarlik, you could scarcely tell the difference.

Quite a lot of it is Muisca, a name that may not mean anything unless you happen to be an anthropologist, or a collector, or at least a Colombian. The Muisca Indians were one of the Chibcha tribes living in the highlands around Bogotá. They were sedentary farmers with no great authority or influence; but for a number of years, nobody knows just how long, until they were deprived of their independence by some Chibcha cousins, they observed a ritual unlike any other in the world.

Guatavitá was their principal village. High above it at an altitude of about two miles is a small circular lake which was formed several thousand years ago when a meteorite plunged into the earth. People were living in the Andean cordilleras at that time and a memory of the phenomenon must have survived, because Chibcha mythology relates how a golden god dropped from the sky to make his home at the bottom of Lake Guatavitá.

Whenever a new Muisca chieftain was elected—or perhaps each year on a certain day—he gave thanks to this radiant underwater deity. After first being anointed with sticky balsam gum he was sprayed with gold dust through cane tubes until he became a glittering living statue. Then he walked from the temple to the lake shore, accompanied by priests wearing black cotton robes and by the Muisca men whose bodies were painted red. At the shore he stepped aboard a raft and was paddled to the center of the lake where—possibly at dawn, just as sunlight illuminated the water—he dove in and washed away the gold. Then the people who had followed him, who now stood all around the perimeter of the lake, hurled emeralds and golden trinkets into the water.

The last performance of this ceremony seems to have taken place about 1480, but when the Europeans arrived they heard stories of a gilded man; and after they had told the stories to each other often enough the Muisca chief became an omnipotent king who ruled a golden empire. Not only did the king himself go about his daily affairs dressed in a golden crust, so did the nobles of his realm; and because it was uncomfortable to sleep in a golden suit they washed it off every night, gilding themselves afresh in the morning. And the warriors wore golden armor. And the buildings were sheathed in gold. That is to say, practically everything in this kingdom except food either was made of gold or was sheathed in gold.

The first European to go looking for it was a young German, Ambrosius Dalfinger—some say Ehinger—who had been appointed governor of Venezuela as the result of a little hanky-panky in the Old World. After Maximilian of Habsburg died three rulers competed for the title of Holy Roman Emperor: Henry VIII, Francis I, and Charles I of Spain. Who was to receive this crown would depend on the Electors; and, as the Spaniards say, Don Dinero speaks with a loud voice. Charles borrowed a wagonload of ducats from two German banking families, Welser and Fugger, in order to bribe the Electors. Dalfinger was related to some Welser officials, Charles owned Venezuela, etc.

Thus, in 1529 young Ambrosius landed at Coro, a settlement of several dozen thatched huts. He was expected to infuse the colony with a more businesslike spirit and speed up the exports—the most profitable being a substance derived from the bark of the guaiac tree which reputedly cured the so-called French disease, morbus gallicus. But the German bankers had misjudged their deputy because Ambrosius Dalfinger-Ehinger-Einguer-Lespinger-Alfinger went marching into the jungle with about 200 soldiers and several hundred reluctant Indian porters to see what he could see. How much he knew of a golden man at this point is uncertain; perhaps not much because the El Dorado legend was just taking shape, although he probably had seen and handled a few seductive ornaments in Coro.

On this march he acquired some gold. Nothing comparable to what Cortés had earlier found at Tenochtitlán, but by force or by trade he did pick up a number of high-carat gold pins, nose rings, diadems, and bracelets. More significant than these gold ornaments, however, was the fact that Venezuelan Indians had not made them. The workmanship was beyond their ability. They came from a place called Xerirá, which was renowned also for emeralds. In Xerirá one could trade seashells and cotton for emeralds and gold.

Dalfinger spent ten months in the jungle searching for this wonderful kingdom and when he got back to Coro he learned that during his long absence a new governor had been appointed. The Welser home office, believing that Ambrosius and all his men must have marched into eternity, sent forth a replacement—Hans Sinserhoffer, or Seissenhoffer, accompanied by one Nikolaus Federmann. It was a bit awkward, having two governors, but Sinserhoffer graciously resolved the problem by dying.

For a while then Dalfinger attended to gubernatorial business, at the same time accumulating supplies and soldiers for another attempt. And he became convinced that the way to locate Xerirá was to terrorize the natives. Sooner or later, he reasoned, they would stop being evasive and lead him straight to it.

In June of 1531 he started off again.

Even by conquistadorial standards he seems to have been unusually brutal and myopic. Indians who welcomed him with gifts and music were stabbed or shot. Rebellious captives were burnt alive. He had linked his porters together by a neck chain and when one died of exhaustion it was at first thought necessary to unshackle them all to get rid of the corpse; then Dalfinger realized it was simpler to decapitate the body, or, in some cases, a living porter who was unable to carry his load.

Meanwhile they were collecting gold. The expedition's accountant listed a great quantity of earrings, brooches, brassards, labrets, and so forth, along with more interesting items such as gold replicas of eagles and humans. Dalfinger loaded it all on a string of Indians and dispatched them to Coro with a guard of soldiers. One man, Francisco Martín, survived. Either he staggered into Coro several weeks later half dead of starvation, or he was adopted by a tribe and told his story long afterward. Historians disagree. In either case, it appears that the convoy got lost and when food ran out the Europeans began eating Venezuelans before being eaten themselves by predators and scavengers. As for the treasure, Martín said they had buried it at the foot of a ceiba tree. Thus, unless some Indians happened to be watching and later dug it up—which seems unlikely—there must still be approximately 100 kilos of gold ornaments at the foot of a ceiba tree somewhere in the jungle.

A little over two years after leaving Coro thirty-five exhausted ragged men tottered back into town. Governor Dalfinger, who had stopped a poisoned arrow with his throat, was not among them. They brought very little gold, but of harrowing stories they had more than enough. Vampire bats. Malaria. Yellow fever, accompanied by black vomit and death. A fever called verruga, transmitted by flies, which disfigured the body with abscesses. Crocodiles, jaguars, a climate where everything rotted, to say nothing of invisible enemies—one torment after another. And as for the soldiers who exercised themselves with native women, they had syphilis.

Those who listened to the grim recital and looked at the survivors grew more than ever convinced that someplace in the jungle a kingdom of inconceivable splendor must exist. As proof, a sizable treasure already had been found—though regrettably lost. Then too, if such a kingdom did not exist why would God create so many obstacles to its discovery? Therefore it must be.

Oveido, an early historian, was equally persuaded. Having asked some experienced conquistadors why the elusive prince should be called *dorado*, he was told that, according to the Indians, this great lord walked about coated with gold as finely pulverized as salt. Oveido continues with blunt practicality that he would rather have the chamber broom of this prince than the gold smelters of Peru, adding that if what he had been told was indeed so, and the great cacique gilded himself afresh each morning, it must follow that he owned some exceptionally rich mines.

After Dalfinger came Gonzalo Jiménez de Quesada, or Ximenes de Casada, an attorney who saw little future in the gloomy Andalusian courts. He sold everything and embarked for Santa Marta on the Colombian coast.

In 1536 he was sent upriver with approximately 900 men to look for a passage to the South Sea. Charles wanted a short route to the Spice Islands, so those were Quesada's marching orders—although everybody in the expedition and everybody in Santa Marta understood that he would be looking for the gilded man.

Quesada's troops hacked their way through some of the most unpleasant territory on earth. Ants, hornets, snakes, ticks, bats, mosquitos, fevers, and tropical rain made their days memorable, with a quick flight of arrows now and then for emphasis. Stragglers caught by Indians were cooked and eaten. Juan Serrano was taken from his hammock by a jaguar, as easily as a cat runs off with a mouse. Others, including the good swimmer Juan Lorenzo, were swallowed by alligators. Graves decorated the trail. Germán Arciniegas reports that sometimes the hand of a buried corpse remained visible, as though waving good-bye to those who struggled on toward the land of gold.

When there was no decent food they scrambled for lizards, rats, insects, bats, and whatever else might sustain them a few hours longer; they gnawed leather shields and the hides of dead horses.

Next came the mountains. They climbed and shivered, chewed on raw corn, and dragged the surviving horses upward.

At last they looked down on a vast cultivated plain. Everything appeared green and peaceful. This was the plateau of Cudinamarca, land of the condor, home of the Chibcha Indians. A year had passed since Quesada left Santa Marta. Three-fourths of his men were dead.

Indifferent now to danger, they descended from the mountain like a company of insects—swarming on what-ever opposed them—and invaded the city of Tunja, where thin sheets of beaten gold dangled from almost every hut, tinkling faintly and shimmering in the sun-light. They found one of the three Chibcha rulers inside a wooden palace. He was very old and fat and was seated on a throne or stool encrusted with emeralds. Quesada, remembering the lesson taught by Cortés and Pizarro, seized the fat old man and never once let go. The city of Tunja quickly surrendered.

It was late afternoon when the Spaniards arrived. Now, after the conquest, they rushed around by torchlight rip-ping sheets of gold from the huts, filling bags with emer-alds and gold dust.

Their next prize was a temple full of royal mummies with parrot-feather headdresses, emerald eyes, and golden ornaments. The temple caught fire while they were strip-ping the mummies, but the treasure was salvaged.

Still they had not found what they were looking for: el hombre dorado.

They were shown the lake above Guatavitá and were told that here the story of a golden man had originated. Here, it was explained to them, the Muisca used to anoint and gild their chief. But that was a long time ago. Now there was no such man. El Dorado no longer existed.

The Spaniards refused to believe it.

Quesada and his men remained on the plateau for two years, relentlessly seeking hidden treasure and gold mines. What they discovered was unquestionably worth stealing in the name of the Spanish crown, but it did not compare with the wealth of Mexico or Peru. So there must be more, Quesada reasoned. Much more. But there was not. The Chibcha had no treasuries, no secret mines. Most of their gold came from trade with Ecuador.

At last, somewhat frustrated because he had expected to rival or surpass Cortés and Pizarro, Quesada began to think about returning to Spain to publicize his conquest and ask for a suitable reward—the governorship of this territory, which he had chosen to call New Granada.

Just then he learned that another expedition led by one of Pizarro's captains, Sebastián de Belalcázar, was on the road to Cudinamarca.

This man's name, in fact, may have been García, but he has ridden down the centuries as Sebastián from Belalcázar. He was a blue-eyed son of Estremadura, home of many conquistadors, and he governed the northern sector of the Inca realm, which we now call Ecuador. Such an office would satisfy most men, but not Belalcázar. Everything in Quito appeared orderly, which is to say boring, and nobody knew what might be disclosed in the lands beyond. On one of those plateaus, it was said, lay a kingdom of gold. He therefore appointed a lieutenant to run the business and, without notifying Pizarro, started off in a northerly direction. If no rich kingdom existed—well, should that be the case one could always plant the seeds of future cities. For this purpose Belalcázar took along a multitude of pigs, cattle, dogs, extra horses, and whatever else seemed appropriate, including fine silver for his table. And if the grand column could proceed no faster than its slowest members—Ay, so be it.

Quesada, awaiting his arrival, grew a bit nervous. He had been told that the invader wore silk clothes and was accompanied by well-equipped soldiers dressed in coats of mail. Quesada's own army was now seriously weakened; his men had very little powder for the harquebuses, few bolts for the crossbows, and their armor was falling apart.

Soon after Quesada got his first report of Belalcázar's host he learned that still another army was approaching. This was led by the red-bearded Nikolaus Federmann, Capitán Barba Roja, who had landed at Coro with Governor Sinserhoffer.

Federmann had no idea that Quesada was firmly planted on the Chibcha plateau, nor did Belalcázar. Nor had Quesada any previous warning that his New Granada would be saturated with armed guests.

So three armies met in the Colombian wilderness. Quesada had come down almost 1,000 miles from the north, Federmann about that same distance from the northeast, and Belalcázar had marched up from the southwest. On a map their routes loosely resemble a Y tilted to the right, converging on the Chibcha realm, for all three —though they knew nothing of one another—all three had heard of El Dorado.

Belalcázar and Federmann arrived at nearly the same time. As fiction it would be impossible, nobody would believe it, yet there they were. Belalcázar with his pigs, soft silk shirts, and well-fed Peruvian conquistadors in plumed steel helmets. Quesada, gone native, his men in

Chibcha cotton. And Federmann's skeletal column, his soldiers racked by fever and dressed partly in animal skins; they had been battling the jungle and the mountains for many months.

Who was most surprised? It's hard to say. Federmann, no doubt, was dismayed. Reaching the goal after such hardship, only to learn you are not the first. As for Belalcázar, he could afford to be philosophic; he would not have minded more gold and glory, but his pockets already were as full as his stomach.

And Quesada? He must have been dumfounded. Not one threat, but two.

Although owning the plateau by virtue of squatter's rights Quesada understood that he was some distance from the courts of Spain and was confronted on one flank by a famished red-bearded German, on the other by an experienced conquistador. Rather than thumping the tub, he decided, it would be wiser to negotiate.

He seems to have approached Federmann first, which is odd. Evidently he considered his countryman, Belalcázar, the greater threat. He gave Federmann a substantial present of gold and emeralds and in exchange was allowed to recruit some of the German's army, which then gave him a military advantage over Belalcázar. That being so, Belalcázar was even less inclined to fight. Besides, he too received a present.

Quesada next put on his advocate's gown. He persuaded the other two that all three captains should return to Spain where the matter of ownership might be legally resolved.

There is disagreement about whether Quesada had formally taken possession of the land in 1538 before an audience of mystified Indians, or in 1539 when Belalcázar and Federmann were present. Either way, it must have been a grand occasion governed by dignified ritual, reminiscent of Balboa wading majestically into the Pacific. Quesada rode into the middle of a field, dismounted, pulled up a handful of grass, and set one foot on the bare earth. He then proclaimed that everything belonged to Charles V. This fact having been established, Quesada got back on his horse, drew his sword, and challenged anybody to dispute his authority. There was no challenge, so he sheathed the sword and again dismounted.

Father Domingo de Las Casas now took charge. The conquistadors knelt in prayer while Las Casas communicated with the ultimate sovereign.

Quesada then marked off the site of a town, specifying twelve huts in honor of the twelve apostles, and the business was concluded.

Bogotá had been founded—named after the reigning chief.

A few weeks later, or perhaps quite a bit later, Captains Quesada, Federmann, and Belalcázar traveled together to Cartagena and from there to Santa Marta, planning to continue as a triumvirate to Europe, each to ask Charles if he might have New Granada.

They landed together at Málaga, but the Spanish wheel of fortune ticked inexorably past them all.

Federmann was accused by his employers—those ever watchful German bankers—of pocketing some gold and emeralds. He died in Valladolid in 1541, vainly waiting for the emperor to help him out.

Belalcázar at first had better luck. He returned to the New World as governor of the northern realm and everything seemed propitious for the foundation of an empire. Accordingly, he was very much surprised to find himself challenged by a long-time comrade, Jorge Robledo. Belalcázar either hanged or beheaded him, executed his followers, and burned down the house containing their bodies. He almost got away with it. Robledo's widow, Doña María, seems to have been the only one seriously troubled by the incident—although it is said that Robledo did have friends at the Spanish court. No matter who was responsible, Belalcázar was ordered back to Spain, but at Cartagena he fell sick and died. Some member of the party bought a length of Rouen muslin for one peso and two reales. Another peso went to the woman who cut his shroud, and twenty pesos to the church that conducted his funeral. Twenty-two pesos, two reales.

Quesada, after depositing in Seville the Royal Fifth— 572 emeralds and a respectable quantity of Chibcha gold —believed that, like Pizarro and Cortés, he would be made governor of the territory he had conquered. But intrigue at court persuaded Charles to reward the financier behind Quesada. Thus the financier's son, who had nothing to do with the discovery and conquest of New Granada, became its governor. Quesada returned to Colombia ten years later with a coat of arms, the meaningless title of marshal, and 2,000 ducats annually. Even then, at the age of fifty, he continued to dream. Having actually found El Dorado—or at least the legend's origin —and found it less than he expected, he thought it must be somewhere else.

He was afflicted with leprosy during his last years, we are told by Flórez de Ocariz, and spent much time in the desert near Tocaima where there was a sulphurous river, "and he rested amid its fumes." He died without a peso, owing 600,000 ducats, in the city of Mariquita in 1579.

His younger brother Hernán, who had been left in charge while the three great conquistadors went to Spain, looked at Lake Guatavitá more intently during their absence. If the legend were true, if Muisca Indians had indeed showered the lake with golden knickknacks, it should be possible to collect some treasure. Hernán therefore lined up a company of Indians, issued empty calabashes, and ordered them to start dipping. An Indian at the edge of the lake would fill a calabash and hand it to his neighbor, who handed it to his neighbor, and so on until the calabash appeared at the rim of the surrounding hill. There it would be emptied and the calabash would start back down the line.

After this had gone on for several months Hernán was able to inspect part of the lake bed and he picked up a few gold offerings—though in fact they were not gold but gilded copper. The pure gold objects, being heavier, had skidded down the muddy slope toward the middle. Nevertheless, these offerings confirmed what the Indians said. Now you would think that after studying these artifacts Hernán would lash his water brigade into furious action until Lake Guatavitá had been reduced to a muddy puddle. Not so. Hernán Quesada had not traveled all the way from Spain to superintend the draining of a lake. Surely this miserable pond, despite a few trinkets in the mud, could not be all there was to El Dorado.

Quite naturally, therefore, he marched away to find it. Several thousand Indians accompanied him, and about 260 Spaniards. Fewer than 100 soldiers got back, all of them afoot, having been obliged to cook their horses. This baroque expedition destroyed Hernán Quesada physically and financially; and soon afterward, while playing cards on a boat on the Río Magdalena during a thunderstorm, he got in the way of a lightning bolt. He was by now very shaggy, reports the chronicler Ocariz, and the lightning burned up his beard, his clothes, and all the hair on his body, leaving him naked and as black as a Negro.

Pizarro's youngest brother, Gonzalo, set out from Quito

—at that time called San Francisco—in 1541, four years after Belalcázar. He, too, had heard rumors. From a tortured Indian he learned that El Dorado actually was to be found in a region known as the Guianas. But before reaching the Guianas, he was told, one comes to the land of cinnamon trees—La Canela.

Now, in those days cinnamon was expensive, and a sixteenth-century physician, Nicholas Monardes, spoke well of American cinnamon in his famous book, *Joyfull Newes out of the Newe Founde Worlde*: "it hath the same pleasantness of taste as the same Cinnamon hath, which they bring from the India of Portugal . . ."

America thus far had provided no spiceries such as the East Indies had given Portugal; perhaps in La Canela they might be found.

Gonzalo recruited 4,000 Ecuadorians, a considerable menagerie of pigs, llamas, horses and dogs, and quite a few Spanish soldiers. According to Garcilaso de la Vega there were 340 Spaniards. Cieza de León says 220. Either way it was a menacing little army.

They struggled across the Andes where dozens of half-dressed Indian porters froze to death. Then at the base of the eastern slope they plunged into a jungle so choked and darkened by frenzied growth that they had no idea where they were going. In this poisonous green twilight, stumbling down a path chopped by macheteros, the expedition began to rot.

At one point, searching for La Canela, Pizarro left his army and went off with seventy men "in the direction of sunrise." They came across a few cinnamon trees. Pizarro thought there must be more, although the natives of that territory said they knew of no others. And where did El Dorado live? Nobody could say. "I took measures to inform myself," Gonzalo later wrote to Charles V, by which he meant that he stretched some Indians on cane racks, roasted them, and threw them to his dogs.

"They decided to return by the way they came," one early historian remarks laconically, "and see if they could not find another track . . ."

At last the demoralized army stopped beside a tributary of the Amazon, which they named the Coca. Here they constructed a brigantine, caulking the seams with their own ragged clothes. Then for two months Pizarro led his bewildered troops alongside the Coca while the brig *San Pedro*, commanded by Francisco Orellana, carried the heaviest cargo and those who were too sick to walk or ride horseback.

Things got worse until at last Orellana with about sixty men continued downstream in the brig and several canoes, the plan being that when they discovered food they would load up the *San Pedro* and return. It was an interesting plan because Orellana could not possibly sail upriver against the current. Nevertheless, away he went. Long afterward he summarized this departure with a line that might have been written by Cervantes: "After boiling our boots in herbs we set off for the kingdom of gold."

Pizarro's army waited and waited beside the Coca, meanwhile enjoying such delicacies as toasted stirrup leather and dogflesh simmered with tree leaves.

A scouting party turned up a plantation abandoned by Indians. It held a crop of *yuca*—little more than roots—which the starving adventurers ate without bothering to wash away the dirt. They began cooking it to make bread. Several men stuffed themselves so full of root bread that they died; others became bloated and had to be roped to their saddles.

The army was now in a bad state, declares Cieza de León: "They all went with bare feet and legs, for they had nothing in the way of shoes, except that a few made a sort of sandal from the leather of the saddles. The road was all through forest and full of prickly trees; so that their feet got scratched all over, and their legs were constantly pierced by the many thorns. In this condition they went on, nearly dead with hunger, naked and barefooted, covered with sores, opening the road with their swords . . ."

At last, their clothes ripped and moldering, they understood what lay ahead.

Two years after he had left Quito, Pizarro returned with seventy-nine men—several of whom soon died because they could not stop eating. How many Indians got back is unknown; by most accounts all 4,000 died. Near the end of this journey Pizarro had a dream in which a dragon plucked out his heart.

Six years later in Peru, after another debacle, Gonzalo Pizarro was beheaded.

A priest who accompanied the Orellana detachment, Father Gaspar de Carvajal, kept a journal and by his reckoning the clumsy brig traveled as much as ninety miles a day. It sounds like a perfectly splendid tour, if you disregard the menu. Foragers saw nothing edible, so that before long they were chewing not only their boots but their belts and leather sword scabbards. Sometimes they crawled ashore—unable to stand erect—and grubbed for roots.

Eventually they saw a village, staggered into it, and gobbled up everything while the Indians fled.

At the next village, not quite so hungry, they built another brig, the *Victoria*, because the *San Pedro* was unseaworthy and before long they would reach the ocean. Then both brigs swept on down the Amazon. There was no thought of returning to Pizarro.

After eight months on the world's most powerful river,

with blankets for sails and vines for rigging, they arrived at the estuary. It is said that one island in this estuary is larger than Switzerland, and so strong is the current that fresh water can be found 100 miles offshore.

Orellana's men followed the coast up to Nueva Cádiz on the island of Cubagua near Trinidad, and from there they reached Santo Domingo. Orellana then returned to Spain where Charles—entranced by his adventures—commissioned him to colonize the florid river basin. It sounds peculiar. You would expect Orellana to be hanged for deserting Pizarro. He must have told his story with great skill.

His triumphant return started badly. An epidemic struck before they left the Canary Islands. Then three of his captains and a number of soldiers objected to crossing the Atlantic, some because they were ill, others because they sensed disaster. At sea the drinking water gave out and had it not been for a rainstorm everybody would have died. On the Amazon they were hit by arrows, toppled by fever, bitten by snakes, spiders, bugs, crocodiles, etc. Orellana died aboard ship. A few of his wretched colonists turned around and got to Margarita Island, their lives indirectly ruined by the Gilded Man.

It would be hard to devise a campaign more starcrossed than Gonzalo Pizarro's, but there was one. The Viceroy of Peru, Don Andreas Hurtado de Mendoza, nobody's fool, having observed that El Dorado hunters invariably were out of town quite a while and frequently never did come back, concluded that searching for the elusive prince might be just the way to get rid of certain redneck soldiers at least temporarily and, with luck, permanently. He therefore encouraged the quest, and no doubt helped to decide who should go, because there were plenty of volunteers.

So it happened that a great butcher of Indians, Pedro de Urzúa, started toward the promised land in 1560 with a regiment of seasoned cutthroats. Like Belalcázar, Urzúa believed that one should dine adequately and travel comfortably while battling the Andes. He took along a swarm of pigs, dogs, cattle and horses, as well as that most valuable commodity, women, notably his mistress—the beautiful young widow Iñes de Atienza.

Deep in the Amazon basin an officer was murdered. Urzúa's response was to execute everybody he suspected. Yet even before this thoughtful display of leadership the expedition had begun to putrefy. And on New Year's Day, in the evening, Pedro de Urzúa was stabbed to death while dozing in a hammock. His lieutenant was skewered with such violence that the sword protruded from his back and wounded a conspirator standing behind him. Cristóbal de Acuña, whose chronicle appeared in 1641, says that Doña Iñes and a mutineer, "thinking they had a favorable occasion to satisfy their Lust and Ambition together," organized the revolt. Other historians doubt this.

In any case, one Fernando de Guzmán now ascended the steamy throne.

The cardinal manipulating Guzmán was a middle-aged gallows bird named Lope de Aguirre who seems to have been a bona fide psychopath. He was small, ugly, about fifty years old, with a black beard and malevolent eyes. What is curious about him is that he never believed in El Dorado. The maddest of a demented lot, he could not be tricked by a luminous phantom in the jungle. He proposed returning to Peru.

Because of the current they would have to float all the way down the Amazon to the Atlantic, sail north around Guiana and Venezuela, march across the isthmus of

Panama, then walk or sail down the Pacific coast. En route they would attack settlements, kill the administrators, and recruit more men for an invasion of Peru. There, after overthrowing the Spanish government, they would divide the kingdom's enormous wealth.

According to Walker Chapman there are certain men "so shaped by birth and breeding that they dedicate themselves to a nihilistic demolition of all human institutions." Now this may be argued; but if it's true, Aguirre was such a man.

Garcilaso de la Vega relates that in 1548, at Potosí, Aguirre received 200 lashes for mistreating Indians, after which he vowed to kill the judge, Esquivel. This threat so alarmed Esquivel that he gave up his post and fled to Lima, but within two weeks Aguirre found him. Esquivel fled to Quito. Twenty days later Aguirre arrived. Esquivel fled to Cuzco, but presently Aguirre arrived, "having traveled on foot and without shoes, saying that a whipped man had no business to ride a horse." For three years and four months Esquivel tried to escape. Aguirre followed him, and caught up with him in Cuzco at noon on a Monday, asleep over his books, and stabbed him.

This was the brain behind Guzmán, the expedition's new commander.

Somewhere along the way Aguirre learned from Indians that it was possible to switch rivers. That is, move entirely by water from the Amazon to the Orinoco because of a stream called the Casiquiare which empties into them both. The Orinoco would deliver them close to a settlement on Margarita Island.

While they were in the midst of this transition the bed of Doña Iñes caused trouble. After Urzúa's death she had become the mistress of one Salduendo, who now rearranged things on the boat for their mutual comfort—

which included an extra mattress. The second mattress infuriated Aguirre; he killed Salduendo and then had Doña Iñes murdered.

The woman's death was especially bloody and unexpected, but there had been others; and Don Fernando de Guzmán, reflecting upon his subordinate's temper, began to think it might be wise to kill Aguirre before Aguirre hollowed out everybody on the boat. However, he was slow getting organized and Aguirre heard about the plot. As a result, Don Fernando with three of his associates quickly joined their ancestors.

Aguirre now proclaimed himself "General of the Marañón"—the Marañón being a tributary of the Amazon —and promised his followers victory in Peru.

They devastated Margarita Island—slaughtering, raping, burning, and looting. The governor and several other officials, having been assured by Aguirre that he meant them no harm, were strangled at midnight in the fortress. Anybody who displeased him was garroted, shot, or stabbed.

Told of a conspiracy against him, he butchered the supposed ringleader and then summoned a longtime friend, Antón Llamoso.

"They also tell me that thou wert one of the party," Aguirre said to Llamoso. "How was this? Was this friendship? And dost thou hold so lightly the love I feel for thee?"

According to Padre Simón, Llamoso was terrified by Aguirre's words. He fell upon the body of the dead conspirator, shouting: "Curse this traitor, who wished to commit so great a crime! I will drink his blood!" And putting his mouth over a horrible wound in the head he began sucking the blood and brains, swallowing what he sucked "as if he were a famished dog."

Before leaving the island Aguirre murdered two priests, various citizens who got in the way, and several of his own men. Then he embarked for Venezuela in three ships flying a black flag with crossed red swords. At the moment of departure he killed his admiral, Alonso Rodríguez, who had suggested that Aguirre go below decks to avoid being splashed by the waves.

He now had approximately 150 insurgents, although when they stepped ashore this number was reduced by one; he shot a Portuguese named Farias who asked whether they were landing on another island or the mainland.

They seized the port of Burburata, and here the touchy general declared war on Philip II. Their next stop was Valencia, a short distance up the coast, where he wrote an irrational vituperative letter to the Spanish king, concluding: "I am a rebel against thee until death." This letter was carried by a priest to Santo Domingo and from there it reached Spain. Whether Philip saw it is not known; probably no one dared show it to him.

After executing a few more of his revolutionaries who did not sound enthusiastic enough Aguirre marched on Barquisimeto, which he found deserted. But the hour had come. Government troops besieged him, his little army melted away, and at last, as wild as Hitler, he stabbed his adolescent half-breed daughter Elvira who had accompanied him all the way from Peru. "Commend thyself to God," he told her, "for I am about to kill thee; that thou mayest not be pointed at with scorn, nor be in the power of anyone who may call thee the daughter of a traitor."

He was shot by two of his own men. His head was then cut off and exhibited in an iron cage. His body was quartered, the pieces tossed into the street like dog food. And in faraway Peru the house in which he had lived was demolished and salt was sprinkled over the earth where it stood so that nothing of him would remain. All of which, provided your mind has a skeptical slope, may cause you to reflect on the nature of madness.

Still, Lope de Aguirre has not been forgotten. Today— or tonight—if a flickering phosphorescence plays above the Venezuelan marshes, a prudent traveler considers it wise to cross himself: he has observed Aguirre's soul flee-ing the approach of man.

Such a repugnant tale ought to conclude the saga of El Dorado, but gold exudes a deadly charm. Only a few years later two roving bands of conquistadors met head on in the jungle and mauled one another for three days in order to decide which group owned the territory. Survivors of this engagement were picked off by Chuncho Indians.

By now it was agreed among El Dorado experts that the fabulous kingdom must be somewhere in Guiana— the name given by Spaniards to the great unmapped basin of the Orinoco. And of those who went hunting for El Dorado in Guiana the most businesslike was Don Antonio de Berrio, who found himself more or less sucked into it.

Berrio was a captain of the guards living comfortably in Granada when his wife's uncle died, leaving the estate to her. Now it happened that Doña Berrio's uncle had been Gonzalo Jiménez de Quesada, and it appeared that after all these years Tío Gonzalo's property in the New World was producing 14,000 ducats annually. Therefore, in 1580, Berrio, his wife, their six daughters and two sons sailed off to the Antilles. Life perhaps could be agreeable in the New World, even more pleasant than Granada, con-sidering those ducats.

However, Tío Gonzalo had left a stipulation in his will

that the heir to his estate must use part of that income to look for El Dorado. Thus, instead of relaxing on a colonial patio, the middle-aged captain of the guards found himself once again on horseback leading a bunch of grubby provincial troops. But before setting out on this distasteful trip he studied the problem: he read the accounts of previous explorers and talked to some who had actually fought their way through the jungle.

And at last, as it had seeped into the blood of earlier men, the legend obsessed him. He spent fifteen years looking for El Dorado. He led three expeditions across the territory, established trading posts, and quarreled with everybody. He knew the kingdom could not be far away. After all, if so many men had destroyed themselves searching—well then, only a fool would claim El Dorado did not exist. Besides, as he explained in a letter to King Philip, the Indians he questioned invariably agreed that in the mountains there was a vast lake and on its far side were cities with many people who had gold and precious stones.

While Berrio was marching back and forth a wild figure emerged from the jungle—Juan Martín de Albujar, last survivor of an expedition that had vanished ten years earlier. Depending on your source, Albujar spoke "perfect Spanish," or he had almost forgotten his native language. Such minuscule discrepancies aren't important, but they are exasperating; one wants to know precisely what happened. Anyway, he was first noticed in or near the Margarita church, dressed like an Indian, and Berrio later talked with him. He said that after being held captive for a long time by Caribs he was taken to see the Gilded Man. He had been led through the jungle blindfolded, and when the blindfold was removed he found himself at the edge of a city which the Indians called Manoa, beside a lake called Parima. This city was so large, said Albujar, that it had taken a full day to walk to the palace. The streets were lined with stone houses, not thatched huts, and in the palace he saw with his own eyes the man they had been looking for, El Dorado, resplendent as the sun.

He stayed seven months in Manoa and was questioned by the Gilded Man about the customs of Spaniards. Then the great ruler presented him with some gold and jewels, after which he was again blindfolded and led into the jungle. Finally the Indians released him and pointed the way to the coast.

Unfortunately, he said, El Dorado's gift had been stolen by some other Indians he met. That's how it is. Something always happens to the treasure. Yet Albujar did have, in fact, a calabash filled with gold beads; and he offered to swear on a Bible that every word he spoke was true—a pledge not lightly regarded in those days. And when he lay dying of fever in Puerto Rico he continued to insist he had told the truth.

Apart from what Albujar saw, or thought he saw, his story reinforced Berrio's conviction that El Dorado must be close by. As a result, though he was no longer young, Don Antonio began to make preparations for one more trip.

But just then—in the spring of 1595—four strange ships dropped anchor at Icacos Point, the southwest corner of Trinidad. A roving English gentleman of fortune had arrived, by name Sir Walter Raleigh, carrying a royal patent from Elizabeth to "offend and enfeeble the King of Spain, and to discover and subdue heathen lands . . ."

Raleigh, like Berrio, had done his homework. He had talked with the captains of vessels that traded in the Caribbean and with men who had spent time ashore. He had read everything he could find on the subject of South

America and he claimed to be familiar with the details of twenty-three expeditions that had searched for El Dorado.

"Guiana is a countrey that hath yet her maydenhead," he wrote, "never sackt, turned, nor wrought, the face of the earth hath not bene torne, nor the vertue and salt of the soyle spent by manurance, the graves have not bene opened for golde, the mines not broken with sledges, nor their Images puld downe out of their temples . . ."

His presence quickly was reported to Berrio—who had been named governor of Guiana and El Dorado, evidently because of his persistence. Berrio dispatched some soldiers to find out what the English pirate wanted. They were assured that the English had stopped at Trinidad only for refreshment.

Berrio mistrusted this. He dispatched a larger party.

Raleigh invited these emissaries aboard. Four Spaniards accepted. And there, beneath Raleigh's flag—five silver lozenges on a blue field—the Englishmen and the Spaniards sat around drinking wine and pretending to be friends, meanwhile subtly pumping each other for information.

Raleigh learned from an Indian that there were less than eighty soldiers on the island. That being so, the hour was ripe. He sent a boatload of food and wine to the Spaniards who had remained ashore and when they settled down to enjoy English hospitality a landing party slaughtered them. Raleigh then murdered his four guests. It might be observed, if one wishes to pick at cause and effect, that during the previous year eight Englishmen who visited Trinidad intending to hunt for meat had been captured by Spanish soldiers who trussed them up like pigs and slit their throats.

Now that the preliminaries were over, Raleigh's men set out for San José. They marched all night and arrived at dawn. The attack was a great success; practically the entire garrison was killed and Berrio was captured. The English then looted the town, set it afire, and marched back to their ships.

Raleigh began to interrogate his prisoner courteously because they both came from good families.

Berrio pretended to be senile. He answered vaguely, talked about how difficult it was to travel up the Orinoco, there were all sorts of wild animals, Indians with poisoned arrows, and so forth. Nobody could reach the land of gold.

But Sir Walter had not crossed the Atlantic for amusement. We regard him as one of Elizabeth's seagoing knights, so it is a surprise to learn that he detested water travel and when aboard ship he usually got sick. John Aubrey remarks that, in order to cross the Thames, Raleigh would "go round about over London Bridge" rather than take the convenient wherry boat.

In any case, now that he had put up with the unpleasant voyage he did not intend to be duped by an elderly Spaniard's nonsense. With Berrio as his prisoner he entered the mouth of the Orinoco—that is to say, one of the mouths—and got lost. The Orinoco delta, 150 miles wide, has fifteen or twenty channels which loop and divide and braid together in such confusion that there are places where the current flows the wrong direction.

Raleigh sounds dismayed:

"We might have wandred a whole yeere in that laborinth of rivers ere we had found any way, either out or in, especiallie after we passed the ebbing and flowing . . ."

Fifteen days after entering the delta they managed to get into the mainstream, which astounded them by its size—four miles across. They rowed upriver, sometimes helped by the wind, and occasionally met native fishermen in dugouts from whom they got not only fresh fish but gourds full of the local palm toddy. Raleigh was smarter than most of the Spaniards when dealing with Indians; he insisted that they not be robbed or abused, with the result that he and his men often were invited to the villages. So well liked was he that he was given a strange little beast "which they call Cassacam, which seemeth to be all barred over with small plates somewhat like a Renocero." The tail of this creature, he noted in his diary, if powdered and blown into the ear would cure deafness. But for all the exchange of gifts and pleasantries he had not forgotten his purpose. By means of Arawak interpreters he asked about a lake called Parima. And did they know of a city or a land called Manoa? A chief who covered himself with gold?

Oh yes! the Indians replied. Yes indeed! Oh yes! Through the jungle. Beyond the mountains.

Raleigh decided he had gone far enough. The directions sounded familiar. Besides, the river was flooding, which made progress more difficult, and there were hints of a Spanish flotilla approaching. But before turning downstream he left behind, 300 miles up the Orinoco, two volunteers named Hugh Goodwin and Frances Sparrey or Sparrow. According to the plan, Raleigh would return someday to pick them up. Until that day Goodwin was to live with the Indians and learn their language. Sparrey's assignment was to find out what truth there might be to the legend of the Gilded Man. With native guides he would proceed through the jungle to the mountains, cross the mountains, locate the city—if it did exist—then draw sketches of its fortifications and otherwise prepare a guidebook on ways and means of capturing it. Then he would return to the Orinoco. If Raleigh was nowhere in sight he would walk to the coast, attract the notice of the first English ship he saw, and thus return to England.

So, having bade his secret agents good-bye, Sir Walter weighed anchor and started home, accompanied by all the debris of the giant river in flood—entire trees now and again roiling past the ship like battering rams. The level of the water rose ominously. In his diary he wrote: "The fury of the Orenoque beganne daily to threaten us with daungers in our return, for no half day passed, but the river began to rage and overflow very fearfully, and the raines came down in terribel showers, and gusts in great abundance: and withall: our men beganne to cry out . . ."

What became of his two benighted emissaries is in wondrous accord with everything else. Goodwin ingratiated himself so thoroughly with the Indians that when a posse of Spaniards came looking for him the Indians declared that he had been eaten by a jaguar. This was good news. The Spaniards therefore went away and for the next twenty-two years Goodwin worked on his assignment. Raleigh located him in 1617, by which time he could hardly speak English.

Sparrey, poking around the jungle, was ambushed by Spaniards. After questioning him they shipped him to Spain where he spent six years observing his fingernails in prison. English authorities eventually negotiated his release on the assumption that he must have learned all about the mysterious city, but Sparrey did not have much news.

Raleigh himself—escaping "the Orenoque's terribel daungers"—returned to his base at Trinidad. There, after failing to obtain any ransom for his distinguished captive, he exchanged Don Antonio for an English prisoner and sailed away to England.

He did not bring back much—some tobacco, a few gold trinkets, specimens of ore, and additional rumors concerning the whereabouts of the ephemeral golden kingdom:

"I have been assured by such of the Spanyardes as have seene Manoa, the emperiall Citie of Guiana, which the Spanyardes call El Dorado, that for the greatness, for the riches, and for the excellent seate, it farre exceedeth any of the world, at least of so much of the world as is known to the Spanish nation; it is founded upon a lake of salt water 200 leagues long . . ."

Raleigh's sponsors, having put up quite a lot of money, were not pleased with the meager result. His enemies, though, were delighted; they claimed that the voyage never took place and said that for seven months he had been skulking off the English coast.

He thereupon wrote his magnificent, preposterous account of what he had seen, as well as much that he had not, entitled *The Discoverie of the Large, Rich, and Bewtiful Empyre of Guiana, with a Relation of the Great and Golden Citie of Manoa (which the Spanyards call El Dorado).*

This is less than the complete title, but it is the important part, even though untrue: Raleigh had discovered nothing that was not already known to the Spaniards. But his narrative was widely accepted and reprinted many times, and his huge saltwater lake began to appear on maps—very like a grotesque insect—between the Orinoco and the Amazon. Cartographers faithfully drew Lake Parima on every map of South America until 1800 when Alexander von Humboldt drained it with a single word: "imaginary."

Sir Walter quite naturally included in his *Discoverie* the legend of a chief "anoynted all over with a kind of white balsamum" and coated with gold dust until he stood forth "al shining from the foote to the head." He included, too, some fairly bizarre creatures such as the topless giants reported by Sir John Mandeville in other parts of the world. These existed, in a sense. One of the Orinoco tribes made enormous ceremonial masks which fitted over their heads and shoulders so that, as Raleigh claimed, their mouths opened in the middle of their breasts. The moral, obviously, is that we should not be too skeptical.

On March 24, 1603, Queen Elizabeth died and a few days later Raleigh woke up in the Tower of London under sentence of death. The charge was old, and it sounds unfair: he had been guilty of negligence in failing to report treasonous talk, which was serious enough, but hardly deserving execution. In any event, he seems to have reasoned that his last hope of emerging from the Tower was Guiana—golden Guiana. If he could lead one more expedition, and if all went well, he would be restored. He may still have believed in the legend of a golden king, or he may have thought only that the mineral wealth of Guiana would save him. Or perhaps he was just pretending.

"It is a journey of honnor and riches I offer you; an enterprise fesible and certayne," he suggested to Viscount Haddington, who might possibly intercede on his behalf. And he went on to say that if he could not lead an expedition to a Guiana mountain alight with silver and gold, "let the commander have commissione to cut of my head ther."

To King James he wrote: "I do therefore, on the knees of my hart, beseich your Majesty to take councell from your own sweet and mercifull disposition, and to remember that I have loved your Majesty now twenty yeares, for which your Majestie hath yett geven me no reward. And it is fitter that I should be indebted to my soverayne Lord, then the King to his poore vassall. Save me, therefore, most mercifull Prince . . ."

And, all hope gone, to his wife:

You shall receave, deare wief, my last words in these my last lynes. My love I send you, that you may keepe it when I am dead; and my councell, that you may remember it when I am noe more ... I trust my bloud will quench their mallice that desire my slaughter; and that they will not alsoe seeke to kill you and yours with extreame poverty. To what frind to direct thee I knowe not, for all mine have left mee in the true tyme of triall: and I plainly perceive that my death was determyned from the first day. Most sorry I am (as God Knoweth) that, being thus surprised with death, I can leave you noe better estate ... I cannot wright much. God knowes howe hardlie I stole this tyme, when all sleep; and it is tyme to separate my thoughts from the world. Begg my dead body, which living was denyed you; and either lay itt at Sherborne if the land continue, or in Exiter church, by my father and mother.

In March of 1616 he was released from the Tower for one last attempt.

Twenty-one years had elapsed since his first voyage. Thirteen of those years he had spent locked in the Tower. He had not been treated badly: he was allowed to walk through the garden, he had visitors such as Ben Jonson, all the books he needed, and paper and ink because he was working on his ambitious *History of the World*. He was nearly as well off as some of our imprisoned politicians. He was permitted to set up an alchemical laboratory where he tinkered about, and when not otherwise occupied he tutored the heir apparent, Prince Henry. His wife shared his bed and his son Carew was born in that sinister place.

Still, despite these comforts, Raleigh had been in prison for thirteen years. He was troubled by headaches, fever, and persistent abscesses on his body, and he walked with a limp. An "ould and Sorroeworn Man," he said of himself, "whom death would shortlye deliver." He was sixty-four.

If the gods had been indifferent to his first voyage they now looked down with disapproval. The expedition had a spectral quality. It started four months later than planned, fights erupted among the crew, supplies were inadequate, the weather turned uncommonly bad, scurvy broke out.

"Gualtero Rale has set forth . . ." wrote the Spanish ambassador, Count Gondomar, to Philip III on June 26, 1617.

Before his flagship *Destiny* reached South America forty-two crewmen were dead. Raleigh himself lay ill with malaria, and so appointed Captain Keymis to take charge of the trip upriver—a disastrous excursion that resulted in a battle with Spaniards, the death of Raleigh's elder son Wat, and Keymis's clumsy suicide.

"I never knewe what sorrow meant till nowe," he said in a letter to his wife, ". . . my braynes are broken, and it is a torment for mee to write, and espetially of misery."

The ships of his fleet returned one by one to England, until only the *Destiny* remained in South America. At last he, too, had no choice but to return. In England again he was called a pirate and doomed, the victim of changing times, reaccused of treason.

On October 29, 1618, about eight o'clock in the morning, he was conducted to the palace yard of Westminster.

Because this was a particular occasion, Raleigh dressed with meticulous care: beneath his black velvet cloak he wore a velvet waistcoat, satin doublet, black taffeta breeches, and ash-colored silk stockings.

En route he paused to chat with a bald-headed old man, then took off a lace nightcap he had been wearing under his hat and gave it to the old gentleman, saying, "Thou hast more need of it now than I."

On the scaffold he delivered his final speech, which lasted half an hour. He then shook hands with the Earl of Arundel and embraced him. "I have a long journey to go," Raleigh said, "and therefore will take my leave."

After having removed his cloak and doublet he asked to see the ax. "This is sharp medicine," he observed while feeling the blade, "but it is a physician that will cure all my diseases."

He knelt on the boards, but faced the wrong direction. Somebody pointed this out.

"So the heart be right," he responded, "it is no great matter which way the head lieth."

These epigrams, instantaneously composed by a man arranging himself for execution, flash across the centuries with such brilliance that average people stand bewildered. Who can explain a quicksilver tongue?

The executioner struck twice and picked up Raleigh's head by the bloody gray hair in order to display it—"with great applause of the beholders." Raleigh's eyes were open.

The head was presented to his wife, who had it embalmed and kept it in a red leather bag.

He left a slim estate: not much money, a sample of ore, two gold ingots, some rough maps of Guiana, and a diamond ring given him by Elizabeth "which he weareth on his finger."

He left also a misty heritage drifting through the Guianas. There is a letter from an English physician, Edward Bancroft, written while traveling on the Río Demerary. It is addressed to Bancroft's brother and is dated October 25, 1766:

The Carribbee Indians are at perpetual variance with the Spaniards, and frequently commit hostilities on their settlements at the River Oronoque. They retain a tradition of an English Chief, who many years since landed amongst them, and encouraged them to persevere in enmity to the Spaniards, promising to return and settle amongst them, and afford them assistance; and it is said that they still preserve an English Jack, which he left them, that they might distinguish his countrymen. This was undoubtedly Sir Walter Raleigh, who, in the year 1595, made a descent on the Coast of Guiana, in search of the fabulous Golden City of Manoa del Dorado . . .

Today in Bogotá's Museo del Oro among those ancient Muisca treasures you will discover a gold raft on which a tiny gold king is riding, no doubt toward the middle of Lake Guatavitá. And should your mind have a certain cast—if, let's say, you believe yourself related to Sir Walter Raleigh, or de Berrio, or Quesada, or Dalfinger, or those others—well then, as you contemplate this miniature tableau it might occur to you that South America is huge, much of it has yet to be explored, and those first adventurers may not have had the right information. And in the archives, as everybody knows, are innumerable musty old documents, some of which should contain new directions.

9

Seven Cities

In A.D. 711 the Berber general Tariq crossed into Spain by way of a rock that carries his name—Jebal al-Tariq, the mountain of Tariq, Gibraltar. On the shore of Lake Janda he was challenged by the Spanish king Rodrigo in what has become known mistakenly, through a misreading of Arabic chronicles, as the battle of Guadalete. Rodrigo was defeated and Tariq's army carved a bloody path across the Iberian Peninsula, scattering terrified Christians in every direction. Some of these refugees boarded ship at Oporto, hoping to find safety on Madeira or the Canary Islands which at that time were vaguely known.

From this exodus arose a legend that seven Portuguese bishops, fearing the end of Christianity, set sail for the mysterious island of Antillia—*ante-ilha*, opposite island—somewhere in the Western Ocean; and there, in order to preserve Christianity until the Moors should be expelled, they burnt their ships and founded seven cities.

Years passed without word from these prudent bishops. Centuries went by. Nevertheless the legend persisted, and sailors far out in the Atlantic kept watch for an island

with seven cities. Or, as it sometimes was told, seven islands, each with a Christian community.

In 1447, according to the Portuguese scholar Galvão,
a caravel bound for Lisbon under the command of Captain Antonio Leone was disabled by a storm and driven
off course to the west. Eventually a flat crescent-shaped
island was sighted where Captain Leone made port—an
island inhabited by people "who spake Portuguese and
inquired if the Moors did yet trouble Spain." Furthermore,
it had seven communities, each with a rude basalt cathedral; and when Captain Leone and his crew attended Mass
they saw gold candlesticks and crucifixes and a gold-
embroidered altar cloth.

They spent several weeks on this island while repairing
their ship, and when they sailed for Portugal they took
along a quantity of sand from the beach, which was good
for scouring decks. In Lisbon they found out that the sand
was streaked with gold.

Now you might think Captain Leone returned at once,
either because of the gold or because he had discovered
the seven cities; but if he did we have no record of it.

The Dominican priest Las Casas mentions that in Columbus's notebooks he came across an account of this
voyage. Las Casas does not say so explicitly, but Columbus
could only have been referring to Captain Leone because
the story is almost identical: a storm-driven vessel anchors at an island where the people speak Portuguese and
the sand is flecked with gold. In this version, however,
Prince Henry heard about it, scolded the captain for failing to learn more, and ordered him to return; but the sailors were afraid and refused. We are not told anything
else about Captain Leone, nor what happened to the
sailors who defied their prince.

Columbus very possibly believed in the medieval legend. One reason for thinking so is that he corresponded with the famous cosmographer Toscanelli—probably on this subject—via the Portuguese court. Toscanelli had included Antillia on his charts, suggesting it as a port of call en route to Japan: "From the island of Antillia, which you call the Isle of Seven Cities . . . to the most noble island of Cipangu is fifty degrees of longitude . . ."

Soon after this a Fleming whose name is given as Fernão Dulmo was authorized by King João II to locate and govern "a large island, islands, or mainland, beyond our shores, presumed to be the island of the Seven Cities." Dulmo went into partnership with a wealthy gentleman from Madeira named Estreito, each of them to provide a caravel. Some historians believe they sailed in March of 1487; others think the caravels were delayed by foul weather and never put to sea. In either event, Dulmo & Estreito are not heard from again.

In 1498 a Spanish ambassador to England, Pedro de Ayala, informed Ferdinand and Isabella that the people of Bristol "fitted out every year, two, three, or four caravels in search of . . . the Seven Cities."

By the early sixteenth century they were thought to be on the American mainland. Why? Nothing could be more obvious. These cities existed—obviously they existed, otherwise men would not be searching for them; consequently, if they did not exist in the Atlantic they must be someplace else, and beyond the Atlantic lay America.

A map in the British Museum, which probably was drawn about 1508, locates them on the eastern seaboard. Who set them there, and why, is unknown.

But they could not be found on the littoral, which meant they must be inland. This brings us to one of history's classic bunglers—a most unpleasant personage even among odious companions, the conquistador Pánfilo de

Narváez. Bernal Díaz tells us that he was very brave, a good horseman, tall and strong, with a red beard, and a voice so deep that it seemed to come from a vault. "He was a captain in the island of Cuba, and a rich man, though reputed to be very mean."

He arrived in Mexico with authority from the governor of Cuba to arrest Cortés. The reasons for this are irrelevant; more interesting is the fact that when it was all over Narváez had lost his soldiers, one of his eyes, and his personal liberty—spending the next three years as Cortés's prisoner.

Cortés at last let him go and Narváez returned to Spain, where he managed to become appointed governor of Florida, which at that time was almost entirely unexplored. Ponce de León had been there, along with a few others, but the peninsula had been so lightly touched that it was still thought to be an island.

Narváez landed on the west side of Tampa Bay in April of 1528, authorized by Charles V "to conquer and govern the provinces which should be encountered from the River of Palms to the cape of Florida." He had 42 horses and about 600 men, but not for long. First he divided his forces, ordering his ships to proceed up the coast. Then he led his cavalry and infantry into the swamps. Accidents, alligators, snakes, dysentery, malaria, hunger, and misanthropic Indians began to pick them off. Nevertheless he kept going, encouraged by traces of gold in some of the Indian huts, until the remnants of his cavalry threatened to desert.

Cabeza de Vaca, the expedition's treasurer, later wrote that a third of their force had fallen sick: "We felt certain that we would all be stricken, with death the one foreseeable way out."

Unable to locate their supply ships, the Spaniards tried

to escape from this labyrinth of lagoons, salt marshes and mangrove-tangled islets by constructing some boats.

"We knew not how to build them, nor had we either the tools, irons, forges, tow, tar, or rigging; nor, in short, a single one of the many things required, nor anyone capable of directing the work, and above all, no food to eat whilst they were being built."

The alternative, though, was to go on plunging through the swamp.

One soldier contrived some deerskin bellows in order to melt just about everything metallic—armor, lances, stirrups, buckles, spurs, conchos—because metal would be needed for nails, axes, and saws. Another soldier had been a carpenter. So it went.

They built five barges, each about thirty feet long, caulked with palmetto oakum and tarred with pine pitch. Sails were made out of shirts. Ropes were braided from horsehair and palmetto husks. Stones served as anchors. Meanwhile they were eating the horses and trying to fashion water bottles out of their hides.

At last they piled aboard, hoping to drift or sail west along the coast to Mexico, which they thought could not be far away. There were nearly fifty men on each barge. The gunwales rode just a few inches above the surface.

Eleven years later Hernando de Soto would be told by captured Indians that other Spaniards had come through the land and had built boats on which they escaped. The Indians did not know what had become of these Spaniards. De Soto found a tree that had been chopped down near Saint Marks Bay. The tree had been cut into rude planks and nearby were the bleached skulls of several horses.

It took the Narváez castaways a month to reach the vicinity of Pensacola. The horsehide bottles were rotting, and their food—supplemented by raiding an occasional thatched-roof village—was almost gone. Why they were unable to catch fish, although they had observed the Indians fishing, has not been explained.

Farther west the miserable flotilla became separated, but de Vaca managed to catch up with Narváez and asked him what they should do. Narváez replied that this was no time for one man to be giving orders to another, each should do as he thought best to save himself; and having offered such good advice, the commandant told his boatmen to pull away. Since he had chosen the healthiest men for his crew he quickly left de Vaca behind. Not long after this, and no doubt because of it, the gods blew Narváez out to sea.

De Vaca says that just five men in his group were strong enough to stand. "At nightfall only the navigator and I remained able to tend the barge. Two hours after dark he told me I should take over; he believed he was about to die."

Next morning a wave hurled them onto an island—possibly San Luis island near Galveston—and when they tried to shove off they capsized. Three men drowned. The survivors crawled ashore naked because they had stowed their clothing on the barge before attempting to launch it.

A few more castaways turned up and they spent that winter as uneasy guests of some exceptionally large Indians who billeted them in various huts. Most of the Spaniards starved to death. Some not only ate the flesh of dead companions but apparently tried to preserve it for future snacks. In one hut de Vaca came across bits of four Spaniards and the untouched corpse of a fifth "whom nobody was left alive to eat."

The Indians too were dying, not from hunger but from

disease—perhaps cholera, or perhaps they had become infected by the Spaniards' dysentery. And either because of the cannibalism or because of this epidemic they began to look upon the Spaniards not as guests but as slaves.

In the spring only about two dozen conquistadors remained alive, sixteen on the island and a few others scattered along the Texas coast, all of them expecting death at any hour. De Vaca himself had become an indentured servant of a tribe he called the Capoques, being shuttled to the mainland whenever his services were required for semiskilled labor: "In addition to much other work, I had to grub roots in the water or from underground in the canebrakes. My fingers got so raw that if a straw touched them they would bleed. The broken canes often slashed my flesh . . ."

Life improved during the next five years, although not much. Consequently, in September of 1534, he and three other men struck out for Mexico. The season was late and the prickly pears upon which they depended for food were nearly gone, but they thought they could get by on acorns. Regardless of what lay ahead, they had resolved "not to live this life, so savage and so divorced from the service of God and all good reason."

The fugitives, in addition to Álvar Núñez Cabeza de Vaca, were Alonzo del Castillo Maldonado, Andrés Dorantes de Carranca, and Dorantes's remarkable Moorish slave, Estebán. Their names are worth recording because, out of hundreds, only these four were obstinate enough to survive.

De Vaca seems to have been the organizer, the demonic spirit, the brightest and most determined. Also, he was the only one who thought enough of their odyssey to write about it. And because he had such an odd name—head-of-a-cow—perhaps this should be explained. One of his ancestors, a shepherd named Martin Alhaja, guided King Sancho VII of Navarre through the Sierra Morena north of Seville, marking the pass with a cow's skull, which enabled the Spanish army to cross over and defeat the Moors at the battle of Las Navas de Tolosa. The shepherd's reward was nobility of a sort, and his descendants were entitled to the honorary name.

The route of this naked, starving quartet after they left the Gulf resembles the track of an undecided snail: northwest through the middle of Texas to the Pecos River which they followed up into New Mexico, south to El Paso, and west to the Gila River in Arizona. At this point they were well over 1,000 air miles from Mexico City—much farther from their destination than when they started. Evidently they thought they were paralleling the coast.

We have the usual scholarly argument about their route; they may not have gotten quite that far north, but it hardly matters.

Along the way they practiced medicine. De Vaca sounds embarrassed: "Our method . . . was to bless the sick, breathe upon them, recite a Pater Noster and Ave Maria, and pray earnestly to God our Lord for their recovery."

This curious treatment seems to have worked more often than might be expected, thanks to the beneficence of God and the strength of suggestion, so that the travelers' reputation began to precede them. As they advanced from one Indian territory to the next they were heralded, followed, and presented with ceremonial arrows, beads, gourds, little bags of mica, deer tallow, dried herbs, spiders, worms, and quail—the native menu varied considerably— as well as cowhides, feathers, blankets, copper trinkets, and whatever else their hosts thought valuable. This must have been awkward, but the Spaniards were shrewd enough to continue the charade, touching and blessing the sick and injured, even attempting minor surgery when the chances of success looked good. And instead of speaking directly to the Indians they made Estebán their intermediary:

"He was constantly in conversation, finding out about routes, towns, and other matters we wished to know."

From the Gila they turned south, and somewhere below what is now the Mexican border they saw an Indian wearing a strange ornament around his neck: a buckle from a sword belt. Where had this come from? From Heaven, replied the Indian. But who had brought it from Heaven? Bearded men on horses with lances and swords.

In March of 1536, guided by other fragments of evidence and by rumors, they caught sight of several Spanish horsemen who had been out raking the provinces for Indians to enslave. So, once again among their own, the weary travelers were escorted southward. They rode into Mexico City on July 24, and were welcomed by the Viceroy.

Eight years had passed since Narváez's expedition began falling apart in the Florida swamps.

The viceroy, Don Antonio de Mendoza, listened to their stories. They had wandered through wretched blistered territory and had met no Indians of any consequence, none whose civilization even remotely approached that of the Aztecs. Still, they had seen copper, iron, a few bits of gold, and other metals, and they were convinced that "pearls and great riches" could be found on the Gulf of California, which de Vaca called the South Sea.

Wild rumors swept Mexico City. The travelers had forded streams whose beds were solid gold. They had seen Indian children playing with rubies and diamonds and emeralds and pearls the size of hen eggs. They had walked past a mountain so studded with jewels that they dared not look at it in bright sunlight for fear of being blinded.

Mendoza, a cautious man, did not want to be held responsible for ordering a disastrous expedition into the unknown north. On the other hand he might be just as much at fault if he neglected an opportunity to benefit the Spanish crown. It was unlikely, yet just possible, that somewhere to the north lay another Aztec treasure house. Pizarro had discovered and captured the incredible wealth of the Incas to the south; there might conceivably be a wealthy nation in higher latitudes.

An Indian called Tejo who belonged to Nuño de Guzmán, governor of the northern provinces, insisted that there were seven flourishing towns up there. He had seen them, he said, when he was a child and went with his father on a long trip. These towns were perhaps as big as Mexico City, their streets crowded with silversmiths and goldsmiths.

The number *seven* also occurred in Aztec legend. Ancestors of the Aztecs had emigrated to Mexico from seven caves somewhere to the north.

Mendoza probably had little faith in the medieval European story, nevertheless it was curious that the number *seven* should reappear; so he decided to send a Franciscan, Marcos de Niza, to look around and take possession of whatever might be worth possessing. Estebán could be his guide. Whether or not an expedition should be organized would depend on the Franciscan's report, because he was thought to be a trustworthy man, "reliable, of approved virtue, and fine religious zeal . . . skilled in cosmography and the arts of the sea, as well as in theology." If the stories told by de Vaca and his companions were fanciful—well, not much would be lost.

Mendoza's marching instructions cautioned the friar also to obtain information about the coast "because the land may narrow and in the country beyond some arm of the sea may enter." That is to say, the Northwest Passage might be discovered.

Fray Marcos and Estebán set out in the spring of 1539.

The farther they traveled the more impatient Estebán became. During the long walk from Texas he had been an important figure, treated with respect by the Indians they had met along the way, admired for his black color and his medical knowledge; but upon entering Mexico he was once again nothing but Dorantes's slave. He was therefore anxious to get out of Mexico and into those northern lands where he had been regally welcomed.

Fray Marcos at last gave him permission to go ahead, with instructions to send back word of his findings by an Indian runner. If he should come upon something noteworthy he should send back a wooden cross the width of his hand. If he came upon something unusual, say a very large town, the cross should be twice that size.

Estebán traveled in style, carried on a litter and accompanied by a pair of greyhounds which may have been given to him by Coronado—the recently appointed governor of New Galicia. His legs and arms were decorated with clusters of brilliant feathers and jingling copper bells. Necklaces of turquoise and coral adorned his chest. He was a big, bearded, powerful man, and he wore plumes to accentuate his height.

Packed among his considerable baggage, which included a tent and plenty of comfortable bedding, were four green pottery dishes on which he was ceremoniously served every meal. Nobody else could use those dishes. He also brought along a sacred medicine rattle made from a gourd; it is said to have been embellished with strands of tiny bells and with two feathers, one white and one red.

Four days after Marcos permitted Estebán to go ahead by himself some Indian runners arrived carrying a cross as tall as a man. They said Estebán had reached people who knew of important cities in the north—seven cities ruled by a lord whose house was several stories high. The first city was called Cíbola. Its buildings were made of stone mortared with lime, the doors abundantly decorated with turquoise, and the people were richly clothed. Beyond Cíbola lay other lands with cities still larger, more influential, and more wealthy.

"So many marvels was I told," Marcos reported, "that I postponed believing them until I could see for myself, or have further verification."

He pushed ahead rapidly, and as he walked he received confirmation of the wonderful news. Pima Indians told him that the houses of Cíbola were indeed very large, and beyond Cíbola lay at least three kingdoms—Marata, Acus, and Totonteac.

A second huge cross arrived from Estebán, urging him to hurry. Then a third great cross.

And while passing through the Sonora valley Fray Marcos met an old man who claimed to be a native of Cíbola, who insisted that despite its wealth, which was very great, the kingdom of Totonteac was the largest, richest, and most populous in the world.

Marcos hurried forward, but it was difficult to catch up with Estebán.

Then another messenger arrived, this time with very different news. Estebán had approached Cíbola at sunset, demanding gifts of turquoise and women. He had not been allowed to enter the city. He and his escort had been confined to huts outside the walls. Next morning, said the messenger, he himself had gone to a nearby stream for a drink and when he looked around he saw Estebán and the others being pursued by the men of Cíbola, who killed them with arrows.

Marcos concluded that he must go forward to find out if what the messenger said was true; and presently he met two other members of Estebán's entourage—both covered with blood. They said the Moor was dead.

Why Estebán was murdered is not known, although his demand for women and turquoise undoubtedly angered the Indians. Perhaps they thought he was a spy from some nation planning to invade their territory. Or the medicine rattle might have alarmed them.

Medicine rattles, unless they came from a tribe hundreds of miles distant, could be identified by the symbols carved or painted on them, by their shape and size, by the feathers or bells or claws or other fetishes attached to them, and sometimes by the gourd alone. The rattle carried by Estebán was picked up in Texas by the traveling quartet; almost certainly it was Comanche or Apache. Whatever it signified, wherever it came from, he miscalculated when he sent it ahead to announce his arrival. The cacique to whom it was offered "flung the gourd to the earth with much wrath" and ordered the emissary to leave.

Estebán, being informed of his ambassador's reception, did not take the hint. He is said to have laughed and remarked that there was nothing to fear. He had been greeted like this before, he said, while traveling with de Vaca.

After he had been killed, to prove that he was mortal and not a man from the sky, the Indians cut his body into very small pieces. Bits of his flesh, bones, and skin were dried and distributed among neighboring tribes as tokens, perhaps to indicate what should be done if any more strangers arrived. The greyhounds and the green dinner plates were confiscated. The rattle was either thrown away or smashed.

So perished the flamboyant sensual overconfident Moorish slave; captured in Morocco, he died in New Mexico during a horizontal rain of arrows without knowing why.

Marcos got close enough to Cíbola to have a look at it. At least that was his claim. He described it as larger than Mexico City and extremely beautiful: "I was tempted to go to it, knowing that I risked only my life . . . [however,] if I should die there would be no account of this land, which, in my opinion, is the greatest and best of all those discovered."

Accordingly, at a prudent distance, he ordered a cairn to be built and surmounted with a cross. Then, after having claimed possession for the king of Spain in the name of Don Antonio de Mendoza, not only of the Seven Cities but of the kingdoms of Totonteac, Marata, and Acus, he started back to safety, "traveling with all possible speed until I came upon the people I had left."

Whether he approached Cíbola is debatable. Most historians doubt it, and the stories he told after his return to Mexico City caused one of them to call him the Baron Munchausen of America.

The fabulous city of Cíbola was, in fact, the pueblo of Hawaiku, now a heap of ruins near Zuñi on the New Mexican plateau. Its name may have been invented by Estebán, but *Cíbola* probably comes from the Zuñi word *Shi'wona*, which refers to their tribal range.

Regardless of Fray Marcos's veracity, he became man of the hour when he got back to civilization. He was elevated to father provincial of his order and everybody repeated what he said. Bishop Zumárraga wrote to a friend: "There are partridges and cows which the father says he saw, and he heard a story of camels and dromedaries and other cities . . ."

The people of Cíbola wear leather shoes and buskins, another priest wrote to somebody in Burgos, and many wear silk clothing. "Of the richness of this country I do not write you because it is said to be so great that it does not seem possible. The friar himself told me this, that he saw a temple of their idols the walls of which, inside and outside, were covered with precious stones; I think he said they were emeralds. They also say that in the country beyond there are camels and elephants."

Marcos, a generous man, did not hoard such nuggets of information. He told his barber that in Cíbola the women wore strings of gold beads. The men wore girdles of gold and white wool gowns. They had sheep, cattle, slaughterhouses, iron forges, and so on.

Mendoza was not a credulous man, but the friar's report plainly demanded further exploration. He commissioned Francisco Vásquez, better known as Coronado.

The expedition assembled at Compostela northwest of Mexico City and started north in February of 1540—a most noble and distinguished assembly, according to the chronicler Pedro de Casteñada.

No doubt the most visible was Coronado, wearing gilded armor and a gilded helmet with a plume, a new manifestation of El Dorado, the legendary gilded man. Behind him rode 225 horsemen, some dressed in chain mail, a few in full armor, others in native buckskin armor, all of them carrying lances and swords. Next came 60 foot soldiers: pikemen, crossbowmen, harquebusiers. Then a swarm of Indian servants and Negro slaves driving the sheep, swine, cattle and pack animals, and dragging six bronze swivel guns called pedreros. Finally came a horde of about 1,300 Indians wearing fantastically colored parrot-feather headdresses, carrying slings, bows, and obsidian-edged maces, their flesh smeared with black and ocher warpaint.

Ahead of this army walked four Franciscans, including Marcos.

They followed the prehistoric trade route out of Compostela, through scrub thickets to the coastal plain. Progress was slow because they could not get very far ahead of the livestock. It took a month to reach Culiacán. Here, impatient to behold the gleaming northern cities, Coronado split his force; he advanced with a squadron of about seventy horsemen, twenty-five or thirty foot soldiers, the artillery, the priests, and a host of Indians. They carried rations for eighty days.

From Culiacán they marched north, this wild and wonderful procession, bearing gradually inland until they crossed what is now the border between Mexico and Arizona. "There are no trees without spines," wrote Casteñada, "nor any fruit . . ."

The monotonous Arizona desert was littered with dry thickets of mesquite, saguaro, gray sage, and the green prickly pear that de Vaca in his extremity had learned to eat. All day the sun reflected from the helmets and shields and breastplates of the armored soldiers. Their swords became too hot to touch. Horses lurched and fell. The desiccated earth shimmered in waves of heat. But ahead of them, they believed, lay Cíbola, first of the Seven Cities. And beyond that? Anything was possible.

Five months later they reached Cíbola—a poor, sunbaked, adobe pueblo on a low bluff overlooking dusty fields. And when at last the soldiers understood that nothing else was to be seen, "such were the curses hurled at Fray Marcos," wrote Casteñada, "that I pray God may protect him from them."

However, they had no choice but to attack the

wretched place, otherwise they would starve. Some of the soldiers already were so weak they could barely lift their weapons, yet Cíbola was captured without much of a fight. Later the subjugated Zuñis said it had been foretold that men such as the Spaniards would arrive from the south to conquer the land. Were the Zuñis revising the myth of Quetzalcoatl? Had they heard rumors of Columbus?

When the job was done Coronado dispatched a letter to Mendoza:

"The Seven Cities are seven little villages . . . within a space of four leagues. Taken together they are called the Kingdom of Cévola. Each has its own name, and no single one is called Cévola, but collectively they have this designation. This one where I am now lodged and which I have called a city, I have named Granada, both because it has similarity to the place, and in honor of your Lordship."

Mendoza was a native of Granada.

The Spaniards saw neither gold nor precious jewels in the adobe pueblos. "Some little broken stones, rather poor, which approach the color of garnet, were found in a paper under some stone crystals."

Coronado knew the viceroy would be interested in native crafts, so he made up a nice collection: "I am sending you twelve small mantas such as the people of this country ordinarily wear, a fabric which seems to me to be very well made . . . I am sending also two canvases showing the animals they have in this country, although, as I have said, the painting is poorly done." And he included fifteen combs, a cowhide, two wicker baskets, a mallet, a shield, a bow and several arrows, and "two pads such as the women customarily wear on their heads when they carry water from the spring, just as they do in Spain. . . . God knows I wish I had better news to write to your Lordship."

Viceroy Mendoza would not be greatly pleased and Coronado could only hope that having the first of the Seven Cities renamed Granada might placate him. "I have decided to send men throughout the surrounding regions to find out if there is anything worthwhile . . ."

These search parties returned one after another to report such interesting but useless things as the Grand Canyon, the Hopi nation, the Rio Grande, and the sky city of Ácoma. It was all very depressing.

Captain Cardenas's sidetrip to the Grand Canyon has been detailed by Casteñada, who says they spent three days trying to find some way to the river "which from above appeared to be only a fathom wide." At last Captain Melgosa and two agile soldiers started down. Late that afternoon they returned. They had descended about a third of the way and from there the river looked very large, just as the Indians had said. The soldiers who stayed on top had estimated that some rocks jutting from a shelf in the gorge must be approximately the height of a man; but when Melgosa and his companions got back they said these rocks "were taller than the great tower of Seville," by which they meant the Giralda, the cathedral tower, 295 feet high. That was remarkable, to be sure, but not likely to excite Viceroy Mendoza or King Charles I.

Good news, however, arrived from Captain Alvarado on the Rio Grande. He had picked up a singular individual wearing a sort of turban, for which reason the Spaniards called him El Turco. The Turk had been captured by one of the Pueblo chiefs along the eastern border of their domain and obviously he knew something about those vast plains to the east.

The Turk "by signs and in the Mexican tongue of which he understood a little" protested that he knew nothing about the region to the east, and urged Captain Alvarado to march northeast because in that direction lay a country called Quivira—very rich in gold, silver, and fabrics. He also said he had a gold bracelet from Quivira, which the Pueblo chief had stolen from him. The chief denied this, insisting he had no knowledge of any such bracelet. Alvarado therefore dressed them both in chains and sent word to the general.

Coronado arrived before long, having left a garrison at Cíbola, and questioned the Turk. One gold bracelet was unimportant; what mattered was the territory ahead.

Quivira, said the Turk, contained a river two leagues wide in which there were fish the size of horses. The name of the gray-bearded king of Quivira was Tatarrax—a Wichita word meaning "chief"—and he prayed to the image of a lady who was the goddess of Heaven. As for gold? Each afternoon he rested beneath a tree hung with tiny golden bells that lulled him to sleep with their music. Every jug in his palace was made of gold, every platter. Even the oarlocks of his canoes were golden. That was how much gold could be found in Quivira. If the Spaniards intended to visit King Tatarrax they should bring many carts to carry away all the gold he would distribute. Furthermore, beyond his kingdom lay the lands of Arache and Guas whose wealth put the wealth of Quivira to shame.

"All this," says the chronicler Jaramillo, "moved us to go in search of that country . . ."

Coronado's army prepared to march as soon as the snow began melting; and so persuasive was El Turco that nobody wanted to stay behind.

Before leaving the Rio Grande valley they picked up two more Pueblo captives. One was named Xabe, a Pawnee, who said yes, yes, there was gold in Quivira, though not quite as much as El Turco claimed. The other captive disagreed; he said the Turk was a liar. His name is

given as Sopete, or Ysopete, and he must have been a
Wichita because he is described as having tattoos encir-
cling his eyes—which gave the Wichita their tribal name
of Kidi Kidesh, Raccoon Eyes.

It is now impossible to follow Coronado's trail with
much precision across eastern New Mexico and the Texas
panhandle because of the flatness of the country. There
are almost no landmarks. Even the Indians who lived there
often got lost. Coronado later wrote that they could not
see a stone, no rising ground, not a tree, not a shrub.
Since there was nothing to guide them, each morning
they looked at the rising sun, then an archer shot an arrow in the direction they wished to take, and before coming to it another arrow was shot to extend the line; and
by this method they were able to avoid marching in
a curve.

They seem to have been mystified by the expanse, by
the insignificance of their expedition. Casteñada wrote:
"Who could believe that 1,000 horses and 500 of our cows
and more than 5,000 rams and ewes and more than 1,500
friendly Indians and servants, in traveling over these
plains, would leave no more trace where they had passed
than if nothing had been there—nothing—so that it was
necessary to make piles of bones and cow dung now and
then to enable the rear guard to follow the army . . . The
country is like a bowl, so that when a man sits down the
horizon surrounds him . . ."

Somewhere in this region Coronado once again decided to ride ahead of the main force. It was now the end
of May, their stock of corn had been exhausted, the horses
were bony, soldiers were getting sick from eating only
meat, and Coronado was troubled by Sopete's insistence
that they would find nothing in Quivira except thatched
huts.

With thirty horsemen, half a dozen foot soldiers, and several guides, including Sopete and the Turk, he angled northeast across the Oklahoma panhandle and entered Kansas near the town of Liberal. Beyond the Cimarron lay the Arkansas—Río de Pedro y Pablo, so named because they came to it on the feast day of Saints Peter and Paul—which they followed for a while and then continued northeast until they could not have been much more than fifty miles from the exact geographical center of the United States. That was early in July, 1541.

At this point Coronado met some buffalo hunters. Sopete was delighted and the Turk was dismayed, because the wretched appearance of these hunters confirmed what Sopete had been saying about Quivira and belied everything the Turk had said. After being interrogated again the Turk confessed that he had lured the Spaniards onto these plains hoping they would die of hunger. He said he had been encouraged in this idea by the Pueblo people who were anxious to see the last of their unwelcome guests. He had planned to slip away from the army when it approached Pawnee territory; he had not expected to be traveling in chains. Now, like an animal that all at once quits fighting for its life, he appeared indifferent to his fate. As for gold, there was none in Quivira.

In spite of the Turk's confession Coronado refused to give up. It seemed to him that the story of King Tatarrax might be true: possibly some member of the Narváez expedition, other than de Vaca and his companions, had survived and moved inland and now reigned over a wealthy tribe. There is another possibility. Coronado may have heard rumors of Hernando de Soto, who just then was only a few hundred miles southeast—although neither of them knew it.

In any event, he wrote a letter in magniloquent Castilian to the gray-bearded Christian monarch Tatarrax—

just as Pope Alexander III had written to the legendary Christian monarch Prester John four centuries earlier. The pope entrusted that letter to his personal physician, Magister Philippus. Coronado, too, had a reliable envoy; he gave his letter to the honorable Sopete, instructing him to deliver it to King Tatarrax somewhere in America. Sopete started off at once, and like Magister Philippus he was never heard of again.

Coronado's army then pushed forward and soon came across six or seven villages where the houses looked like grass and dirt beehives. They saw no canoes with golden oarlocks, no Christian king taking his siesta beneath a tree hung with golden bells. No golden platters or jugs, only drab clay water jars.

Still they could not give up the dream. This might not be the kingdom of Tatarrax, maybe it lay just a little farther.

They marched on, demanding that their guides lead them to other villages, until at last they came to a miserable settlement beside a river—probably the Kansas—which their guides said was the end of Quivira. Upon being asked if there was anything beyond, "they said there was nothing more of Quivira, but there was Harahey, and it was the same sort of place."

By Coronado's order the Turk was strangled; and late that summer, anxious to avoid being caught by snow on these desolate plains, the army marched southwest.

But before leaving they raised a cross, "at the foot of which some letters were cut with a chisel saying that Francisco Vásquez de Coronado, general of the army, had reached this place." No doubt the cross has vanished, being made of wood; but the inscription—because we are told it had been chiseled—almost certainly was cut in stone and might still be there, someplace in the middle of Kansas.

In this area, too, links of sixteenth-century chain-mail armor have been found, and shards of Pueblo pottery.

That second winter they spent in familiar territory and the general addressed a letter to his sovereign, Charles V: "I have done all that I possibly could to serve Your Majesty and to discover a country where God our Lord might be served and the royal patrimony of Your Majesty increased, as your loyal servant and vassal. For since I have reached the province of Cíbola, to which the viceroy of New Spain sent me in the name of Your Majesty, seeing that there were none of the things there of which Friar Marcos had told, I have managed to explore this country for two hundred leagues and more around Cíbola, and the best place I have found is this river of Tiguex where I am now, and the settlements here."

On All Fools' Day, 1542, began the long march home.

That autumn Coronado led what remained of his army across the deserts and mountains into Sinaloa where, at Culiacán, it was disbanded. The army consisted of about ninety men dressed in animal hides and rusty, dented mail. Later, during a period of several weeks, a few more soldiers straggled in. Those who were present to observe this ignominious spectacle have reported that the feeling in Mexico was not of bitterness but of disappointment.

Casteñada, musing on the adventure, reflects that so long as we have a thing we take it for granted, and the longer we have it the less we value it. But once we have lost it we begin to suffer, and look for ways of getting it back again. This is what happened, he writes,

to all or most of those who went on the expedition which, in the year 1540 of Our Saviour Jesus Christ, Francisco Vásquez de Coronado led in search of the

Seven Cities. Granted that they did not find the riches of which they had been told, they found a place in which to search for them, and the beginning of a good country to settle in, from which they could go on further. Since they returned from the country which they conquered and abandoned, time has given them a chance to understand the direction and locality in which they were, and the borders of the good country they had in their hands, and their hearts weep for having lost so favourable an opportunity.

Coronado himself was broken by the experience, although he was just thirty-two years old. He had been injured in New Mexico when a saddle girth broke during a race, and he never quite recovered from this; but the failure of his exploration seems to have weakened him more than the accident. He resumed his post as governor of New Galicia but handled the job carelessly and before long the king's auditor filed thirty-four charges against him, including neglect of duty, short accounts, accepting bribes, favoritism in appointments, and inhumane treatment of the natives. Although absolved of some of these charges he was arrested, fined 600 gold pesos, and removed from the governorship. Ten years later he died, and with his death the legend began to fade.

In 1571 the renowned cartographer Ortelius noted Sept Cités in the ocean, thus continuing the tradition that they would be found on an island.

They reappeared on the American mainland when Hakluyt published the *Relation of Henry Hawks, merchant, who lived for five years in Nova Hispania.* This is the testimony of merchant Hawks: "The Spanyards have notice of Seven Cities, which old men of the Indians show them should lie toward the North-east from Mexico.

They have used and use daily much diligence in seeking of them, but they cannot find any one of them. They say that the witchcraft of the Indians is such that when they come upon these townes' they cast a mist upon them, so that they cannot see them . . ."

A few years later Mercator's map returned them to the ocean.

And in 1639 a party of Franciscan monks arriving in Lisbon swore that while en route from Madeira they were blown off course by a storm and had been saved by the miraculous appearance of an unfamiliar island. They said in their deposition, which strangely echoes the fifteenth-century tale of Captain Leone, that on this island was a city with very few inhabitants, with no sign of a priest or a monk. They were greeted by people who spoke Portuguese, who escorted them to a circular palace with a lighthouse rising above it, where they saw paintings of battles between Portuguese and Moors, and statues of many kings, and a chapel guarded by lions in which they beheld a statue of the Virgin holding a sword. They thought the island was not far from Madeira, no more than a day's sail—although because of the storm they were not sure in which direction. But it is said that nobody believed their statement.

The myth was fading, gradually losing color, retaining only its texture and dignity, like those stiff frayed tapestries from the Middle Ages that now and again we meet in the corridors of great museums.

10

GoldGoldGold

Atahualpa, after being captured by the Spaniards, tried to buy his freedom. Through an interpreter he said to Pizarro, meanwhile indicating the apartment in which they stood, that he would cover the floor with gold. Pizarro did not respond immediately; he and the other Spaniards who were present when Atahualpa made this offer merely listened with incredulous smiles.

Then the Inca, misinterpreting their silence, thinking they wanted more, said that if they would release him he would fill the room with gold as high as he could reach. And standing on tiptoe, he touched the wall.

Pizarro accepted. He had not planned to release the hostage so his reasoning can only be surmised, but the Spaniards had heard tremendous rumors—Atahualpa himself had described Cuzco, where the temple roofs were plated with gold and the floors were inlaid with golden tiles. It is thought that Pizarro reasoned simply: There might be truth to these rumors, let us see. Atahualpa remains my captive. If he delivers all this gold, so much the better.

Pizarro ordered a line to be drawn around the room at the height Atahualpa had indicated, and the terms of the proposal to be recorded. The gold need not be melted into bars, it might retain the form into which it had been cast. But the Inca should, in addition, twice fill a small adjoining room with silver.

The dimensions of the principal room are given differently by various chroniclers. According to the notary Xerez, who was Pizarro's secretary, the room measured twenty-two by seventeen feet. Hernando Pizarro, Francisco's half-brother, said it was seventeen or eighteen by thirty-five. Another contemporary account gives it as fifteen by twenty-five. Whatever the true dimensions it was no closet, and trying to imagine such a room filled with gold is difficult.

As to the depth of this treasure, again there is some discrepancy. Prescott, a most respected historian, says the mark on the wall was nine feet above the floor. Yet how could Atahualpa, who probably stood not much more than five feet, have reached that high? Hernando Pizarro states that the ceiling was nine feet above the floor, which makes more sense. By the account of some anonymous conquistador this room was to be filled up to a white line "which a tall man could not reach." Jonathan Leonard says that the stone-walled room where the offer was made can still be seen in Cajamarca, and the line—which has been renewed—"is about four inches below the level that a six-foot man can reach."

No matter. Atahualpa promised something like 3,000 cubic feet of gold, not to mention the silver. Quite a lot even by Inca standards. The job would take a couple of months, he explained, because it would have to be brought from all over the empire.

Pizarro agreed to this.

Couriers went out.

The empire was not wide, but from north to south it covered thirty-six degrees of latitude, from what is now Colombia to the middle of Chile. A highway ran the length of the realm, almost 3,300 miles, which would take you from Maine to California and beyond.

Soon the treasure began to arrive, some of it in the form of solid gold slabs weighing twenty pounds. We hear no more about incredulous smiles. Incredulity, perhaps, but neither a sixteenth-century Spaniard nor anybody else would respond with amusement to what was being deposited in that room.

Pizarro had Atahualpa strangled while the gold was still pouring into Cajamarca—but that's another story. As to the amount delivered, we know exactly, because Xerez was a meticulous accountant: 1,326,539 pesos of gold and 51,610 silver marks.

In those days a peso de oro was not currency but a unit of measurement, equal in weight to the coin known as a castellano. There were about six castellanos to an ounce, although numbers do not suggest the value of the Inca's ransom. It was, of course, millions of dollars—perhaps sixty million on the basis of today's gold price. And more was on the road. Much more. We will never know how much more.

If you want to evaluate what was delivered not in terms of weight, as though it were cotton or beans, but as high-carat gold artworks to be priced accordingly and marketed at posh galleries in New York, London, Geneva, and Paris—well, my friend, on that basis an apartment stuffed with fifteenth- and sixteenth-century Inca treasure could save a middle-sized nation from bankruptcy.

Look at it like this: the famous hammered gold masks, et cetera, that Schliemann dug from the ruins of Mycenae weighed, altogether, thirty-three pounds.

There never has been a collection of gold artwork, with

perhaps one exception, remotely equal to that brought to
Cajamarca by the Inca's command. And Pizarro, impatient to get on with the conquest, did not even let him
finish. All told—which is to say, Atahualpa's ransom in
addition to the rest of the gold the Spaniards carted off
during the sixteenth century—all together it is thought
to have totaled about nine tons. Nine tons of gold. Schliemann's thirty-three pounds made him an international
celebrity.

The exception could be the treasure hauled away from
Persepolis by Alexander. We are told that 5,000 camels and
10,000 pairs of mules were required, but we have no idea
how much of this was gold. Alexander might have
loaded the beasts with rolls of silk, carpets, embroidered
shawls, and pistachio nuts.

And besides, the Inca's treasure train may have equaled
or surpassed Alexander's. "We hold it to be very certain,"
wrote Cieza de León, "that neither in Jerusalem, nor in
Rome, nor in Persia, nor in any other part of the world, by
any state or kings of this earth, was such wealth of gold
and silver and precious stones collected . . ."

As to what the Spaniards missed, S. K. Lothrop says
there is a Peruvian tradition that 11,000 llama loads of
gold dust were buried near Jauja. Another 500 loads of
silver and gold are said to be buried in the Casma valley.
And 4,000 loads in a vault beneath the plain that faces the
Sacsahuaman fortress. Now, whether such tales are true,
we can't be sure, but there is no doubt that prodigious
quantities of gold and silver were hidden as soon as
word got around the countryside that Atahualpa had been
strangled.

Among the fantastic creations reported on the imperial highway was a gold chain about 800 feet long—
either a chain or a multicolored rope embellished with

gold plates—which was so heavy that 200 Indians carried it. This chain, or rope, was held by dancers during important festivals, and is said to have been cast into a lake just south of Cuzco. But a thing like that—how could you throw it into a lake? How far could 200 men throw it? My own opinion is that it was buried.

Unfortunately the Incas left no written records, which might tell us where to start digging; they communicated information by means of a knotted string, the quipu, and although a good many of these strings have survived nobody knows how to decode them. But tomorrow, perhaps, or the next day, after enough rain or a landslide in the high Andes a Peruvian farmer crossing the imperial road might pause to look at a gleaming oval in the mud.

Such things happen. A while ago in the Mimbres Mountains of New Mexico a sheepherder who sat down to rest beneath a cottonwood tree saw a length of metal protruding from the roots. He dug it out and found it was the hilt of a Spanish sword inlaid with gold. It must have lain there since 1540 when Coronado passed that way.

And the Bolivian mines at Potosí—the most fabulous source of silver the world had known—Potosí, too, was discovered by chance. An Indian pursuing a llama on a mountainside caught hold of a bush, the earth crumbled, and the Indian suddenly held in his hand a bush festooned with silver nuggets. It sounds implausible, like cheap fiction, yet that seems to be what occurred.

Now, what became of Atahualpa's stupendous ransom?

"Segun Dios Nuestro Señor le diere á entender teniendo su conciencia y para lo mejor hazer pedir el ayuda de Dios Nuestro Señor..." In other words, Francisco Pizarro with the fear of God in his eyes invoked the assistance of Heaven to do the work before him conscientiously and justly.

Thus fearing God, Pizarro took for himself 57,222 gold pesos, the Inca's gold throne which was valued at 25,000 pesos, and a hefty slice of silver.

His captains drew less, even so they were at once transmogrified into Peruvian millionaires. And it is said, with perhaps a little exaggeration, that ordinary foot soldiers grew as rich as Spanish dukes.

What happened next was inevitable.

At that time in Castile you could buy several acres of choice land for ten gold pesos. What could you buy in the New World for that?—a few sheets of writing paper. Did a conquistador want a bottle of wine?—the price would be sixty gold pesos. A warm cloak?—one hundred pesos. Or say he wanted to buy a horse. Provided the owner could be talked into selling, a horse would cost thousands.

Debtors, followed by Indian slaves wearing preposterous necklaces of gold—gold pots, gold plates, gold urns, gold statuettes—debtors visited their creditors in the hope of settling accounts, but would be told that the debt was not due. Or the creditor would hide so that he would not be obliged to accept any more gold.

As for silver, in Peru during the sixteenth century they shod horses with silver. They used it to mortar the walls, which explains why the Spaniards tore apart so many walls. They had no tapestries, wrote Garcilaso de la Vega, because they decorated the interior walls with gold and silver. And listen to this: in one palace the Spaniards saw three rooms filled with gold furnishings, five rooms furnished with silver, and 100,000 gold ingots—each ingot weighing five pounds.

Pedro Pizarro says that while looking for something to eat he wandered into a native hut and found ten silver slabs. Each slab was twenty feet long—twenty feet!—and one foot wide, and three fingers thick. The Indians were carrying these slabs to Trugillo where they meant to build a shrine for their idol, Chimo.

And in Cuzco there was a massive gold image the size of a ten-year-old boy.

There was even a stack of firewood reproduced in gold.

And the priest who officiated at important ceremonies wore an immense headdress with a golden replica of the sun on his forehead, with a silver moon beneath his chin, and he was crowned with macaw plumes.

But where is it now? What became of the treasure?

Those conquistadors, being practical men, decided to ship it to Spain in the form of ingots. All the baroque shapes—goblets, salvers, ewers, masks, birds, serpents, crickets—such things would be difficult to pack into the hold of a galleon. Only a few of the most remarkable specimens would be preserved and delivered to Charles V so that he might obtain some idea of native ingenuity.

Very often the objects were demolished by the same artists who had conceived them. "They toiled day and night, but such was the quantity to be recast, that it consumed a full month." And when the job was finished the gold and silver ingots weighed several tons.

Pizarro, contrary to what you might expect, made sure that Charles was not swindled: "He would often rise from his seat while watching the melting down of the gold and silver to retrieve a small piece of the king's share, which had fallen to one side as it was being broken down, and in so doing he remarked that he would pick up the king's property with his mouth if need be."

On January 9, 1534, the galleon *Santa María del Campo* carrying Hernando Pizarro and an incomprehensible load of treasure sailed heavily up the Guadalquivir to Seville. Pizarro was escorting one consignment of the royal fifth.

Albrecht Dürer did not live quite long enough to see

what was aboard the *Santa María del Campo,* but he did see the Aztec goldwork that Moctezuma had sent to Charles thirteen years earlier and he described it in his diary: "all sorts of marvelous objects for human use which are much more beautiful to behold than things spoken of in fairy tales. These things were all so precious that one has appraised them worth one hundred thousand guilders. And in all the days of my life I have seen nothing which so rejoiced my heart as these things. For I saw among them wondrous artful things and I marveled over the subtle genius of these men in strange countries. And I know not how to relate all of what I saw there before me."

The court historian, Peter Martyr, if less emotional than Dürer, also enjoyed the Moctezuma exhibit: "I do not marvel at gold and precious stones, but am in a manner astonished to see the workmanship excel the substance. . . . I never saw anything whose beauty might so allure the eye of man."

Charles, however, was unimpressed by native ingenuity. An imperial *cédula* published in 1535 directs that all gold and silver objects from Peru shall be melted in the royal mints at Seville, Toledo, and Segovia. Thus we have only the chronicles to describe what we shall never see:

Replicas of Indian corn, each gold ear sheathed in silver, with tassels of silver thread. Innumerable gold goblets. Sculpted gold spiders, gold beetles, gold lobsters, gold lizards. A gold fountain that emitted a sparkling jet of gold while gold animals and gold birds played around it. Twelve splendid representations of women, all in fine gold, as lovely and complete as though they were alive. And the sandals, or slippers, that women like—these also were reproduced in gold. The Inca's throne—which Pizarro claimed.

The list goes on and on, as Dürer said, until one can

hardly relate all of what was there. Nevertheless, after the death of Atahualpa, some Inca nobles poured a bucket of corn in front of the Spaniards, and one of them picked up a grain and said, "This is the gold he gave you." And then, pointing to the heap on the ground: "This much he has kept."

But the most spectacular agglutination of wealth seen by the Spaniards was at Cuzco, 600 miles south, when they entered the Coricancha—the Golden Enclosure. This temple complex occupied the site where according to legend the first building of the empire had been erected by Manco Capac, the first Inca.

A Dominican monastery now occupies this site, although some of the original Inca masonry peeps through. The entrance was by a side door of the present church, and around the inner patio stood thatched-roof chapels consecrated to various plenipotentiaries.

The most important shrine was that of the sun. Just what it held is a matter for scholarly dispute because sixteenth-century writers describe it differently. Garcilaso de la Vega mentions an altar on which there was an image of the sun fashioned from pure gold: "The face of the god was adorned with flames, extending from one wall to the next, in the same way that our painters often represent the Sun. The whole temple contained just this one idol, since the Incas have but one god, the Sun. On both sides of the Sun were ranged the mummified bodies of the Inca kings, so artfully embalmed that they seemed to be alive. They were seated on golden thrones . . ."

Another report has the mummies seated on stone benches encrusted with emeralds.

In addition to the central image of the sun there seems to have been a representative disc on the western wall "looking forth from amidst innumerable rays of light

230 / A LONG DESIRE

which emanated from it in every direction." According to Cieza de León, the sun's face was engraved on a gold plate thickly powdered with jewels: "muy primamente engastonada en muchas piedras ricas." This plate was so situated that through the east portal the rising sun illuminated it like a shimmering cymbal, reflecting upon a variety of silver and gold ornaments, warming and filling the shrine with an unearthly effulgence. Twelve immense silver vases were supposed to have been discovered in this chapel, each taller than a good lance—"mas altos que una buena pica"—and of such circumference that two men with outstretched arms could scarcely reach around one.

In the shrine dedicated to the moon, mother of the Incas, the planet was personified just as the sun was personified, except that the disc was larger: a great silver platter nearly hid the wall. And every object in this room had been fashioned from silver, which best complements the pallid lunar light.

Other shrines were dedicated to the rainbow, to the stars, and to thunder and lightning—ministers of vengeance.

Sarmiento writes that in the Coricancha every utensil, every ornament—everything—was either silver or gold: religious censers, ewers that held sacrificial water, the pipes that conducted water through subterranean channels, even the agricultural implements used in the temple gardens.

And at the heart of this spectacle, surrounded by the various shrines, stood a perfect replica of a field of maize, each stalk carefully contrived of gold and planted among golden clods. Here, too, on good authority, stood at least twenty-three life-size llamas with their young, all made of gold, with life-size Indian shepherds to guard them, each shepherd fashioned from gold, each with a golden sling and a golden crook. Miguel de Estete, an inspector for Charles V, was present and his account has survived. After summarizing what he saw he tells us that if he were to recount everything that the Incas had made of gold his story would never end.

Now the Coricancha has disappeared, except for a few plastered walls, replaced by the church of Santo Domingo. Prescott puts it like this: "Fields of maize and lucerne now bloom on the spot which glowed with the golden gardens of the temple; and the friar chants his orisons within the consecrated precincts once occupied by the Children of the Sun."

Gone, too, is Atahualpa's throne. Pizarro undoubtedly seated himself on it, at least once. After that? Probably it was melted.

And the massive gold lid of the sun-god's chicha basin —what happened to that? It was awarded to the redoubtable conquistador Mansio Serra de Leguizano, who lost it the same night in a game of dobladilla. The proverb *Juega el sol antes que amanezca*—gamble the sun before dawn—is thought to have originated with this conquistador's bad luck. But we do not know who won it, nor what the winner did with his prize. We assume it was melted.

Then what became of the ingots?

Most of them reached Spain where they were melted again and cast into coins, although many bars of Peruvian and Mexican gold settled on the bed of the Atlantic.

In 1622, for example, nine ships stuffed with bullion from the New World went down in a hurricane near Fort Pierce, Florida. Hundreds of Spaniards drowned, along with an undetermined number of Indians and Negroes whose deaths were not listed on the casualty report. As for the value of the cargo, it cannot even be estimated, but according to documents in the Archiva General de Indias in Seville, one galleon—*Nuestra Señora de Atocha* —had been loaded with 250,000 freshly minted silver coins, 901 silver ingots, and 161 bars of gold, in addition to an unknown amount of contraband.

The wreck of the *Atocha* has been found and much that is valuable brought to the surface—silver coins, a gold chalice, a bronze astrolabe, a gold boatswain's-whistle, small gold bars. But if all of her cargo could be recovered the *Atocha* would be one of the world's richest prizes.

In 1702 a fleet of twenty-three heavily loaded galleons escorted by French men-of-war sailed from Havana toward Cádiz. News of this wallowing treasury reached England and Sir Cloudisley Shovell—for that was his name—set out to capture them, because the War of the Spanish Succession had just begun. However, news of the English force got back to Spain and a friendly Genoese vessel sailing from Cádiz to Portugal warned the approaching galleons. The Spanish commander therefore changed course and arrived safely at Vigo in northern Spain. But here the bureaucrats took charge. Cádiz did not want the treasure unloaded at Vigo; being destined for Cádiz, it should be delivered to Cádiz.

And while this point was being argued the English learned where the galleons were hiding.

When the Spanish admiral, Don Manuel de Velasco, realized that his French protectors were being defeated he ordered the treasure thrown overboard; and then, to save the ships themselves from capture, he ordered them scuttled. He gave this order almost in time. The English seized only three galleons. The two smaller ones—*Santa Cruz* and *Tauro*—eventually got to England "with a mighty freight of bullion," but the largest, which held as much as the other two combined, struck a submerged rock and went down just outside Vigo Bay.

"We do not, as yet, exactly know the amount of booty taken at Vigo," says a contemporary English account. "We are sure that they have taken a value of 1,200,000 pounds Sterling in silver, with a great quantity of gold ingots . . ."

Whatever it came to, this was the produce of two unimportant ships plus a certain amount collected ashore. Twenty-one galleons, including the largest, went down.

All the same, it was a great victory and the English government celebrated by issuing coins minted from this New World wealth—gold guineas and silver crowns with VIGO stamped below the portrait of Queen Anne. The procedure was supervised by Sir Isaac Newton, master of the mint, and today the very least of these silver crowns is a treasure by itself.

As for the remaining gold and silver, worth an incalculable fortune, it rests in fifty feet of mud at the bottom of Vigo Bay.

In 1715 a much smaller fleet set sail from Havana, but was annihilated by a hurricane off the east coast of Florida not far from where the *Atocha* sank. More than 1,000 men drowned. Of eleven ships in this fleet, ten were lost. Aboard were 2,290 chests packed with freshly minted silver and gold coins from Vera Cruz and a cargo of emeralds, pearls, and gem-studded jewelry from Cartagena. Don Juan del Hoyo Solórzano, sergeant major of Havana, was assigned to salvage whatever he could.

After having located several of the wrecks Solórzano camped on the beach and put his Indian divers to work. It is said that about a third of them died, but that was unimportant; the rest brought up four million pesos of silver which the honest sergeant major dispatched to Havana.

Word of this got around and an English privateer named Jennings led two brigantines and three luggers from Port Royal to Florida where he lay offshore, observing things through a spyglass, until the Spaniards accumulated another heap of pesos. Then, as we learn from *A General History of the Robberies and Murders of the Most Notorious Pyrates:* "The rovers came directly upon the place, bringing their little fleet to anchor, and landing 300 men, they attacked the guard who immediately ran away; and thus they seized the treasure which they carried off, making the best of their way to Jamaica."

Solórzano did what he could for the crown, despite several such interruptions, and it is thought that altogether he retrieved about six million pesos, leaving another eight million in the shallow sandy water. Very little of this has been recovered.

At the beginning of the nineteenth century a surveyor picked up hundreds of escudos and doubloons on the beach near Fort Pierce inlet.

And there was an old man who had been postmaster in the nearby town of Sebastian who kept a cigar box full of Spanish coins; but one night he was murdered and the coins were stolen.

And there was said to be another man who found a strangely heavy brick in the surf, which he used when he built a fireplace, and the brick melted.

But these stories may have been discolored by time, or by the long human dream of treasure.

Much more recently, just a few years ago, a building contractor who was walking along this beach picked up a copper maravedi dated 1649. He then borrowed a metal detector and began finding silver pieces of eight—so many that he melted a number of them to make bracelets for neighborhood children.

Later, having read about attempts to salvage the 1715 treasure fleet, the contractor located Solórzano's camp. Here he dug up some cannonballs, a pair of cutlasses, broken porcelain, a gold ring set with a diamond, and thirteen more pieces of eight.

Next he decided to look offshore, and while paddling around on a surfboard he saw five ship's cannon and a huge old anchor. In the shallow water nearby he found a cluster of coins as big as his fist. The shape of this cluster indicated that the coins had originally been in a pouch.

He organized a company and very soon his divers were bringing up hundreds of blackened silver coins, some of which had undergone a sea change—fused by the water into rocklike greenish black clumps. One clump was so large that a diver sat on it, using it for a stool while he probed the sand.

And the treasure multiplied, as though the sea were a great alchemist. They scooped up handmade silver forks, plates, buckles, a pewter jewel box, and more.

While inspecting the beach after a storm they came upon a superb gold chain glittering in the sand—a chain eleven feet long—with more than 2,000 flower-shaped links. It had a dragon pendant, a whistle, which served also as a gentleman's grooming tool: a toothpick swiveled out of the dragon's belly, and the dragon's tail was a tiny spoon which aristocratic Spaniards used for cleaning their ears.

One day the divers brought up a clump of coins that weighed seventy pounds. Then five more clumps.

Twenty-eight valuable K'ang Hsi ceramic pieces were found unbroken, packed in clay for shipment. And another gold chain—although not as elaborate as the first. And two gold discs, each weighing seven pounds. And a gold doubloon dated 1698.

Something else they found was a pocketknife with this inscription: SIBO A MI DUEÑO Y SR. DON DIEGO PENALOSA Y PICAZO. Don Diego himself disintegrated; but that trusty uncomplaining servant, his knife, remained to honor him.

In another place the divers blasted a trench through the sand and were almost blinded by a sudden gleam. The trench appeared to be paved with gold. It is said that they swam to the surface with their hands full of gold doubloons, spilling fifty or sixty at a time on the deck of their boat.

Ten discs eighteen inches in diameter—an alloy of gold, copper, platinum, and silver—ten such discs were recovered at one site. Then eight more, along with several thick bars and wedges of solid silver. So much wealth had been flung across the bed of the sea that after a while they swam above loose coins, pausing only to collect the discs and clusters.

They saw a black wooden chest. Its top had rotted away, but the interior had been lined with lead and was filled to the brim with Spanish silver and gold.

Now, have you heard enough? Or do you want more?— because what I've described represents only a fraction of the cargo. For example, vacationers walking along the nearby beach after a storm sometimes pick up coins from that doomed fleet, flung ashore by General Juan Estéban de Ubilla, the drowned commander.

We hear of such things—sunken galleons, the Inca's golden enclosure, a mountain veined with silver. We hear about these luminous treasures, or read about them, just as we learn that somebody somewhere has won the Irish Sweepstakes. Then for a moment we feel vaguely baffled and resentful, wondering why the ponderous wheel of fortune has once again ticked slowly past us. Why, we ask, should our good luck be limited to picking up a nickel on the pavement?

One evening several years ago a professional treasure hunter knocked at my door—a pleasant, brown-bearded man with rather stagnant breath. He said he had been told by mutual friends that I was interested in antique objects such as coins and manuscripts and prehistoric pottery, and he wanted to show me something. I invited him in and gave him a glass of wine and listened while he talked about his adventures, and then he took out of his shirt pocket a triangular gold lump—three Spanish doubloons which had been in the sea for so many years that they could not be separated.

I weighed this curious object in my palm—this heavy warm triangle as smooth as velvet. I turned it over and over between my fingers and stared at the royal lettering.

I asked what he planned to do with it.

He said he knew of a galleon that had never been explored and he meant to sell this gold piece along with some others he had found in order to finance the expedition. This was what he always did. He cared very little about treasure; what excited him was the search.

At last he dropped the gold triangle into his pocket as though it had no more significance than a cigarette lighter. He stood up, shook hands, thanked me for the wine, and slipped away into the night. I've not seen him since. He told me where he found that lump of doubloons, but I've forgotten—someplace in the Caribbean. Maybe Bermuda.

Now that I've had several years to think about our conversation I believe that everything he told me was true. If I had made an appropriate offer he would have sold the piece. Undoubtedly he had a sale in mind when he came to visit; but I made no suggestion, so he took back his treasure and disappeared.

Once in a while I dream of finding coins, although I doubt if the gold he showed me was responsible because in my dream—which never varies—the coins are silver. I have two Spanish pieces of eight, which might possibly explain a dream like that, yet I don't think they account for it either.

I bought these pieces of eight at an auction. One is counterfeit, the other authentic. The authentic coin, blackened and worn, carries a portrait of Ferdinand VII and is dated 1820. The fake looked very much the same at first, but then it began turning yellow. It never did ring as sweetly when I dropped it on the table and its surface is pocked. The inscription—CAROLUS IIII DEI GRATIA 1791—looks irregular when compared to Ferdinand's inscription, and the milled edges are not well delineated. Some previous owner, frankly suspicious, had drilled a tiny hole beneath the king's chin. I inspected this hole through a jeweler's glass and the metal appears to be lead.

I doubt if they have anything to do with my persistent dream because, if I remember correctly, it began sometime after I had read about Potosí. The symbolic image of an Indian pulling up a shrub spangled and trembling with silver nuggets—that image must be the origin of this recurrent dream because I always see the coins among bushes or on dusty ground. I become aware of myself floating toward them with the splendid buoyancy we all have experienced while we sleep. I float toward them with the intention of picking them up. But just then the dream concludes.

My most sensuous dream of money—and it has materialized only once—concerned ordinary American paper dollars. It began while I was infinitely high in the air, floating gently downward—weightless as a mote of dust. I remember floating down beside a tree where bunches of dollars grew in the forks like cabbages or heads of lettuce. I remember myself wrenching these tough, crisp, fat bunches out of the tree. I seized them with both hands.

I twisted them and wrenched them loose, these bundles of dollars, one after another, but I don't know what became of them.

Then I was rising swiftly upward as though I had touched the earth and bounded hundreds of feet into the air, because in a little while here I came floating down again, pausing once more at this tree among trees where I promptly resumed harvesting those excellent leafy green tufts. I remember being surprised at the silence. The dollars were fresh and crisp, yet when I wrenched them out of the tree they made not a sound. However, I could be wrong about that. Maybe it was sometime later when I felt surprised by the silence. Perhaps, too, the dollars weren't green, for it is said that men seldom are conscious of color in their dreams. I might have added the green later, I can't be sure. As to what became of these handsome cabbages, I have no idea; the instant I caught them they vanished. This didn't bother me. I was always reaching for the next fine bunch.

Every so often when I feel sleep approaching I remind myself of that dream because it was pleasant, to say the least, and I wouldn't mind dreaming it again. But of course the inner being who directs our lives pays no attention to what we want.

The contemplation of money usually leads me to think about my father, who worked industriously for sixty years to accumulate as much of it as possible. In this respect I suppose he wasn't unusual; he differed from most men only in that he put together a larger packet. More than enough to feed the family. Now, any man who has gotten himself into that situation must figure out what to do with the surplus—which is not as much fun as you might think. After the sensible investments and a few luxuries, if there still remains a little extra, what do you do?

My father used it to become a millionaire. He was a

millionaire for several weeks. He told me how this happened a long time ago, when I was a child. It was during
the Depression. He and some friends who also had a bit
of extra money decided to finance an Oklahoma oil
prospector.

Well, sometime after they had done this they got a
telegram.

There are things I would ask my father now, but it's
too late. I would ask how they behaved when they got the
news—whether he and his friends pounded each other on
the back and roared and danced a little jig. I suppose
they did. I would ask, too, why he told me this amazing
story only once; I should think he would have told it
again and again, until my mother and my sister and I
were unspeakably bored.

It's too late, as I say, and all I know is that they chartered a railroad car for the trip to Oklahoma and they sat
up all night drinking champagne. And my father said
that when they reached Tulsa they were driven out to a
field where they had to put on rubber boots and raincoats
and rubber hats because in those days it was difficult
to cap a gusher and the air was saturated with oil. Everything everywhere was oily, he said. You couldn't touch
anything without getting oil on your hands. The entire
field was soaked. They walked through pools of oil up to
their ankles. "Great Lord!" my father said to me, wagging
his head as he remembered. "Great Lord, I never saw
anything like it!"

So all at once they became grotesquely rich, the prospector and his middle-class financiers. Then the Oklahoma legislature cooked up some sort of a bill to prevent
the money from leaving the state.

My father sold his share and I believe he said his part-
ners did the same. They made money, quite a lot for

those days, but nothing like the million or two or three or five or ten or twenty that each man expected would be his.

As he told me this story I thought about the black mist in the air, the dangerous black column of spouting oil, and the pools in the field. I don't remember thinking about anything else. Nor do I recall what questions I asked. Maybe I asked if he had to take a bath afterward, or if they were still drinking champagne, or whether anybody slipped and fell. But now, if I had the chance, I would ask what went through his mind when he learned that the Oklahoma legislature had seized his fortune. Although, because he was my father and I knew him so well, I think I could answer for him. He would have been angry. He would have felt that he was being cheated.

At first I would have felt the same, I suppose. And yet, unlike my father, I would have decided very soon that what occurred was inevitable. I doubt if we are meant to get our hands on unreasonable wealth.

For instance, now and then an orange comes floating down a certain river in the Sierra Madre of Mexico, and each time this happens the people who live along the banks of the river stop whatever they are doing and look upstream because they know that the orange has come from El Naranjal.

Not much has been learned about this fabulous mine, except that it is in the country of the Tepehuane Indians, probably in Sinaloa near the Durango border, and that during the seventeenth century, according to church records in Guadalajara, it produced millions of dollars worth of gold and silver. Then, around 1810, the Tepehuane laborers revolted, killed their Spanish overseers, destroyed the haciendas, and concealed the entrances to the huge mine which had been the cause of their suffering. Since that time nobody has been able to locate El Naranjal—whose name means "the orange grove"—although a great many men have spent years searching the archives for clues, and others have lost their lives exploring the tremendous barrancas of the Sierra Madre.

It is thought that some of the Indians who live in that country know the location of the mine, but even today they are not anxious for it to reopen.

The historian J. Frank Dobie states that in Mazatlán he once met a German assayer who showed him a reproduction of an eighteenth-century road sign. The sign had been carved on the face of a rock. This is what it said:

DEPARTEMENTO

DE

CAMINOS

CAMINO A LAS MINAS

DE ARCO

Y

NARANJAL

The sign, therefore, was inscribed by the department of roads to indicate the way to the mines of Arco and Naranjal.

One gringo prospector may actually have seen El Naranjal. A white-haired old man who lived in the mountains pointed out a trail to him. The prospector traveled for several days and then came to a precipice. Looking down thousands of feet he was able to make out a river, the white ruins of a hacienda, and some bright green foliage unlike any other growth on the canyon floor—which could only have been the orange grove. He was unable to find a path down the cliff and on the way back he almost starved. He reported that there must have been a trail to the canyon floor, but probably some act of nature had annihilated it. Whether or not anyone could descend from someplace farther along the cliff, he did not know.

Seventy or eighty years have passed since then, perhaps more. The prospector is long dead, and of course everything may have happened in his imagination. Nevertheless, an orange occasionally does come floating down the river from somewhere in the mountains and orange trees do not grow by chance in the Sierra Madre. Thus, if it were possible to identify the tributary that empties into this river—if you could do that, my friend, you might be able to locate El Naranjal. But each tributary is fed by smaller tributaries, and each of these by lesser ones. Look at the problem this way: given a gigantic tree, could you find a particular leaf if you began at the trunk and followed one limb after another upward and outward, each smaller than the last, returning again and again to your starting point?

In other words, asleep or awake we dream of treasure, we search for it in numberless directions, and perhaps for an instant we see it from a distance—as blindingly white as the ruins of a hacienda, as green as the foliage of an orange grove. We might even touch it, just as I held three gold doubloons from the bed of the sea. Or, as my father did during the Great Depression, we may slosh ankle-deep through spreading pools of oil. But ultimately some power intervenes.

It may be that treasure exists for the purpose of tantalizing us. If so, how strange. Why should something we passionately desire be subtly withheld?

11

Philippus Theophrastus Aureolus Bombastus Ab Hohenheim & Co.

During the Middle Ages it was held that God bestowed a knowledge of alchemy upon Adam, who passed along this wisdom to Abraham, who gave it to Moses, who gave it to Job—who septupled his assets before handing over the secrets to certain illustrious disciples. Other legends concerning the origin of alchemy are more appealing, such as the belief that Nature's ineffable mysteries were betrayed by angels who fell in love with earthly women. But no matter how this art originated, the goal of almost every alchemist was to equal or surpass the accomplishment of Job.

It is true that many of those who spent their lives diddling with retorts and alembics considered the search twofold—philosophic as well as material. That is, they hoped to realize not just the transmutation of common metals but some method by which unhappy Man could shed his greatcoat of imperfections. "False alchemists seek only to make gold," wrote Becher, "whereas true philosophers desire knowledge. The former produce mere tinctures, sophistries, ineptitudes; the latter enquire after the principles of things." Even so, the initial objective from which all subsequent iridescence came streaming was the pot at the rainbow's end: a crucible bubbling thickly with gold.

How was this to be achieved? By the discovery or development of an elusive substance known by various names—stone of Egypt, elixir of quintessence, tincture of gold, powder of projection—but which most often was called simply the philosophers' stone. As to its appearance, whether in fact it was a stone, a liquid, or a powder, every alchemist had his opinion. In short, nothing could be said with certainty about this vital substance except that it represented potential gold, which meant that its color should be red, deep orange, or possibly yellow.

Raymond Lully described it as a small coal, or carbuncle, glowing like fire; though he says that, like a coal, it might first be black, then red, and finally yellow before reaching a state of whiteness. It might even turn green, if necessary. Indeed, the stone might take on any color of the universe, yet it could never be mistaken for anything else because it shone like the eyes of fishes.

Berigard of Pisa, who taught physics during the seventeenth century, said it had the color of a wild poppy and gave off an odor of scorched salt.

Jean-Baptiste van Helmont claimed to have seen the stone and handled it frequently. He said it had the color of saffron, "yet weighty and shining like unto powdered glass."

As to just how this substance was to be concocted,

distilled, or perfected—"Poor idiot!" exclaims the alchemist called Artephius. "Could you be so simple-minded as to believe that we would teach you clearly and openly the greatest and most important secrets?"

So the ingredients, their proportions, and the intricate alchemical procedures were expressed vaguely, or in cabalistic language. We are told by Rhazes: "Take of some unknown thing any quantity that you wish." And according to Morenius: "From several things make 2, 3 and 3, 1, 1 with 3 is 4 . . ."

Even when you unscramble alchemical directions they don't make sense. *M. the azothi aoefth epuhiloqosophersa lisati ptheiruri imeracurerty* sounds like Etruscan, but can be restructured to read "The azoth of the philosophers is their mercury." Wonderful. We seem to be making progress. Now what is "azoth"? It comes from the Arabic *al-zāūq*, meaning "quicksilver," which, as everybody knows, is another word for mercury. All right, what have we? The mercury of the philosophers is mercury. So is a rose a rose.

However, nobody said making a pot of gold would be easy. Quite the opposite; the alchemist flings as many obstacles as possible in front of us. The German monk who called himself Basil Valentine took the trouble to write "Visitetis Interiora Terrae, Rectificando Invenietis Occultum Lapidem" in order to avoid writing "vitriol." And once you have translated his Latin you find yourself no nearer the fabulous stone. It's someplace in the bowels of the earth. Good luck.

At times the alchemist refuses even to title his manuscript because the title might provide a clue. Everything must be masked. Everything. Still, there was more than militant perversity in these fantastic circumlocutions: a good many alchemists were murdered—strangled in their sleep—because word got around that they had achieved the miraculous transmutation, and not only would heaps of gold be found in the laboratory but also the recipe. And perhaps a bit of the stone itself. So there was a degree of logic, a not wholly unnatural desire to avoid being strangled, that encouraged him to clothe his works in the rich brocade of allegory and symbol.

Nor were manuscripts the only textbooks: medieval paintings and tapestries are not necessarily what they seem. The diabolic visions of Bosch, for instance, are alchemically precise; and in Paris, in the Cluny museum, you will find a tapestry called "The Lady and the Unicorn," which has to do only incidentally with the relationship between a lady and a unicorn.

In this same museum, bolted to the wall beside a staircase, is the tombstone of Nicolas Flamel who knew how to change lead into silver and mercury into gold. His tombstone, by the way, is not as cold as you might expect; it is oddly warm. I've touched it.

Flamel probably was born at Pontoise, the birthplace of Francois Villon, just north of Paris, about the year 1330. He received education enough to set himself up as a notary or public scribe in Paris, and is known to have worked in a small wooden booth near the church of Saint-Jacques-la-Boucherie. He lived close by, in a house called At the Sign of the Fleur de Lys, where he gave calligraphy lessons and where he and several assistants produced illuminated manuscripts. His reputation was sufficient to attract ladies and gentlemen of the court who wanted to learn how to write their names. He died March 22, 1417, and was buried in the church, most of which was demolished soon after the French Revolution. At this point Flamel's tombstone disappeared, but turned up years later in the shop of an herbalist on the Rue des Arcis. The shopkeeper was using the smooth back side of Flamel's tombstone as a chopping block for dried herbs. A pet-shop owner, Monsieur Guérard, then got hold of it, expecting to make a profit, and consigned the stone to a Monsieur Signol who sold antiques. Some years after this the Cluny museum bought it for 120 francs. All of which may seem irrelevant, but is required to prove the existence of Monsieur Flamel.

Our hero displayed no interest in alchemy until he purchased, for two florins, "a guilded Booke, very old and large" whose leaves were made of bark or papyrus instead of parchment. The text was beautifully inscribed with an iron point in clear Latin, supplemented on every seventh leaf with symbolic paintings. Flamel then discovered that he had bought an important book, the *Asch Mezareph* of Rabbi Abraham, which Jewish cabalists thought had been lost forever; and from a converted Jew known as Maître Canches he learned enough to interpret some of it. The book revealed to Jews the art of transmuting ordinary metals into gold so that they could pay the tribute demanded by Roman emperors.

Flamel began a series of experiments that went on for three years and at last believed he had produced the catalytic substance. On January 17, 1382, with his wife Pernelle as witness, he melted half a pound of lead and added to it the white elixir he had devised. The lead promptly turned to silver.

On April twenty-fifth, about five o'clock in the evening, again with Pernelle as witness, "I made proiection of the Red Stone upon the like quantity of Mercurie . . . which I transmuted truely into almost as much pure Gold."

Flamel achieved only three more transmutations—or perhaps three altogether—yet he acquired gold enough to build three chapels, to endow fourteen hospitals, and to make substantial gifts to various churches not only in Paris but in Boulogne, where scholars think his wife was born. According to Jacques Sadoul, "some forty deeds have been found, legally drawn up, showing evidence of the considerable gifts made by the one-time humble Public Scrivener." And apparently it is a fact that Flamel's wealth caused Charles VI to send his chief tax inspector, the Sire de Cramoisy, to investigate. How this investigation ended is unclear, but Monsieur de Cramoisy may have been bribed.

Even so, the size of Flamel's fortune has been disputed. The provisions of his will totaled only about 800 pounds and much less than that was found in his house—an amount not be kicked aside, but hardly what his heirs expected. And whether he was just a frugal scribe, or whether he actually distilled the philosophers' stone, is another matter not yet settled. We are free, therefore, to believe or disbelieve.

In the spring of 1602 a wealthy Scot named Alexander Seton, who was touring the Continent, got into an argument with a professor of medicine at Freiburg, Johann Wolfgang Dienheim. The two men were on a boat going from Zürich to Basle. Dienheim scoffed at the possibility of alchemical changes and Seton replied by offering to give a demonstration, saying there should be an additional witness, preferably a skeptic. In Basle a test was arranged with several slabs of lead, a crucible borrowed from a jeweler, and some sulfur bought at a shop. Seton, who did not touch either the materials or the apparatus, ordered the lead and sulfur put into the crucible and the crucible placed over a fire. Fifteen minutes later he took out of his pocket a small paper in which there were a few grains of heavy, greasy, lemon-colored powder. He told Dienheim to throw this into the crucible, which was done.

250 / A LONG DESIRE

Then the lid was put back on. About fifteen minutes later Seton ordered the fire quenched, and when the lid was lifted it was found that the lead had turned to gold. The jeweler attested to its purity. The witness, Dr. Jakob Zwinger, from a prominent Swiss family, wrote a letter to Professor Emmanuel König in Basle supporting the incident in every detail. Zwinger's letter also states that Seton performed another transmutation before resuming his tour of the Continent, this time for the goldsmith André Bletz.

Seton next appeared in Strasbourg during the summer of 1603, where he worked his magic at the shop of a goldsmith named Gustenheover. Not long afterward he concocted gold in Offenbach, then in Cologne, then in Hamburg—always in front of witnesses, some of whom were given gold souvenirs. However, he made the mistake of demonstrating his art before the Duke of Saxony, Christian II, who had him imprisoned and tortured in an attempt to get the secret. Although he was smuggled out of prison by a sympathizer, Michael Sendivogius, he had been so brutalized that he soon died.

Johann Friedrich Schweitzer was born in Köthen in the duchy of Anhalt in 1625 and became a famous doctor, personal physician to the Prince of Orange. He is better known as Helvetius. Professor E. J. Holmyard has this to say about him: "A man of culture, education, and discernment, he can scarcely be suspected of having lied, or wilfully misreporting the remarkable events he describes."

Helvetius reports that in December of 1666 "came a Stranger to my house in the Hague, in a plebian habit, honest Gravity, and serious authority; of a mean Stature, a little long face, with a few small pock holes . . ." After discussing transmutation the homely stranger displayed three lumps of the philosophers' stone "each about the bigness of a small walnut, transparent, of a pale brimstone colour." Helvetius asked for a piece and was given a crumb. The visitor then promised to return the next morning to demonstrate how it should be used. At half past nine a message arrived saying he would be there at three in the afternoon "but [he] never came, nor have I heard of him since; whereupon I began to doubt the whole matter."

Nevertheless, being urged by his wife to attempt a transmutation, he cut a small amount of lead which he melted in a crucible. Then the crumb, wrapped in wax, was added to the pot. The mixture began to hiss and bubble and "within a quarter of an hour all the mass of lead was totally transmuted into the best and finest gold, which made us all amazed as planet-struck . . . Truly I, and all standing about me, were exceedingly startled, and did run with this aurified lead (being yet hot) unto the goldsmith, who wondered at the fineness, and after a short trial of touch, he judg'd it the most excellent gold in the whole world, and offered to give me most willingly fifty florins for every ounce of it."

Helvetius refused to sell the gold, and word soon got around The Hague. Master Porelius, controller of the Dutch office of assay, came to see him, inspected the hermetic gold, and demanded that it be tested in a government laboratory. Under his personal supervision it was subjected to the usual tests, after which Master Porelius declared that it was indeed gold of very high quality.

Helvetius then took it to a silversmith named Brechtel who melted it, mixed it with silver, and finally separated the two components. During this process some of the silver turned to gold. The philosopher Spinoza was in The Hague at about that time, and in March of 1667 he wrote to a friend:

When I spoke to Voss about the Helvetius affair, he
made fun of me, and said he was surprised to find me
interested in that sort of nonsense. To make sure of my
facts, I went to see Brechtel, the man who did the assay. He told me that while it was being melted, the
gold had actually increased in weight when they
dropped some silver into the pot . . . Not only Brechtel,
but other people who were present when the tests were
made have told me that this is a true account of what
occurred. After that I went to see Helvetius himself,
who showed me the gold and the crucible, that still
had some traces of gold on the inner surface. He told
me that he had used a piece of the Philosopher's Stone
about a quarter the size of a grain of wheat in the
melted lead, and he added that he was going to tell
everyone in the world about it.

A Swedish general named Paykull, convicted of treason
and sentenced to death, offered Charles XII one million
crowns a year in exchange for his life, saying that he
could make gold artificially. He had learned the secret,
he said, from a Polish officer named Lubinski. Charles
agreed to a test, supervised by an independent observer,
General Hamilton of the British Royal Artillery. All of the
materials were examined and every precaution taken
against fraud; nevertheless, General Paykull created a
lump of gold which subsequently was coined into 147
ducats. A medal was struck to commemorate the event. It
is inscribed: O.A. VON PAYKULL CAST THIS GOLD BY CHEMICAL
ART AT STOCKHOLM, 1706.

What should we think of such implausible stories?

One might suggest that they be accepted verbatim; after all, not many of us dispute the Christian miracles. But
if this answer seems unsatisfactory then we must say that

in many cases of "transmutation," probably in most, the miracle was accomplished by sleight of hand. A certain Geoffrey the Elder wrote in 1722: "They often used double-bottomed crucibles or culpels, lining the bottom with oxides of gold or silver, then covering it with an appropriate paste. They also sometimes made a hole in a lump of coal and poured gold or silver into it; or sometimes they soaked coals with solutions of these metals and pulverized them before projecting them on the substances to be transmuted . . . They stirred fused substances with wands or little wooden batons; these had been hollowed out at one end, filled with gold or silver filings, and then stopped up again . . ."

Apart from fraud, what explanations could there be?

Self-deceit? At times, yes.

Credulity? Yes.

Ignorance? Of course. In this enlightened age, for example, we know all sorts of things our predecessors did not, such as the fact that many copper ores contain gold. You see what might happen. The alchemist, unaware that gold had been present from the start, deduced incorrectly when he found a trace clinging to the sides of the pot that his own efforts were responsible.

So it's hard to be sure after six centuries just what took place on the seventeenth of January, 1382, in Paris. Or on that day in Stockholm when a treacherous general supposedly coined a lump worth 147 ducats. And Helvetius? One feels a bit uncomfortable discrediting such a man. Even more uncomfortable when it comes time to laugh at Sir Isaac Newton—for Newton, that supreme scientist, thought transmutation was quite possible. His annotated copy of a famous alchemical text, *The Open Door,* is now in the British Museum. As a matter of fact, he and the chemist Robert Boyle were so convinced of alchemical truths that they urged Parliament to prohibit disclosure of the process for fear the gold market would collapse.

Today, plucking details from brittle documents, how do we isolate the truth? What good is Newton's opinion? Who cares that Helvetius was honorable and distinguished? Nor does a medal in a Swedish museum reveal much, no more than Flamel's tombstone or Spinoza's letter.

We do know there were plenty of charlatans, just as engaging and industrious as their descendants. We know they gulled the public, the nobles, and the kings because some were a trifle heavy-handed and if you care to muck about in the archives you can find out what happened to many of those who were caught. And follow the paths, at least for a while, of some who were caught but contrived to escape. How slippery they were in the good old days.

Our own masters of deceit—presidents, congressmen, generals, industrialists—seem merely vulgar when compared to the Comte de Saint-Germain, alias the Marquis de Montferrat, alias Prince Rakoczi, and so on. Or to Giuseppe Balsamo, who might not have gone far with his own name but did very well as Comte Alessandro di Cagliostro. Or to Jean de Gallans, alias the Baron of Pezerolles, who took the bona fide Duke of Anjou for 120,000 pounds—although, sad to say, Monsieur Jean bowed out of the ducal presence a moment too soon and concluded his performance by imitating a tap dancer high above the ground.

Then there was that slick Neapolitan, Domenico Manuel Caetano. Born in the provinces, he was apprenticed to a goldsmith but seems also to have studied the art of legerdemain—an ominous mixture. Before long he was demonstrating his alchemical skill by producing gold from dross, saying he had learned the science from an old manuscript. And so spectacular were these conversions that he was invited to perform in Brussels before Maximilian Emmanuel, governor of the Spanish Netherlands. Domenico's act must have been impressive because he received 60,000 gulden, either to perfect his art or to arrange a massive transmutation. With this honorarium in his pocket he tried to skip town, but not being as fast with his feet as with his hands he spent the next six years in prison.

Somehow he escaped and popped up in Vienna where he dazzled Emperor Leopold.

Next he appeared in Berlin, conducting a successful experiment before Frederick I and promising to make a generous supply of the philosophers' stone. Frederick, against the advice of suspicious counselors, rewarded him with a variety of gifts and "lucrative offices"; but after a couple of months when the magic stone was not forthcoming the king grew peevish and Domenico decided to visit Hamburg—which he did without bidding his imperial host good-bye. Frederick found out where he was, though, and abruptly changed his address to the Kostrzyn fortress. Domenico, aggrieved at such rude treatment, complained that nobody could make gold in these drafty quarters so he was escorted back to Berlin. However, he once again chose to leave in the middle of the night. He was caught at Frankfort and returned to Kostrzyn; and Frederick, having mulled things over, decided that the Neapolitan was less than impeccably honest. On August 23, 1709, therefore, dressed in a cloak glittering with tinsel, Domenico Manuel Caetano was suspended from a gilded gallows.

So much for swindlers. They come and go, parasitic, imaginative, voracious as locusts, otherwise meaningless.

Most alchemists, like a fair majority in any age, were not crooked; however unlikely their goal and however pe-

culiar their approach to it, concealing hollow secrets behind a screen of cryptic nonsense, they seem to have been
passionately sincere—although at times they wandered
sincerely down questionable paths.

For instance, Rudolph von Habsburg, that indecisive,
dreamy, optimistic ruler of the Holy Roman Empire. Being convinced that not only his private troubles but all
the world's problems could be solved alchemically, Rudolph ordered a large silver coin to be struck which por-
trayed him with mysterious symbols attached to his coat,
and he began assembling a team of highly regarded alchemists at his court in Prague. He built each of them a
little house—living quarters and a smelter. These houses,
nearly 200 munchkin houses, were situated within the
outer wall of the palace, convenient to Prague's apothe-
cary shops, and all day and all night alchemists scurried
back and forth, each persuaded that at the appointed
time his crucible would yield the magic stone.

Rudolph himself did a certain amount of experimenting
and is said to have become engrossed in the work while
his authority as emperor was being subverted by his
brother, Archduke Mathias. This erosion of power did not
trouble him until too late. Then, in a frantic effort to
blunt the challenge, he attempted to blend alchemy with
sorcery. Hans Holzer states that a Jesuit, Father Damiano,
left a diary describing an event that took place in the
cellar of the Belvedere adjacent to Hradshin Palace:

> I was summoned by His Majesty to help him with the
> preparation for the magical invocation His Majesty had
> in mind in relation to the attacks directed towards him
> by the Archduke Mathias. I was to secure a small dog
> which would form part of the experiment.
> I did not know what use the animal was going to be

put to . . . His Majesty, dressed in his long cloak and wearing the five-pointed silver star around his neck, seemed unusually grim that evening. Promptly at the stroke of midnight, another man joined us in the enterprise. This was the alchemist Christopher Hauser, lately arrived from Regensburg . . . Hauser brought with him certain tools, which I recognized as being a brazier, a short knife, a salt cellar, a silver candlestick, and a vial of oil. In addition, I noticed a leather whip, a tool I had never seen before in any of His Majesty's magical evocations.

After His Majesty had consecrated the magical circle in the usual manner with his Spanish sword, and sprinkled salt, then water into the four corners of the room, carried the candle aloft and the brazier around the circle, setting them all down again on a small table in the center which served as altar, His Majesty sat back and allowed Christopher Hauser to take the center of the circle.

Hauser began to invoke the powers of light, at which point, says Father Damiano, the little dog grew frightened and started howling and pulling at the leash. Hauser led it to the center of the circle, touched its head, and the animal sat down, moaning, but otherwise strangely silent.

Hauser then said: "In the name of the Holy Trinity, and in the name of that which is above and also below, I hereby baptize thee, O creature, to the name of Mathias." He sprinkled a few drops of oil on the dog's head, which caused it to let out a dismal howl.

Rudolph stood to one side, ignoring the procedure, gazing straight ahead.

Hauser then began beating the dog with a leather whip. Father Damiano says that he himself could hardly

endure this and wanted to leave, but was afraid of anger-
ing Rudolph. So, instead of leaving, the priest "sent
thoughts of a pleading nature to His Majesty . . ."

After having beaten the dog for several minutes, during
which time he referred to it as Mathias, Hauser picked
up a knife and cut off its head.

So much for the wretched dog, so much for Rudolph.
Archduke Mathias soon controlled the Holy Roman
Empire.

It should be noted that this crossbreeding of alchemy
with black magic was rare; the adept usually was closer
in spirit to the mystic than to the sorcerer. In fact there
were some who looked down not only on wizards and
mountebanks but upon all those who devoted themselves
to fabricating gold—calling them "puffers" because of the
bellows they used to fan the fire. And of these alchemists
one in particular emerges with archetypal clarity—that
quasi-genius who proclaimed himself Philippus Theophrastus Aureolus Bombastus ab Hohenheim.

Few recognize him by that grandiloquent title, but as
Paracelsus he may sound familiar.

"Many have said of alchemy," he wrote, "that it is for
making gold and silver. For me such is not the aim, but to
consider only what virtue and power may lie in medi-
cines." And he continues: "The art of medicine is rooted
in the heart. If your heart is just, you will also be a true
physician . . . one for whom the ultimate instance is man's
distress. Privilege and lineage pale to nothingness, only
distress has meaning."

All of which is a long way from decapitating a dog or
relieving a simpleminded countess of her gold florins. It is
equally distant from those curious "transmutations" ef-
fected by Flamel, Seton, Helvetius, Paykull, and nobody knows how many others. In those cases the subject

was unashamedly material; Philippus Theophrastus focused on Man.

His medical philosophy grew from the belief that astral influences determine sickness and health, and these influences must be countered by secret alchemical prescriptions. Treatment was intended to restore harmony between the private "astrum" of the patient and the heavenly astrum, implying that the essence of a remedy should be celestial. That is to say, the medicine itself would be earthly stuff but its nature should be celestial. A physician, therefore, must acquaint himself with the stars.

For example, he recommended a drink made from black hellebore to patients over fifty years of age, advising them to gather the plant under a full moon. Now you may not think such a brew would do much for a fifty-year-old who feels poorly, but it happens that the dose he prescribed is just right to alleviate certain symptoms of arteriosclerosis. And eventually we may discover that he also happened to be right about the full moon. In short, how do you evaluate this man?

It may or may not help to know what he looked like and where he came from. Several portraits of him exist. He resembles Immanuel Kant, with the skull deformation characteristic of rickets—from which Kant also suffered —but in Paracelsus' case it was the result of desperate poverty, although the Hohenheims once had been rich. His grandfather, in fact, had been a commander of the Teutonic Knights and lord of Hohenheim castle near Stuttgart but lost the estate after a serious political miscalculation.

So Paracelsus grew up poor and sickly. And it is thought, although this cannot be verified, that he was a eunuch. There are at least two stories of how this came about, if it did. In one version he was attacked by a wild boar; in the other, which sounds curiously plausible, a group of drunken soldiers decided to operate on him. In any event, he never associated with women; and he advocated continence, insisting it was better to be a castrate than an adulterer. Nor is there an authentic portrait of him with a beard, which doesn't prove anything—and yet it does, so to speak, fit the picture. He made enemies enough, who salted him with just about every imaginable vice, but he never was accused of lechery. Still, he grew bald, which eunuchs seldom do. Anyway, what we see is an intelligent, somber, middle-aged man with troubled eyes sunk in a huge, domed head.

From the beginning he had been restless. His mother drowned herself in the Siehl River when he was nine, but how this affected him we have no idea. His father then moved to a Tyrol mining community where the boy was put to work in the metallurgy shops, but at fourteen he left home to become a traveling student—drifting from school to school, wearing the traditional velvet hat and yellow scarf.

In Heidelberg, he said, the students devoted themselves more to pleasure than to knowledge. Freiburg he labeled "a house of indecency." Nor did Ingolstadt please him, the lessons were unimaginative. At Cologne the instruction was obscure.

In 1509, aged sixteen, he enrolled at the University of Vienna where he lasted two years, studying the high arts of the time: arithmetic, geometry, music, and astrology. But he grew impatient. "At all German schools," he wrote, "you cannot learn as much as at the Frankfort Fair."

He resumed wandering. The great teachers were known to be in Italy, so he went to Ferrara but his studies were interrupted by war. He fled south and became an army surgeon. It was customary to dress wounds with a poultice of feathers, dung, snake fat, and whatever else looked appropriate. The result usually was gangrene. Paracelsus, with nothing to support his heretical opinion, refused to apply these poultices and to everybody's amazement quite a few of his patients recovered. Though he did on occasion use frog's eggs as a disinfectant—without knowing that they contained iodine. At the same time he thought frost blisters should be treated with children's hair boiled by a red-headed person.

On his way home, tired of army life, he stopped at Würzburg to visit the famous alchemist Johannes Heidenberg, known as Trithemius, whom he seems to have revered all the rest of his life. Yet not even Trithemius could satisfy his deep hunger for knowledge, and in 1517, as Martin Luther nailed that reverberating document to the church door in Wittenberg, Paracelsus set out again:

"No man becomes master while he stays at home, nor finds a teacher behind the stove . . . I traveled on to Granada and Lisbon through Spain, England, Brandenburg, Prussia, Lithuania, Poland, Hungary, Walachia, Transylvania, Croatia . . ."

It is now impossible to trace much of this obsessive circuitous journey, but beyond doubt he traveled thousands of miles, staying nowhere very long, telling himself that the next town or the next school or the next master might hold the key to enlightenment.

He turned up in Sweden, then in Russia where he was captured by Tartars. A Tartar prince took him to Constantinople where he either escaped or was freed, because he appears next in Egypt, amazed and alarmed by the sight of "monsters so fearful you would jump right back into your mother's womb"—presumably hippos and crocodiles.

In 1524 he was home again, at his father's house in Villach, and somewhere he had acquired the huge sword that he carried for the rest of his life and slept with every night. People said that in the hollow pommel of the sword he kept a devil, though it was more likely a supply of his greatest treasure—the drug laudanum.

After a while he moved to Salzburg, but got involved in a peasant rebellion and just escaped the gallows, leaving town with such speed that he did not even pack his belongings. An actuary's inventory at the time lists one compass, one magnetic needle, a portrait of his father, several Oriental garments, fur-lined coats, and a variety of medical unguents.

On the road again, peddling drugs, promising health and long life, he met the duke of Bavaria, who was interested in the possibility of manufacturing gold. The duke already had an alchemist named Kilian on his payroll, but he hired Paracelsus and the two of them went to work in the basement of the duke's castle. Their laboratory was adjacent to the wine cellar, which evokes some images; but after a few months, despite the proximity of the wine, Paracelsus moved along—arguing, belittling, boasting, studying.

He became a citizen of Strasbourg where he promptly entangled himself in a debate with the celebrated surgeon, Dr. Vendelinus Hock. Hock knew anatomy, a subject Paracelsus hated and knew nothing about. The result was inevitable. Humiliated and ridiculed, he was driven from the lecture room.

Such a brutal exposure ought to have ruined him; but the great publisher Froben, lying ill in Basle with an infected leg, sent for him. Froben's doctors were ready to amputate, which in those days very often meant the end of the patient. Paracelsus contrived to save the publisher's leg, probably by intuition rather than by knowledge, and at the same time met Erasmus who was living on the upper floor of Froben's house.

The contrast between Erasmus and Paracelsus could hardly be more graphic. As Henry Pachter, a biographer of the alchemist, puts it: "One was the most refined Latinist, the other sought to make his coarse Swiss dialect a language of science. One was fastidiously neat; the other wore an alchemist's smeared apron. One was a master of innuendo, the other given to outspoken abuse. One was the most balanced mind of his time, scrupulously weighing each word, the other a mystic, rash of judgment and fond of speculation. The one lived with books, the other considered life the only book of value."

Several letters between them have been preserved. The two did not care much for each other, yet there was mutual respect; and when Erasmus did not feel well he wrote to Paracelus for advice. "I cannot offer thee a reward equal to thy art and knowledge—I surely offer thee a grateful soul. Thou hast recalled from the shades Frobenius who is my other half: if thou restorest me also thou restorest each through the other."

What doctor could resist such a gracious, elegant patient?

Paracelsus diagnosed the ailment and prescribed a cure.

Erasmus responded courteously, thanking him, but declined the treatment: "At present I have no time for a cure, indeed I have no time either to be sick or to die, for I am engaged in exacting studies. . . ."

Paracelsus stayed in Basle longer than he had anticipated, forcing himself like a splinter into its midst. When he was appointed municipal doctor and given a university professor's office a new quarrel blossomed—which he encouraged by being rude not only to his antagonists but to his friends. He was told that, although he might be a professor, no lecture halls were available. He retaliated by scheduling class off campus, and appeared for his first lecture dressed in the traditional academic robe; then with a melodramatic gesture he tore off the robe to reveal his sooty old alchemist's apron. The students, of course, loved it.

So he went about his affairs in Basle, seeing patients, writing outrageous pamphlets, experimenting with drugs and herbs and distillations, lecturing, drinking prodigiously, insulting everybody.

To a citizen who offended him, his reply began: "So then, you wormy and lousy Sophist..."

According to one Johannes Herbst, who worked for Paracelsus:

The two years I passed in his company he spent in drinking and gluttony, day and night. . . . Nevertheless, when he was most drunk and came home to dictate to me, he was so consistent and logical that a sober man could not have improved upon his manuscripts. . . . Often he would come home tipsy, after midnight, throw himself on his bed in his clothes wearing his sword which he said he had obtained from a hangman. He had hardly time to fall asleep when he rose, drew his sword like a madman, threw it on the ground or against the wall, so that sometimes I was afraid he would kill me. . . . He was a spendthrift, so that sometimes he had not a penny left, yet the next day would show me a full purse. I often wondered where he got it. . . . He did not care for women and I believe he never had doings with any. In the beginning he was very modest, so that up to his twenty-fifth year, I believe he never touched wine. Later on he learned to drink and even challenged an inn full of peasants to drink with him and drank them under the table, now and then putting his finger in his mouth like a swine.

"He is said to have received the philosophers' stone during his 28th year," wrote Jöcher in the *Scholar's Dictionary,* "and knew how to go about making gold, which is why he spent money like hay, often not having a penny left at night but loaded with bags of money next morning. . . . The rumor is, he made a pact with the devil."

On Saint John's Day, June 24, 1527, Paracelsus surpassed himself. Into the traditional campus bonfire went the accumulated rubbish of a year, whatever the students did not need or like. And into the fire this year— at his command—went a gigantic book, the greatest of all medieval medical books, the *Canon* of Avicenna. It was too big to be carried; it had to be dragged to the ceremonial fire.

"There is more wisdom in my shoelaces," said Paracelsus, "than in such books."

He, and he alone, Philippus Theophrastus Aureolus Bombastus, henceforth should be regarded as the supreme authority.

"I am a rough man, born in a rough country," he wrote later. "I have been brought up among pines, and I may have inherited some knots."

The Basle establishment was of that same opinion. After he publicly accused the clergy and magistrates of corruption they decided the best way to silence the knotty professor was to imprison him. Some friends at last convinced him of the danger and he left Basle in the middle of the night, hours ahead of the police.

He fled to Neuenburg, then to Colmar in Alsace where he was given a temporary resident's permit. But his permit was not renewed; he had become too controversial.

He moved to a village in Württemburg where he resumed studying astronomy; years later the house where he had lived was renovated and the chimney and roof were found to be covered with astrological signs.

Nuremberg was the next stop. Sebastian Franck in *Chronica of Our Times* wrote: "Item Dr. Theophrastus ab Hohenheim, a physician and astronomer. Anno 1529, said doctor came to our town; a peculiar and wondrous man . . ."

Here, as usual, he antagonized influential citizens, especially the doctors, and once more was obliged to flee. It had become the pattern of his life. He would arrive, impress himself with overpowering strength on a community, challenge its authorities, alienate those whose support he needed, and be expelled. "They drove me out of Lithuania and Prussia," he complains, "and from Poland, and still it was not enough for them. The Dutch did not like me either, nor the schools, neither Jews nor monks . . ."

But constant rejection, instead of depressing him as it does most men, seems to have stimulated him. One observer, struck by his furious energy, noted that he seldom slept: "he never undresses, throws himself on his bed with boots and spurs, rests for three hours, then gets up and continues to write."

What he was writing about were matters never before discussed—"invisible diseases"—leading toward modern concepts of gynecology and human psychology: "I am not embarrassed to be the first who dares to write on the diseases of women . . ." Martin Luther, whose name always has outshone that of Paracelsus fifty times over, was commenting at about the same time: "If women die in childbed, that does no harm. It is what they were made for."

And he understood, as perhaps no one else did, that the cause of erratic behavior might not be a devil but an emotional crisis. In the sixteenth century he was explaining that weak personalities could be shaken by the force of their instincts. Such people should not be condemned, he argued; instead, they deserved treatment.

He wrote of faith healers: "It is not the curse or the blessing that works, but the idea. The imagination produces the effect." Man's imagination, he said, "is like the sun, whose light cannot be touched and yet may set a house on fire. It guides man's life."

"As we desire things in our hearts," he said, "so they appear to us in dreams."

The name he suggested for the disease we call Saint Vitus's dance was "chorea lascivia," indicating that he realized its sexual origin.

Yet his cures might include camphor and mandrake mixed with "quintessence of gold"—medieval remedies prescribed by a man whose intellect was centuries ahead of his time.

Germany in 1532 was disrupted by religious disputes; and Paracelsus, congenitally unstable, resumed wandering, almost aimlessly, always searching. But he has changed; now he worries about personal salvation: "The time of geometry has come to an end, the time of art is over, the time of philosophy has come to an end. The snow of my misery has thawed. The time of growing has ended. Summer is here and I do not know whence it came. It is here. Now is the time to write of many things on which I have ruminated for years, namely of blessed life. . . ."

Then he continues: "The world cannot be gained by astronomy, which has little value except for its own sake, nor by medicine, which lacks power over all diseases, nor by philosophy, which is held in contempt. . . . Where I had seen flowers in alchemy, there is but grass."

The deterioration of belief so affected him that not only

his temperament but his appearance changed. He paid little attention to insults, he fasted, he began to give away his clothes and money, and he abandoned alchemical experiments. He meditated, tried to help the poor, preached, wrote incoherent moralistic tracts. Dramatic conversions are not unusual but they are always unexpected, and in this case the resemblance to Leo Tolstoy is startling.

He decided there were two kinds of wisdom, one eternal, the other mortal. "I started out in the Light of Nature ... and finished in the Light of Eternity."

He subsisted by begging, complained about those who would not give him a bowl of soup, and found himself an outcast. Wherever he went, the door slammed.

"I have sickness in me, my poverty and piety."

And, of course, the more he was ignored or abused the more desperate became his message. If the wealthy and powerful would not listen to him they must ultimately hear the message of the Apocalypse.

And lo!—it arrived.

Plague.

The town of Sterzing was struck. Most of its citizens fled, leaving sick relatives and friends to rot. Paracelsus, indifferent to his own safety, hurried to Sterzing where he helped care for the victims. Yet as soon as the plague subsided the town burghers ordered him to leave. So he left, meanwhile bestowing a fresh title on himself: Professor of Theology. And, very much like his old self, he addressed a letter to the authorities of Sterzing, denouncing them for bigotry, stupidity, and hypocrisy, railing especially against the Catholic priests whom he considered responsible for his eviction. He scorned all ecclesiastics. Luther and the pope, he said, were two whores discussing chastity.

From Sterzing to the village of Merano, where he seems to have been treated with respect; but his private crucifixion forced him to leave. He moved to Saint-Moritz, but once again was unable to find a home.

He returned to the Tyrolean metallurgy shops where he had worked as a boy, and the result of this visit was the first essay ever written on an occupational disease: *Von der Bergsucht,* concerning respiratory infections suffered by miners. Tradition ascribed such sickness to the displeasure of mountain spirits who guarded the veins of ore; Paracelsus attributed the problem to metallic vapors.

In 1536 he published a book on surgery. Ambroise Paré usually gets credit for being the first to emphasize cleanliness after surgery; but Paracelsus, a generation earlier, offered the same advice.

Other books followed. *Occult Philosophy. Explanation of Universal Astronomy.* And his masterpiece: *Sagacious Philosophy of the Great and Small World,* which considers man, salvation, geometry, the healing power of stones, meteorology, phrenology, witches, ghosts, sorcerers, and just about everything else. Someday, he prophesies, the human voice will be carried long distances "by the aid of pipes and crystals." He speculates on mirrors to project images across mountains, or even into the future. "Man possesses the capability of seeing his friends and how they live, though they are 1,000 miles away."

He reveals his formula for creating the homunculus:

"If the sperm, enclosed in a hermetically sealed glass, is buried in horse manure for about forty days and properly 'magnetized', it begins to live and to move. After such a time it bears the form and resemblance of a human being, but it will be transparent and without a corpus. . . ."

While he wandered across Europe his father died. Paracelsus returned to Villach to claim the estate but the townspeople did not think he was a reputable successor. He departed meekly, without his inheritance. Then the prince bishop of Salzburg offered him asylum, so there he went and there he lived until his death the following year. He was forty-eight. The cause of his death is not known. Enemies said he was killed during a tavern brawl; friends believed he died from an overdose of that great elixir he carried in the pommel of his sword.

He left very little: ten guilders to one of his mother's relatives, twelve guilders to the executors, some surgical instruments and ointments to the Salzburg barbers, and several boxes of manuscripts. He did not bequeath his manuscripts to anybody; he did not think anybody deserved them.

"I have traveled throughout the land," he wrote, "and was a pilgrim all my life, alone and a stranger feeling alien. Then Thou hast made grow in me Thine art under the breath of the terrible storm in me."

Not long after his death a legend began to take shape—that of man's infinite desire for knowledge—and Dr. Faustus was born.

Bibliography

Arciniegas, Germán. *The Knight of El Dorado.* Translated by Mildred Adams. New York, 1942.

Ashe, Geoffrey. *The Quest for America.* New York, 1971.

Bakeless, John. *The Eyes of Discovery.* Philadelphia, 1950.

Baring-Gould, Sabine. *Curious Myths of the Middle Ages.* Boston, 1904.

Berlitz, Charles. *Mysteries from Forgotten Worlds.* New York, 1972.

Berrill, N. J. *Journey into Wonder.* New York, 1952.

Bolton, H. E. *Coronado.* Albuquerque, N.M., 1949.

Brandon, S. G. F. *Ancient Empires.* New York, 1973.

Brebner, John Bartlett. *The Explorers of North America.* New York, 1937.

Brundage, B. C. *Empire of the Inca.* Norman, Okla., 1963.

Burgess, Robert. *Sinkings, Salvages & Shipwrecks.* New York, 1970.

Calvin, Ross. *Sky Determines.* Albuquerque, N.M., 1948.

de Camp, L. Sprague. *Lost Continents.* New York, 1975.

———— and Catherine de Camp. *Citadels of Mystery.* New York, 1973.

Caron, M., and Hutin, S. *The Alchemists.* Translated by Helen R. Lane. New York, 1961.

Cary, Max. *Ancient Explorers.* London, 1963.

Casson, Lionel. *The Ancient Mariners.* New York, 1959.

Ceram, C. W. *The First American.* Translated by Richard and Clara Winston. New York, 1971.

Chapman, Walker. *The Golden Dream.* New York, 1967.

Cleator, P. E. *Lost Languages.* New York, 1962.

Clissold, Stephen. *The Seven Cities of Cíbola.* London, 1961.

Cohen, Daniel. *Mysterious Places.* New York, 1969.

Columbus, Christopher. *Journal.* Translated by Cecil Jane, New York, 1960.

Cousteau, Jacques. *Diving for Sunken Treasure.* Translated by J. F. Bernard. New York, 1971.

Crone, G. R. *The Explorers.* New York, 1962.

Crow, John A. *The Epic of Latin America.* New York, 1971.

Daniel, Glyn. *Myth or Legend.* New York, 1968.

Day, Arthur Grove. *Coronado's Quest.* Berkeley, Calif., 1940.

Debenham, Frank. *Discovery and Exploration.* Garden City, N.Y., 1960.

Descola, Jean. *The Conquistadors.* Translated by Malcolm Barnes. New York, 1957.

Divine, David. *The Opening of the World.* New York, 1973.

Dobie, J. Frank. *Apache Gold and Yaqui Silver.* New York, 1939.

Engl, Lieselotte, and Engl, Theo. *Twilight of Ancient Peru.* Translated by Alisa Jaffe. New York, 1969.

Federmann, Reinhard. *The Royal Art of Alchemy.* Translated by Richard Weber. Philadelphia, 1969.

Fernández-Armesto, Felipe. *Columbus.* New York, 1974.

Gaddis, Vincent. *Invisible Horizons.* Philadelphia, 1965.

Gardner, Martin. *Fads and Fallacies.* New York, 1957.

Gay, Carlo. *Xochipala.* Princeton, N.J., 1972.

Goodman, Edward J. *The Explorers of South America.* New York, 1972.

Gould, Rupert. *Oddities.* New York, 1965.

Gray, George Zabriskie. *The Children's Crusade.* New York, 1972.

von Hagen, Victor. *Realm of the Incas.* New York, 1957.

———. *The Golden Man.* London, 1974.

Hakluyt, Richard. *Voyages.* New York, 1965.

Halliburton, Richard. *His Story of His Life's Adventure.* New York, 1940.

Hart, Henry. *Sea Road to the Indies.* New York, 1950.

———. *Venetian Adventurer.* London, 1942.

Heer, Friedrich. *The Medieval World.* Translated by Janet Sondheimer. New York, 1969.

Hermann, Paul. *Conquest by Man.* Translated by Michael Bullock. New York, 1954.

———. *The Great Age of Discovery.* Translated by Arnold Pomerans. New York, 1958.

Herring, Hubert. *History of Latin America.* New York, 1968.

Holmyard, E. J. *Alchemy.* Baltimore, Md., 1957.

Holzer, Hans. *The Alchemist.* New York, 1974.

Hordern, Nicholas, et al. *The Conquest of North America.* Garden City, N.Y., 1973.

Humble, Richard. *Marco Polo.* New York, 1974.

Janvier, Thomas. *The Aztec Treasure House.* New York, 1918.

Kirwan, L. P. *A History of Polar Exploration.* New York, 1960.

Lacey, Robert. *Sir Walter Raleigh.* New York, 1973.

Landström, Björn. *Bold Voyages and Great Explorers.* Garden City, N.Y., 1964.

Leithäuser, Joachim. *Worlds Beyond the Horizon.* Translated by Hugh Merrick. New York, 1955.

Leonard, Jonathan. *Ancient America.* New York, 1967.

Ley, Willy. *Another Look at Atlantis.* New York, 1969.

Lothrop, S. K. *Inca Treasure.* Los Angeles, 1938.

Luce, J. V. *Lost Atlantis.* New York, 1969.

Mahn-Lot, Marianne. *Columbus.* Translated by Helen R. Lane. New York, 1961.

Manley, Seon, and Lewis, Gogo, eds. *Polar Secrets.* Garden City, N.Y., 1968.

Maple, Eric. *Domain of Devils.* London, 1969.

Marx, Robert. *The Lure of Sunken Treasure.* New York, 1973.

Middleton, Dorothy. *Victorian Lady Travelers.* New York, 1965.

Mirsky, Jeannette. *To the Arctic.* New York, 1948.

———. *The Great Chinese Travelers.* New York, 1964.

Moore, Patrick. *Suns, Myths & Men.* New York, 1968.

Morison, Samuel Eliot. *Admiral of the Ocean Sea.* Boston, 1942.

———. *The European Discovery of America.* New York, 1971.

———. *The Caribbean as Columbus Saw It.* Boston, 1964.

———. *Christopher Columbus, Mariner.* Boston, 1955.

Mountfield, David. *A History of Polar Exploration.* New York, 1974.

Mowatt, Farley. *Ordeal by Ice.* Boston, 1961.

Munro, Dana C. "The Children's Crusade," *American Historical Review,* vol. XIX. New York, 1913.

Neatby, L. H. *In Quest of the Northwest Passage.* New York, 1962.

Nesmith, Robert. *Dig for Pirate Treasure*. New York, 1958.

Newby, Eric. *World Atlas of Exploration*. New York, 1975.

Norman, Charles. *Discoverers of America*. New York, 1968.

Outhwaite, Leonard. *Unrolling the Map*. New York, 1972.

Pachter, Henry. *Magic into Science*. New York, 1951.

Penrose, Boies. *Travel and Discovery in the Renaissance*. Cambridge, Mass., 1952.

Prescott, W. H. *The Conquest of Peru*. New York, 1963.

Quinn, David B. *North America from Earliest Discovery to First Settlements*. New York, 1977.

Rackl, Hanns-Wolf. *Diving into the Past*. Translated by Ronald J. Floyd. New York, 1968.

Ramsay, Raymond. *No Longer on the Map*. New York, 1972.

Rasky, Frank. *The Polar Voyagers*. New York, 1976.

Read, John. *Through Alchemy to Chemistry*. London, 1957.

Renault, Gilbert. *The Caravels of Christ*. Translated by Richmond Hill. New York, 1959.

Runciman, Steven. *History of the Crusades*. Cambridge, Eng., 1954.

Sadoul, Jacques. *Alchemists & Gold*. Translated by Olga Sieveking. New York, 1972.

Sanderlin, George. *Across the Ocean Sea*. New York, 1966.

de Santillana, Giorgio. *The Age of Adventure*. New York, 1956.

Schreiber, Herman. *Vanished Cities*. Translated by Richard and Clara Winston. New York, 1957.

Severin, Timothy. *The Golden Antilles*. London, 1970.

Silverberg, Robert. *The Realm of Prester John*. Gorden City, N.Y., 1972.

———. *Empires in the Dust*. New York, 1966.

———. *Sunken History*. New York, 1964.

Smith, William. *Northwest Passage*. New York, 1970.

Snow, Edward. *Ghosts, Gales & Gold*. New York, 1972.

Stefansson, Vilhjalmur. *Northwest to Fortune*. New York, 1958.

———. *Unsolved Mysteries of the Arctic*. New York, 1937.

———. *Great Adventures and Explorations*. New York, 1952.

Strayer, Joseph Reese. *The Middle Ages*. New York, 1959.

Sykes, Percy. *A History of Exploration*. New York, 1961.

Taylor, F. Sherwood. *The Alchemists*. New York, 1962.

Terrell, John. *Journey into Darkness*. New York, 1962.

———. *Pueblos, Gods & Spaniards*. New York, 1973.

Treece, Henry. *The Crusades.* New York, 1962.

de Vaca, Cabeza. *Adventures in the Unknown Interior of America.* Translated by Cyclone Covey. New York, 1961.

de la Vega, Garcilaso. *Royal Commentaries of the Incas.* Translated by Harold Livermore. Austin, Texas, 1966.

Wagner, Kip. *Pieces of Eight.* New York, 1966.

Wauchope, Robert. *Lost Tribes & Sunken Continents.* Chicago, 1962.

Winton, John. *Sir Walter Ralegh.* New York, 1975.

Wood, H. J. *Exploration and Discovery.* London, 1958.

Wright, Louis. *Gold, Glory, and Gospel.* New York, 1970.

von Wuthenau, Alexander. *Unexpected Faces in Ancient America.* New York, 1975.